SOCIAL POLICIES IN
WESTERN INDUSTRIAL SOCIETIES

RESEARCH SERIES/NUMBER 61

361.61
An24s

Social Policies in Western Industrial Societies

CHARLES F. ANDRAIN

INSTITUTE
OF INTERNATIONAL
STUDIES
University of California, Berkeley

Library of Congress Cataloging in Publication Data

Andrain, Charles F.
   Social policies in Western industrial societies.

   (Research series, ISSN 0068-6093 ; no. 61)
   Bibliography: p.
   Includes index.
   1. Social policy—Evaluation. 2. Social accounting—
Cross-cultural studies. 3. Economic policy—Cross-
cultural studies. 4. Education and state—Cross-cultural
studies. 5. Medical policy—Cross-cultural studies.
I. Title. II. Series: Research series (University of
California, Berkeley. Institute of International
Studies) ; no. 61.
HN18.A628 1985   361.6'1   85-10840
ISBN 0-87725-161-4

CONTENTS

85-3647

LIST OF TABLES

vii

PREFACE

The chapters in this monograph are based on three Royer lectures that I presented at the University of California, Berkeley, on 2-4 May 1983. These lectures, sponsored by the Department of Political Science, the Department of Economics, and the Institute of International Studies, gave me the opportunity to describe, explain, and evaluate policy performance in seven modern industrial societies: the United States, Canada, Britain, Sweden, West Germany, France, and Italy. In this monograph I stress the interaction between the political and economic sectors of society.

The monograph analyzes different dimensions of economic, education, and health policy performance, with a focus on the impact of these policies. Chapter 2 assesses the contemporary crisis of the welfare state by examining the effect of economic policies on growth rates, unemployment, inflation, and voting behavior. Chapter 3 considers how education policies affect students' cognitive performance, political participation, social mobility, and attitudes toward civil liberties. Chapter 4, which explores health policies in six Western nations, evaluates health care systems according to several criteria: equality, efficiency, popular satisfaction, and effectiveness in lowering infant mortality and raising life expectancy. Chapter 5 presents an overview of policy performance by describing the longitudinal trends in policy contents, explaining these policies, and evaluating economic, education, and health policies.

I have used the institutionalist approach to explore policy performance in these industrialized nations. Several assumptions underlie the institutionalist approach to policy analysis.* First, it views institutions rather than individuals as the primary units for investigation. Particularly in the contemporary modernized, democratic areas of Western Europe and North America, governments, political parties,

*See Jerry L. Petr, "Fundamentals of an Institutionalist Perspective on Economic Policy," *Journal of Economic Issues* 18 (March 1984): 1-17.

business corporations, professional associations, and labor unions exercise the dominant power over the policy process. By helping to formulate and implement public policies, they shape individual choices.

Second, although institutions determine policymakers' behavior, political leaders still retain some choice over public policies and methods of implementation. From this perspective, both policy contents and their impacts depend not only on the power of dominant institutions but also on the policy preferences of key political elites: political party heads, business executives, professionals (physicians, teachers), labor union leaders, and government officials, especially cabinet ministers and civil servants.

Third, the institutionalist approach takes a dynamic view of the policy process. Rather than tending toward a static equilibrium, the policy process reveals changes through time. As the power of particular institutions changes, as elites articulate changing policy priorities, and as technological developments transform production methods, the content and impact of public policies also change. Thus policy analyses must rely on a historical, longitudinal, and time-series orientation.

Fourth, institutionalists stress the need for empirical observations of policy consequences rather than axiomatic assumptions about individual motivations. Instead of assuming that business executives seek to maximize their profits and then using mathematical reasoning to deduce the behavioral conclusions that derive from these motivational assumptions, institutionalists empirically examine the power of dominant institutions and the policy preferences actually held by institutional leaders, such as corporate executives. Together these two variables—organizational power and elite policy preferences—best explain policy contents and their impacts.

Fifth, from the institutionalist perspective policy analysis rests on a holistic base. Rather than divided by tight disciplinary boundaries, the political world revolves around public decisions that affect the whole society. To understand the policy process, investigators should remain open to the research findings from different fields, including political science, sociology, economics, public health, and education. Synthesizing information from these academic disciplines, the monograph highlights the political dimensions of public policies, especially their impact on social groups within a nation.

Producing a book, like making public policies, is a collective enterprise. Although authors must take responsibility for the finished product, they owe a debt of gratitude to all those who helped with the research project. I began this work as a research associate in the Institute of International Studies, Berkeley, in 1974. Since then I have spent an additional three years at the IIS gathering material and writing preliminary drafts. I especially appreciate the intellectual encouragement that Professor Carl G. Rosberg, director of the Institute, offered to me. William K. Muir, chairman of the Political Science Department in May 1983, made my visit to the Berkeley campus to deliver the Royer lectures an enjoyable, stimulating experience. Several faculty have read drafts of the manuscript; these include Harold Wilensky, Bernard Hennessy, Alexander Groth, C. Richard Hofstetter, and Ibrahim Poroy. The quantitative data analysis in Chapter 2 was carried out at the San Diego State University Computer Center. I am grateful for the computer time made available by the computer facilities committee and staff. David Selover, a proficient computer programmer with a background in both political science and economics, helped me analyze the time-series multiple regression data. I appreciate his support in unraveling the complexities of computer routines and printouts. This manuscript represents the fourth one that Peggy McCroskey has typed for me during the last decade. As usual, she handled the typing responsibilities in an efficient manner.

C. F. A.

Chapter 1

THE PURPOSES OF POLICY ANALYSIS

Throughout Western industrial nations the problems of unemployment, inflation, ineffective education, and expensive health care have recently become more severe than at any time since the Great Depression. In the late 1970s there was a simultaneous rise in both the jobless rates and inflation as economic stagflation befell North America and Western Europe. Although inflation decreased during the early 1980s, double-digit unemployment became more widespread. Not only unskilled blue-collar workers but also college graduates experienced growing difficulties finding a job. Faced with deteriorating economic conditions, they began to question the effectiveness of their formal education. Older citizens felt the painful impact of inflation on their health care costs. As a result, many people became skeptical about the ability of public economic, educational, and health policies to meet their needs. As the limits of public policies became more apparent, alienation toward government mounted.

Confronted by such social crises, policy analysts can help clarify the issues involved in the government decision-making process. In particular, they can fulfill three general purposes: accurate description, explanation, and evaluation of policies.[1]

DESCRIPTION OF POLICIES

We shall concentrate on describing three dimensions of economic, educational, and health policies: (1) *Structural administration*. Policy contents and outcomes involve the decision-making power of central, regional, and local governments and such private groups as business firms, labor unions, and medical associations. (2) *Costs*. Information about a policy's expenditures and finances discloses the resources needed to attain policy objectives. In this regard we need

1

to ascertain the degree of reliance placed on government tax revenues and private fees. (3) *Services and benefits.* From the typical citizen's perspective policy outputs become a crucial consideration for judging governmental competence. How extensive are old-age pensions, family allowances, and unemployment benefits? What values, information, skills, and role behaviors do youths learn in public schools? What kinds of health care benefits do public health programs offer the population, and how accessible are these services?

Policy analysts describe not only policy contents but also policy consequences. They seek to ascertain policy impacts on the national well-being as well as on specific ethnic and economic groups. What are the inflation and unemployment rates in different nations? How do they affect middle-aged male professionals compared with young female service employees? How do educational policies shape political values, knowledge, and participation? What are the outcomes of health policies on infant mortality and life expectancy, both nationwide and among various groups?

Public policies have exerted diverse impacts. Investigators have distinguished between intended and unintended, short-run versus long-range, and benign versus malign outcomes. For example, in attempting to deal with inflation, policymakers may intend for a decrease in the money supply to reduce escalating prices, but such a monetary policy may unintentionally cause soaring bankruptcies, lower growth rates, and raise unemployment levels. Higher interest rates will probably curb aggregate demand and thus lead to lower inflation over the long range; however, during the short run they may increase business costs, thereby pushing up prices. Foreign exchange policies that halt inflation usually favor some groups at the expense of others. For instance, an overvalued currency reduces the prices of imports but raises the prices of exports. Even though import purchasers benefit, the currency appreciation may cause falling profits and higher unemployment for those working in the export industries.

EXPLANATION OF POLICIES

Explanatory statements specify some effect that needs explaining (e.g., inflation), a general proposition that links certain "causes" (e.g., expansion of aggregate demand) to the effect, and information about the particular conditions to which the general propositions apply (e.g., the level of industrial development, plant capacity usage, and reliance on imported raw materials).[2]

To explain policy contents in the economic, education, and health fields, we stress beliefs and power as the crucial explanatory conditions—in particular the beliefs and power of four structures: the national electorate, interest groups within a population (especially business organizations, professional associations, and labor unions), political parties, and government agencies.

Policy-relevant beliefs revolve around assumptions about social problems. What specific problems do the electorate, interest groups, parties, and governments regard as most important? What are the causes of the problems? Policymakers may blame high unemployment on fate, individual laziness, or a collectivity such as labor unions, monopoly capitalism, Japanese auto firms, or the government. To what extent should the government try to resolve a social problem? We assume that those who place the major blame on the individual rather than on the government will show less support for public policy solutions. For them, market mechanisms should make the binding choices for society. If people do seek a government decision to alleviate social distress, what policy preferences do they express? If double-digit unemployment plagues the society, should the government expand information about available jobs, grant tax credits to firms that hire jobless workers, establish more public-service employment, or cut interest rates? Policy preferences will derive from conceptions about desirable conditions and from expectations about feasible alternatives. The policies chosen for implementation will thus depend on policymakers' value priorities and their assessment of the probable consequences of the policies.

If leaders are to transform their policy preferences into government decisions, they need to wield power over the policy process. Political "power" means the effective use of resources (information, money, weapons, status) to secure binding public consequences. To ascertain the political power of groups, organizations, institutions, or individuals, we need to know the resources they possess, their will to shape public policies, and their skill in using resources.

In Western industrial democracies the electorate, interest groups, political parties, and government agencies play a powerful role in the policy process. The "mandate theory" of voting assumes that voters

3

can impose their will on legislators. Motivated by a desire to gain reelection, legislators will supposedly frame policies that at least a plurality of the electorate prefers. Interest group leaders, political party activists, and government officials more directly participate in the decision-making process than do rank-and-file citizens. The power of trade unions and business associations depends on their degree of internal solidarity, coalitions with other groups, dominance over rival organizations, and representation in government agencies. Like effective interest groups, political parties need high solidarity, a dedicated commitment to particular policy concerns, and access to government officials to exercise power. Government institutions such as legislatures, cabinet ministries, and the civil service have the primary responsibility for making public policies; thus they are crucial in determining what decisions ultimately emerge from the policy process. Government agencies with high centralization, clear coordination, and extensive autonomy from social groups wield the most power in shaping the content of policies.

This explanation of government decision-making assumes an interaction between voluntarism and determinism. From the voluntarist perspective, individual policymakers enjoy some freedom to translate their policy preferences into binding policies. The decisions accepted for implementation reflect policymakers' conceptions about the public well-being, salient social problems, causes of these problems, and the most desirable and feasible solutions to them. If policymakers can effectively wield power, they can attain certain policy objectives.

From the determinist viewpoint, both cultural beliefs—e.g., ideologies, formal laws, informal customs—and the distribution of power hinder the realization of certain policies as well as particular outcomes. For example, commitment to a laissez-faire ideology may inhibit policymakers from taking actions that will expand governmental control over capital investment, increase aggregate demand, and perhaps lower unemployment. Dedication to socialist principles may deter government leaders from placing greater reliance on market mechanisms to promote efficiency, productivity, and economic growth. Particularly in a federal system, the constitution deters central government leaders from implementing policies that run counter to the preferences of regional governments. At the same time, policies often stem from traditions, conventions, and customary ways of making decisions, rather than from a rational calculation of costs and benefits.

4

A lack of power in both the political system and the economy limits policymakers' choices. The fragmentation of political institutions, the restricted scope for public actions, and limited resources (especially tax revenues) pose political restraints. The level of industrialization, growth rate, ownership of capital goods, resources of corporate firms and labor unions, and conditions in the world economy (e.g., supply shortages, dependence on imported oil, demand for exports, and expansion of currency by multinational banks) also restrain the achievement of policy goals.[3] By explaining the causes of policy contents and their effects, policy analysts clarify the limits of public choices.

EVALUATION OF POLICIES

Policy evaluation involves three steps. First, a policy analyst specifies the criteria of worth—that is, the standards used to judge a policy process. In this study I shall use four general criteria: equality, efficiency, public satisfaction with programs, and institutional goal attainment—that is, the success in reducing unemployment, decreasing inflation, raising the economic growth rate, increasing student competence, lowering infant mortality, and lengthening life expectancy.

Second, the analyst devises empirical indicators to measure such abstract criteria as equality and efficiency. Since these criteria are general and ambiguous, they cannot easily be measured appropriately. Formulating verbal definitions presents few difficulties. For example, we can define "efficiency" in terms of cost/benefit ratios: the number of beneficial outcomes that result from the input of each dollar (or other relevant monetary unit).[4] However, devising "operational indicators" that measure the same value in different countries poses problems—especially if we want to assess the efficiency of an entire national economy compared with a single firm's performance. When we evaluate education and health care systems, the problems of finding satisfactory operational indicators mount. Investigators find it difficult to establish empirical linkages between expenditures and certain impacts of education like political values, knowledge, and participation.

Third, the analyst matches empirical observations to the criteria of worth, thereby rank-ordering different political systems on their

5

policy performance. Assume that we choose to evaluate Western nations on their equality of access to policy benefits. If we secure empirical evidence on the degree to which all individuals gain similar access to social services, post-primary education, and health care benefits, we can rank various societies on an equality scale.

Obviously the evaluation of policy performance arouses controversy, primarily for three reasons. First, analysts do not agree on the specific criteria that should constitute the evaluative standards. Some attach the highest value to efficiency, whereas others assign greater importance to equality. Thus evaluations based on efficiency criteria may rank countries differently from those based on equality criteria. For analysts committed to a free market economy, efficiency also takes priority over public satisfaction with programs. Second, disagreements arise about the best ways to measure some general criteria. For example, equality is difficult to measure across nations. It may mean similar access to policy benefits, or it may denote similar outcomes, like levels of income, knowledge, or health. Third, evaluation of policy performance is difficult because variables other than public policies influence individual well-being. By examining infant mortality and life expectancy rates among groups, analysts can secure cross-national information about the distribution of good health. Yet they cannot so easily measure the empirical linkages between national health care policies and equality of health because good health partly stems from individual behavior and environmental conditions that lie beyond policymakers' direct control.

CONCLUSION

Description, explanation, and evaluation depend on each other. Just as researchers must base their explanations on accurate descriptive information, so they should evaluate different political systems according to valid explanations. Without accurate descriptions about specific effects and their assumed policy "causes," we cannot accept the credibility of the pertinent explanations. Unless we study several countries, we cannot affirm that explanations of causes apply beyond a single case. Evaluation rests on valid explanations that specify the relationships between organizational power and cultural beliefs. For example, if we fail to explain the linkages between low infant mortality and health care programs, we cannot claim that the health policies implemented in (say) Sweden more effectively lower the infant death rate than do those in Britain.

In the following chapters we shall describe, explain, and evaluate various aspects of economic, education, and health policies in seven industrialized nations—Canada, France, West Germany, Italy, Sweden, the United Kingdom, and the United States. Chapter 2 explores the current crisis of the welfare state, probes the impact of economic policy performance on electoral outcomes, and analyzes the reasons for unemployment, inflation, and economic growth in seven countries from 1960 through 1980. Chapter 3 describes and explains the effects of education policies on democratic values, cognitive achievements, political participation, and occupational mobility. The fourth chapter evaluates public health policies according to the four criteria noted above. Chapter 5 surveys policy performance in the seven industrialized societies. It describes the content of policies by analyzing three dimensions: structural administration, costs, and benefits. Then I explain the different policy contents in these nations, guided by the hypothesis that there is an interaction between policymakers' beliefs and the structures in which they operate. Finally, I evaluate policy performance according to the criteria of equality, efficiency, public satisfaction, and institutional goal attainment.

Chapter 2

ECONOMIC POLICIES AND THE CRISIS OF THE WELFARE STATE

When the economic slump hit the United Kingdom during the late 1970s, factory workers faced a desperate situation. From 1974 through 1981 inflation rates soared to double-digit figures in every year except 1978. By 1981 over 11 percent of the total labor force was unemployed, including Joe Greenhill, a steel worker. When he lost his job, his family suffered financial hardship. The Conservative government had raised council rents, increased prices of prescription drugs, lowered unemployment benefits, and imposed higher fees for school meals. As a result, the Greenhills's disposable income fell to half the amount that Joe made when employed. At first he expected to find another job fairly quickly, but after looking for over a year—often competing with two hundred applicants for the same low-paying pick-and-shovel job—Joe became increasingly despondent. Unemployment lowered his sense of political efficacy and disrupted his social contacts with other persons, so his political involvement declined. He stopped attending meetings of his local union and Labour party organization. Although still voting for the Labour party candidate in the 1983 election to the House of Commons, Joe did not blame Conservative Prime Minister Margaret Thatcher for the high unemployment. Instead he held the world economic situation responsible for Britain's economic mess. Joe's teenage son lent some verbal support to the neo-Fascist National Front party that links the dire economic situation to people with Asian and West Indian ethnic backgrounds, but Joe himself felt no inclination to join either the National Front or the Communist party. For Joe Greenhill, as for most other jobless workers, unemployment and the growing crisis of the British welfare state brought political quiescence, not a popular backlash against democratic government.[1]

During these hard times how can we best understand the impact of public policies on aggregate economic performance and individual well-being? Policy analysts seek to understand whole political and economic systems, yet they participate in only a part of the whole. Most political economists live in the United States; how can they explain economic performance in other nations? Since we all live in the present, we may exaggerate immediate problems. When talking about the "crisis of the welfare state," we must take a cross-national and historical view. Only by looking beyond the United States and the present time can we gain an overview of a whole system's performance. In this sense the task of the policy analyst resembles the calling that Czeslaw Milosz ascribes to the poet: "He is the one who flies above the earth and looks at it *from above* but at the same time sees it in every detail."[2]

THE GROWTH OF THE WELFARE STATE

Particularly since the end of World War II there has occurred a rapid growth of the "welfare state," a term that refers to the social service programs implemented by Western industrialized societies. The major benefits include education, health care services, and income maintenance payments—pensions for the old, family allowances for the young, public assistance for the needy, and unemployment compensation for the jobless. For all these programs expenditures have risen rapidly—especially during the 1970s in Sweden, West Germany, and France. As the worldwide economic recession deepened after 1973, unemployment rates escalated in many countries to double-digit figures. Thus unemployment compensation also increased. More people applied for public assistance. Workers who lost their jobs or who feared unemployment retired early, causing higher spending on pensions. As societies became more urbanized, industrialized, technologically advanced, and impersonal, the family and church retained fewer responsibilities for helping to meet individual needs. Policymakers faced greater pressures to provide education, health care, and steady levels of income.

However great the growth of the welfare state throughout Western industrial societies, some governments administer more comprehensive, generous programs than others. We can compare different growth rates in the welfare state by examining three policy dimensions: (1) expenditures on government programs; (2) levels of taxes for financing these programs; and (3) the percentage of the total labor force employed by government agencies, including public corporations. On all three dimensions, Sweden has the most "developed" welfare state. By contrast, the United States has the least developed.

Total government outlays include three types of expenditures. Final consumption expenditures refer to government purchases of public administration services (salaries for civil servants), defense, health care, and education. Current disbursements include all these expenditures, besides spending on social service transfers (pensions, family allowances, unemployment compensation, disability benefits, public assistance, aid to war victims), business subsidies, and interest on the public debt. Total government outlays consist of current government disbursements as well as investment expenditures for gross capital formation—that is, additions to the stock of buildings, plant, and machinery.

During the 1960s and 1970s total government expenditures as a share of the gross domestic product (GDP) showed a rapid growth (see Table 2.1). The steepest increases were for current disbursements, especially for social service transfers. Except in Sweden, final consumption expenditures showed only a modest rise over the 1960-80 period. Spending on capital formation varied across nations, decreasing in Canada and the United States, growing larger in Italy, remaining the same in West Germany, and reaching the highest share of the GDP from 1967 to 1973 in France, Sweden, and the United Kingdom.

Swedish and U.S. leaders implement the most divergent expenditure policies. Since 1967 Sweden has shown the highest government spending in all areas, and the United States has ranked lowest in government expenditures, at least for social service transfers and capital formation. The French, German, Italian, and British governments spent about the same share of the GDP on current disbursements and total outlays—a higher percentage than Canada or the United States but lower than Sweden. Because of large outlays for defense and education, U.S. government leaders maintained comparatively high expenditures on final consumption, particularly between 1960 and 1973. Yet the modest spending for social service transfers and capital investment meant that U.S. current disbursements and total outlays remained the lowest throughout the 1960-80 period.

Government expenditures in Western industrialized countries revolve around three major programs: defense, social services, and

10

Table 2.1

GOVERNMENT EXPENDITURES AS PERCENTAGES OF
GROSS DOMESTIC PRODUCT (GDP),[a] 1960-80

Country	Type of Expenditure	1960-66	1967-73	1974-80
Canada	Final consumption expenditure[b]	14.9%	18.2%	19.7%
	Current disbursements[c]	25.6	31.1	36.5
	Total outlays[d]	29.5	34.9	39.9
France	Final consumption expenditure	13.2	13.3	14.6
	Current disbursements	32.8	34.6	40.4
	Total outlays	37.1	39.0	44.0
West Germany	Final consumption expenditure	14.8	16.6	20.1
	Current disbursements	29.4	33.1	40.7
	Total outlays	35.0	38.6	46.2
Italy	Final consumption expenditure	13.8	14.9	15.5
	Current disbursements	27.9	32.0	39.0
	Total outlays	31.6	35.7	43.3
Sweden	Final consumption expenditure	17.1	21.5	26.5
	Current disbursements	28.9	37.5	50.9
	Total outlays	34.0	43.7	56.8
United Kingdom	Final consumption expenditure	16.9	17.9	20.8
	Current disbursements	30.7	33.6	40.3
	Total outlays	34.5	39.8	44.9
United States	Final consumption expenditure	17.5	18.7	18.1
	Current disbursements	26.1	29.5	32.1
	Total outlays	28.7	31.5	33.6

Source: OECD Economic Outlook, no. 31 (July 1982): 147-49.

[a]GDP measures the national income of goods and services produced in a country; it excludes income deriving from investments and possessions owned abroad.

[b]Final consumption expenditures include current purchases of goods and services for public administration, defense, health, and education at all levels of government. Figures are annual averages of the GDP during each seven-year period.

[c]Current disbursements refer to final consumption expenditures, as well as interest on the public debt, subsidies, and social security transfers to households.

[d]Total outlays consist of current disbursements and gross capital formation expenditures.

education. As Table 2.2 indicates, spending on these three programs constituted between two-thirds and three-fourths of current disbursements. During the 1970s expenditures for social services consumed the largest share of the GDP. Governments spent fewer funds on education, while the defense budget took the lowest fiscal priority. In all seven nations defense expenditures as a percentage of total domestic income declined from 1960 through 1980, at the same time that social service spending rose. Education expenditures showed a less consistent longitudinal pattern across nations. In France, West Germany, Sweden, the United Kingdom, and the United States education spending grew larger during each successive seven-year period between 1960 and 1980. Canada spent more on education from 1967 through 1973 rather than during the late 1970s. Italy maintained the same ratio of educational spending throughout the twenty-year period.

From a cross-national perspective the funds allocated to various programs reflect both policymakers' value priorities and a nation's location in the geopolitical environment. As the most militarily powerful member of the North Atlantic Treaty Organization (NATO), the U.S. government has given the highest priority to defense expenditures. During the 1960s spending on defense took a larger share of the GDP than did expenditures on either social services or education. Over the 1960-80 period U.S. officials spent less on social services than did leaders from the other six countries. By contrast, Canadian policymakers, relying on U.S. nuclear forces for protection, allocated fewer funds for defense. Even though social service spending remained low in both North American nations, education assumed a higher priority in Canada. Expenditures in the United Kingdom more closely resembled the U.S. pattern than that of continental Europe. Defense spending was higher than in any other country except the United States. Expenditures for social services ranked third lowest, just ahead of the United States and Canada. Spending on education lagged slightly behind the U.S. figures. Policymakers in France, West Germany, and Italy stressed social service expenditures, especially for old-age pensions. Sweden accorded the highest priority to both social services and education; particularly during the late 1970s it ranked highest on these expenditures. Again Sweden and the United States displayed the greatest budgetary contrasts, with U.S. policymakers concentrating on defense and Swedish officials placing greater emphasis on social services.

Table 2.2

DEFENSE, SOCIAL SERVICE, AND EDUCATION EXPENDITURES AS PERCENTAGES OF GDP, 1960-80

Type of Expenditure

Country	Defense			Social Service[a]			Education[b]		
	1960-66	1967-73	1974-80	1960-66	1967-73	1974-77	1960-66	1967-73	1974-80
Canada	3.7%[c]	2.4%	1.9%	9.5%	12.4%	14.1%	6.0%	8.2%	7.8%
France	5.7	4.3	3.9	14.4	15.1	21.0	3.8	4.6	5.2
West Germany	4.4	3.6	3.4	16.1	17.0	21.7	3.3	3.9	4.7
Italy	3.3	2.9	2.4	12.6	16.0	20.5	4.9	4.9	5.0
Sweden	4.1	3.7	3.3	12.9	18.6	26.5	5.8	7.8	8.4
United Kingdom	6.1	5.1	4.8	10.8	13.0	15.4	4.9	5.6	6.0
United States	8.6	7.9	5.5	7.0	9.4	12.5	5.0	6.3	6.7

Sources: Stockholm International Peace Research Institute (SIPRI), *World Armaments and Disarmament: SIPRI Yearbook 1979* (New York: Crane, Russak, 1979), 36-40; *World Armaments and Disarmament: SIPRI Yearbook 1983* (London: Taylor and Francis, 1983), 171; Olof Palme et al., "Military Spending: The Economic and Social Consequences," *Challenge* 25 (September/October 1982): 8; International Labour Office (ILO), *The Cost of Social Security*, 1961-77 (Geneva, 1967, 1972, 1976, 1979, 1981), table 2; *UNESCO Statistical Yearbook*, various years (Paris, 1964-83).

[a] Social service expenditures include spending on pensions, employment injury benefits, health (sickness-maternity) services, unemployment compensation, family allowances, and public assistance, including aid to war victims.

[b] Education expenditures refer to total public expenditures (current and capital spending) as a percentage of the gross national product (GNP).

[c] Figures are annual averages of the GDP during each seven-year period.

13

In the typical social service state—more developed in Western Europe than in North America—policymakers stress the importance of health care and income maintenance. During 1977 the largest social service expenditures were for medical care and pensions (see Table 2.3). Old-age pensions as a proportion of the GDP were particularly high in West Germany, Italy, and Sweden, but low in Canada, the United Kingdom, and the United States. Canadian officials gave higher priority to comprehensive universal health care services; U.S. leaders, however, downplayed both medical care and pensions. The French government stressed family allowances, a program under which parents with one or more children received a cash grant for child support. Spending for unemployment compensation partly depended on the national jobless rate. Whereas Sweden had low unemployment (under 3 percent), the Canadian unemployment rate never fell below 3.4 percent during the 1960-80 period. Therefore Canadian policymakers spent a larger share of the GDP for unemployment compensation than did Swedish officials. The two major contenders in World War II—Germany and the United States—spent the largest proportion of their national incomes on aid to war victims. General public assistance grants were the highest in Sweden, the United Kingdom, and the United States.

As illustrated by the fairly high expenditures for public assistance but low spending on family allowances, U.S. leaders have preferred means-tested social service programs, whereby claimants must demonstrate a low income before receiving a cash benefit. The other six governments grant child allowances to all families regardless of income, but in the United States these benefits are allocated under public assistance programs. Thus recipients of Aid to Families with Dependent Children (AFDC) are mainly unemployed, poor women in urban areas. In 1977 AFDC benefits totaled about 0.6 percent of the GDP—less than half the family allowance expenditures in continental Europe.[3]

When we examine social service benefits accruing to individuals, Sweden again emerges as the most generous provider (see Table 2.4). In 1980 Swedish public expenditures for health care totaled over $1,000 per individual—the highest figure in the world. During 1981 the typical married manufacturing worker with two children received family allowances that amounted to 12 percent of his disposable

Table 2.3

SOCIAL SERVICE EXPENDITURES AS PERCENTAGES OF GDP, 1977

Country	Type of Expenditure						All Social Services[a]
	Medical Care	Old-Age Pensions	Family Allowances	Unemployment Compensation	Public Assistance	Aid to War Victims	
Canada	5.3%	2.9%	1.0%	1.8%	2.3%	0.3%	14.2%
France	5.6	7.7	2.5	0.6	2.1	0.0	22.5
West Germany	6.5	9.1	1.1	0.9	1.0	1.0	22.4
Italy	4.9	9.9	1.0	0.5	1.1	0.4	20.5
Sweden	8.9	9.2	1.5	0.3	4.7	0.0	29.7
United Kingdom	4.7	5.5	0.5	0.5	2.8	0.2	16.3
United States	3.2	4.6	0.0	0.7	3.1	0.7	12.9

Source: ILO, *The Cost of Social Security: Tenth International Inquiry, 1975-1977,* tables 1, 2, 5, 8, and appendix.

[a] All social expenditures include medical care benefits, pensions, family allowances, unemployment compensation, public assistance, aid to war victims, benefits for public employees (military and civilian), employment injury benefits, and maternity benefits.

Table 2.4

SOCIAL SERVICE BENEFITS FOR INDIVIDUALS

Country	Health Care: Government Expenditures per Individual in U.S. dollars 1980	Family Allowances: Percent of Disposable income[a] 1981	Old-Age Pensions: Percent of Earnings in Year before Retirement[b] 1980
Canada	$ 515	3.4%	49%
France	743	12.4	75
West Germany	884	7.8	49
Italy	418	7.5	69
Sweden	1035	11.7	83
United Kingdom	443	10.4	47
United States	439	0.0	66

Sources: Ruth Leger Sivard, *World Military and Social Expenditures, 1983* (Washington, D.C.: World Priorities, 1983), 37, 39; Organization for Economic Cooperation and Development (OECD), *The 1981 Tax/ Benefit Position of a Typical Worker in OECD Member Countries* (Paris, 1982), 33, 36, 37, 40, 48, 50, 51; Jonathan Aldrich, "The Earnings Replacement Rate of Old-Age Benefits in 12 Countries, 1969-80," *Social Security Bulletin* 45 (November 1982): 5.

[a]The data refer to the family allowance received by a married manufacturing worker with two children. Disposable income indicates annual gross earnings minus income and social security taxes.

[b]The data refer to a retired couple whose wage-earner worked forty years in the manufacturing sector.

income (gross earnings minus income and social security taxes); only a French married couple obtained a slightly larger children's benefit. The Swedish pension system also provides generous retirement benefits. In 1980 a married man who had worked forty years in the manufacturing sector secured a pension equalling 83 percent of his earnings the year before retirement—a higher ratio than in any other Western industrial country. Swedish workers pay taxes on the pension benefits, but employers and the government, rather than the employee, finance the retirement program. Most Swedes retire at age sixty. Those who wish to work a part-time schedule (usually twenty hours a week) from ages sixty through sixty-four receive a partial pension, which amounts to one-half the earnings foregone when an employee transfers to part-time status.[4]

Like government expenditure programs, tax policies express value priorities about government's role in the economy. High taxes and high expenditures imply that policymakers prefer a wide scope of public authority. Lower taxes and expenditures indicate that they seek to restrain government involvement in the economy and to rely on market mechanisms.

The Swedish and U.S. governments are at opposite poles on tax policies, as shown by Table 2.5. Committed to a strong public sector, Swedish officials impose the highest total taxes as a percentage of GDP. These taxes finance the expansive role played by the Swedish government in the economy. Personal income taxes in Sweden raise twice the revenues collected in the United States. Swedish social security contributions and goods and services taxes are also higher. However, taxes on corporate profits and capital gains as a proportion of the GDP are only half as great in Sweden as in the United States. Thus Swedish government leaders try to gain support from both business and labor. Although businesses must pay high social security taxes, comparatively low corporate income taxes help stimulate capital investment. Employees pay high income taxes, but they receive comprehensive, generous social service benefits.

West German officials extract lower personal income taxes from the citizenry, but other features of the German tax system resemble the Swedish pattern. For example, corporate income taxes are a small share of the GDP, and total revenues from social security contributions and value-added taxes, which are levied at each stage of the production and distribution of a good or service, are similar to Sweden's.

Although the United Kingdom raises higher overall tax revenues than does Canada, the two countries implement similar tax policies. They collect the highest revenues from personal income and taxes on goods and services. Corporate income taxes are higher than in continental Europe. Social security contributions remain the lowest among the seven nations.

17

Table 2.5

TAX REVENUES AS PERCENTAGES OF GDP, 1960-80

Country	Type of Tax	1960-66	1967-73	1974-80
Canada	Personal income	5.9%[a]	9.5%	10.8%
	Corporate income	3.9	3.7	3.9
	Social security	1.7	2.8	3.4
	Goods and services[b]	10.2	10.4	10.6
	Total tax revenues	25.3	31.0	32.4
France	Personal income	3.9	4.1	5.0
	Corporate income	1.9	1.9	2.2
	Social security	11.2	13.0	16.3
	Goods and services	12.8	13.3	12.5
	Total tax revenues	33.7	35.5	39.4
West Germany	Personal income	8.0	9.3	11.2
	Corporate income	2.5	2.0	1.9
	Social security	8.6	10.0	12.5
	Goods and services	10.6	10.4	9.7
	Total tax revenues	32.0	33.6	37.0
Italy	Personal income	3.1	3.2	6.0
	Corporate income	2.0	2.0	2.2
	Social security	9.2	10.5	12.1
	Goods and services	10.7	10.4	8.8
	Total tax revenues	27.0	28.1	30.3
Sweden	Personal income	15.1	19.0	20.7
	Corporate income	1.9	1.8	1.6
	Social security	3.5	6.2	11.8
	Goods and services	10.9	12.5	11.8
	Total tax revenues	32.3	40.7	48.2
United Kingdom	Personal income	9.2	10.9	12.0
	Corporate income	2.2	2.8	2.5
	Social security	4.3	5.1	6.2
	Goods and services	10.2	10.1	9.4
	Total tax revenues	30.0	34.7	35.1
United States	Personal income	8.6	9.8	10.5
	Corporate income	4.5	3.8	3.3
	Social security	4.3	5.7	7.5
	Goods and services	5.4	5.6	5.3
	Total tax revenues	26.8	29.1	30.3

Sources: OECD: *Revenue Statistics of OECD Member Countries, 1965-1981* (Paris, 1982), 68-79, 203; *Revenue Statistics of OECD Member Countries, 1965-1980* (Paris, 1981), 79-86; *National Accounts of OECD Countries, 1960-1977*, vol. 2 (Paris, 1979), table 9 for each nation.

[a]Figures are annual averages of tax revenues during each seven-year period. Data refer to all levels of government (central, state/provincial, local), social security agencies, and public enterprises.

[b]Taxes on goods and services include general sales taxes, value-added taxes, excise taxes, and taxes on the import and export of goods.

By contrast, France and Italy place the greatest reliance on social security taxes; neither personal nor corporate income taxes constitute an important revenue source. These two governments depend on value-added taxes to finance most government programs except pensions, health care, and unemployment compensation. The major contrast between French and Italian tax policies stems from the relative strength of the two states. French officials have long directed a more centralized, coordinated government, whereas Italians live under a relatively weak one. Hence total tax receipts are far higher in France than in Italy; indeed from 1965 through 1980 France had the highest tax revenues of any nation except Sweden. Italy, along with the United States, had the lowest overall taxation.

Between 1960 and 1980 total tax revenues rose in all seven countries. Sweden faced the largest increases, while the United States and Italy had the smallest. Particularly in Canada, the United Kingdom, and the United States the greatest growth in overall tax receipts occurred during the 1960s. As the recession grew more severe after 1973, anti-tax sentiments among the citizenry deterred officials from enacting large tax increases, although in France and West Germany taxes increased more during the 1970s than in the previous decade. In all seven countries throughout the 1960-80 period both personal income and social security taxes showed the steepest growth; taxes on goods and services either remained the same or fell slightly. In five countries corporate income taxes held about constant over this period; in West Germany and especially the United States taxes on corporate profits and capital gains declined sharply.

Besides rising taxes, increasing employment in government agencies has marked the growth of the Western welfare state. The "public sector" includes government agencies at all levels (central, regional, local), public financial institutions, and public corporations (enterprises that are both owned and controlled by government institutions and that sell goods on the market). As Table 2.6 shows, Sweden has the highest proportion of the labor force employed in the public sector—over 37 percent during the late 1970s. Sweden has also experienced the fastest rise in public employment: from 13 percent of the labor force in general government (i.e., all levels of government) in 1960 to over 30 percent in 1980. By contrast, the United States has had a much smaller growth in public employment; indeed during the 1970s it was the only nation in which the public sector diminished.

19

Table 2.6

PERCENTAGE OF TOTAL LABOR FORCE EMPLOYED BY GOVERNMENT,
1970 AND 1978

Country	General Government[a]		Public Corporations[b]		Total Public Employment	
	1970	1978	1970	1978	1970	1978
Canada	19.5%	19.8%	4.3%	4.6%	23.8%	24.4%
France	12.4	14.2	8.0	9.0[c]	20.4	23.2[c]
West Germany	11.2	14.5	7.7	7.8	18.9	22.3
Italy	10.9	14.2	4.9	6.3	15.8	20.5
Sweden	20.6	29.0	6.6	8.2[d]	27.2	37.2[d]
United Kingdom	18.0	21.4	8.2	8.3	26.2	29.7
United States	18.0	16.8	1.6	1.5	19.6	18.3

Sources: OECD, *Employment in the Public Sector* (Paris, 1982), 9, 12, 79;
"Big Government—How Big Is It?" *OECD Observer*, no. 121 (March
1983): 9, 10; Göran Therborn, "The Prospects of Labour and the
Transformation of Advanced Capitalism," *New Left Review*, no. 145
(May-June 1984): 34.

[a]General government includes central, state/provincial, and local departments
and agencies that produce nonmarket goods and services, such as public administration, defense, health, education, and welfare.

[b]Public corporations are government-owned enterprises that produce and sell
goods and services in the market.

[c]Figure for 1979.

[d]Figure for 1977.

In 1960 nearly 16 percent of the total labor force was employed in
general government, primarily in local and state agencies. In 1970 that
share rose to 18 percent, but it fell in 1980 to less than 17 percent.
During the late 1970s only 1.5 percent of U.S. employees worked in
public enterprises—compared with over 8 percent of Swedes.

The other European nations and Canada have seen only modest
rises in public employment. In Canada total public employment in
both general government and public corporations remained about

constant (22-24 percent) from 1960 through 1980; the most marked trend was a decline of federal government workers as a share of total employment and a growing proportion of municipal and especially provincial government employees, most of whom worked in education, health care, or public enterprises. In Western Europe the public sector gradually increased during the 1970s, although after 1975 the growth in total government employment began to decelerate. By 1980 nearly 30 percent of the labor force worked for the public sector in the United Kingdom, as did around 20-25 percent in France, West Germany, and Italy.[5]

CRITIQUES OF THE WELFARE STATE

The growth of the welfare state has provoked challenges from both neoclassical market economists and Marxist theorists. In the following two sections we shall analyze each challenge in turn.

THE NEOCLASSICAL CRITIQUE

Taking an individualistic perspective, neoclassicists support price competition, private enterprise, free trade, and a laissez-faire economic policy; for them government intervention in the competitive market brings harmful results. Market theorists like Friedrich Hayek, Daniel Usher, and Milton Friedman perceive that the welfare state leads to lower economic efficiency and less individual political freedom. By enacting high taxes, authorizing large expenditures for social services, establishing overmanned bureaucracies, formulating detailed regulations over private market activities, making plans for the total economy, and pandering to particularistic interest group pressures, welfare state officials decrease savings, deter industrial investment, diminish growth rates, and reduce the incentive to work hard. According to Hayek, certain features of the contemporary welfare state—central economic planning, public ownership of enterprises, an egalitarian redistribution of wealth through progressive taxes, and high government expenditures for social services—lead down "the road to serfdom." He has written:

> Though we may have speeded up a little the conquest of want, disease, ignorance, squalor, and idleness, we may in the future do

worse even in that struggle when the chief dangers will come from inflation, paralyzing taxation, coercive labor unions, an ever increasing dominance of government in education, and a social service bureaucracy with far-reaching arbitrary powers—dangers from which the individual cannot escape by his own efforts and which the momentum of the overextended machinery of government is likely to increase rather than mitigate.[6]

The Conservative Thatcher government in the United Kingdom and the Reagan administration in Washington view the crisis of the welfare state in neoclassical terms.

How valid is this neoclassical critique of the welfare state crisis? To what extent does the welfare state actually undermine economic efficiency and civil liberties? Economic efficiency is difficult to define and measure for an entire economy rather than for a particular firm. Generally it refers to input/output ratios—that is, the greatest output (manufactured goods) vis-à-vis input (labor time). Applied to the manufacturing sector of Western industrial societies, efficiency designates labor productivity, as measured by output per employee-hour.* According to this criterion, from 1960 through 1980 Italy, France, West Germany, and Sweden—all nations with high expenditures for social services—attained the highest manufacturing labor productivity, averaging yearly increases in output per hour of 5 percent and more (see Table 2.7). By contrast, the welfare state "laggards"—Canada, the United Kingdom, and especially the United States—achieved the lowest gains (between 2.6 and 3.6 percent). During the 1960-80 period all seven nations had declining labor productivity, especially after 1973. Sweden and the United Kingdom faced particularly steep drops. Yet even during the recessionary period (1974-80) gains in output among Swedish manufacturing workers were nearly twice as high as among workers in the United States.

Falling productivity and cross-national variations in efficiency stem from variables other than government expenditures for social services. Manufacturing productivity declined in all seven nations mainly because of the recession after 1973: sluggish demand for manufactured goods meant that factories operated at less than full capacity (under 80 percent of potential), and unemployment rose.

*Labor productivity depends on plant capacity usage, managerial performance, workers' attitudes and skills, capital investment, and energy use.

Table 2.7

CHANGES IN MANUFACTURING PRODUCTIVITY, 1960-80
(Percent)

Country	1960-66	1967-73	1974-80	1960-80
Canada	4.3%[a]	5.0%	1.6%	3.6%
France	5.5	6.0	4.6	5.4
West Germany	5.9	5.3	4.6	5.3
Italy	7.3	7.1	3.7	6.1
Sweden	5.8	6.7	2.3	5.0
United Kingdom	4.1	4.7	1.7	3.5
United States	3.4	3.0	1.3	2.6

Source: U.S. Department of Labor, Bureau of Labor Statistics, *Handbook of Labor Statistics*, Bulletin 2175 (December 1983), 426.

[a]Figures are average annual percentages of changes in output per hour for each seven-year period and for 1960-80 era.

The price of oil charged by the Organization of Petroleum Exporting Countries (OPEC) escalated after 1973.* Decreasing plant capacity use, growing unemployment, and soaring oil prices led to declining efficiency. Rising expenditures for social services played a relatively unimportant part.

Managerial attitudes and the use of physical capital are the crucial factors explaining cross-national variations in labor productivity. In contrast to managers in France, West Germany, Italy, and Sweden, Canadian, British, and U.S. executives have placed less emphasis on worker consultations with management. Manufacturing workers there have lower job security than on the European continent; they have less influence over job training, occupational responsibilities, and ways to improve productivity. Rather than seeking suggestions from workers about techniques for raising efficiency, North American and British managers concentrate on disciplining and controlling the labor force. They also devote less attention than continental European managers to using capital investment effectively in promoting export

*In the 1970s OPEC increased its prices for crude oil—in 1973-74 (from $2.50 to nearly $12 a barrel), and in 1979-80 (from $14.55 to $26 a barrel).

sales.[7] The evidence suggests that the neoclassicists exaggerate the deleterious effects of the modern social service state on economic efficiency.

Neoclassical theorists like Friedrich Hayek also mistakenly assume that the welfare state is headed down "the road to serfdom" and political dictatorship. If we equate civil liberties with universal suffrage, electoral competition, lack of press censorship, a nondictatorial police and military, and rights for an opposition to speak, assemble, and organize, then the contemporary social service states rank highest on worldwide civil liberties scales. According to a study conducted by Ivo K. Feierabend, Betty Nesvold, and Rosalind L. Feierabend on seventy-three nations, the countries with the lowest government coercion between 1945 and 1966 were (in rank order) Iceland, Luxembourg, New Zealand, Norway, Sweden, Finland, Ireland, the United States, the Netherlands, Belgium, Canada, the United Kingdom, and Italy. All these societies are highly industrialized, and Social Democratic parties are strong in most. In all thirteen, social service expenditures in 1977 amounted to over 10 percent of the GDP; in all cases except Canada, Iceland, and the United States they averaged over 15 percent. Rising expenditures for social service benefits have hardly diminished these governments' commitment to political freedom. Research during the 1970s confirms the civil liberties rankings found by Feierabend, Nesvold, and Feierabend.[8]

Neoclassical critics of the welfare state exaggerate the dangers from an oppressive government bureaucracy. Except for the Italian senior civil servants who entered the government during Fascist rule, most bureaucrats in these seven countries support political liberty, pluralism, and political equality. They seek to mediate policy differences among legislators, citizens, and interest group leaders. They rule by consensus, not coercion. For example, although the Swedish civil servants play an important role in both formulating and implementing economic policies, they hardly oppress other participants. Instead they try to accommodate group conflicts. They consult widely with legislators, citizens, and representatives from both business organizations and labor unions. Rather than ruling arbitrarily, as Hayek fears, they make decisions through orderly procedures. Local government in Sweden remains powerful. County and city governments retain fiscal independence from the central government; locally raised taxes finance health and education programs. Rather than imposing their will on local leaders, the Swedish civil servants negotiate with the elected local leadership. Even the much maligned French bureaucracy does not rule in an arbitrary or oppressive way. Despite the stereotype of the centralized French state, the national bureaucracy is pluralistic—indeed riven with factions. French regionalism and local ties remain strong. The civil servants mediate between powerful local leaders and central cabinet ministers. These bureaucrats want to keep the support of local leaders like mayors, who often retain power for longer periods than cabinet ministers.[9]

THE MARXIST CRITIQUE

Like the neoclassicists, Marxist theorists perceive a severe crisis stemming from the growth of the welfare state, although they view the welfare state differently. Whereas neoclassical economists assume that the welfare state marks a retreat into feudalism, Marxists view it as a transition between capitalism and socialism. They consider that democratic socialism will bring enhanced employee participation at the workplace and will involve control over basic economic activities: the investment of money and capital, the use of capital equipment, and the performance of the labor force. Unlike laissez-faire economists, who perceive the welfare state in negative terms, Marxists like James O'Connor and Ian Gough see both positive and negative features. On the one hand, the health services, educational opportunities, and pensions in a welfare state enhance individual well-being; on the other hand, the state seeks social control, discipline over the labor force, and mass conformity—mainly in abortive attempts to maintain high growth rates, capital accumulation, and favorable profits for the private business sector. Marxists dispute the neoclassical contention that the burgeoning welfare state alone has caused the capitalist crisis, but they concede that it partly contributes to the economic stagnation now affecting Western industrial societies.

According to the Marxists, the dilemmas or "contradictions" faced by capitalist systems became more severe during the 1970s. ("Contradictions" refer to conflicts that maintain an economic system in the short run but lead to systemic disintegration over the long run.) Expanding social service benefits helped maintain social peace and high total demand for goods and services sold by capitalist firms. Yet growing social welfare expenditures also caused lower profits, lower investment, and hence lower growth. In O'Connor's view, the capitalist state became subject to a contradiction between opposing needs: capital accumulation vs. legitimation. On the one hand, government leaders must create the conditions that facilitate high profits and investment, especially for oligopolies. These conditions can be met through business subsidies and low taxes on business. On the other hand, the government must promote social harmony and pacify those who bear the burdens of capitalist growth—e.g., the unemployed, the marginal workers, and the poor. Pension, unemployment compensation, and health care policies can help retain popular support for the capitalist economy. Yet these policies arouse resentment—not only from big businesses, who fear that lower profits will ensue from overly generous concessions to the working class, but also from smaller, more competitive businesses, who can less easily charge higher prices to cover increased social service contributions. Moreover, social service policies can also lead to a backlash by voters who feel overburdened by high taxation. Particularly if regressive taxes are the major means to raise revenues, even working poor people will join the backlash against the welfare state. Under such pressures government leaders will be reluctant to increase taxes but will continue to finance expenditures. Deficit budgets will result. Even in social democracies leaders cannot easily reconcile this contradiction between accumulation and legitimation.[10]

How valid is the Marxist claim that the welfare state leads to high fiscal deficits, diminished investment, and a populist backlash against increased social service expenditures? Marxists exaggerate the dilemmas faced by the contemporary welfare state. After 1974 most Western governments experienced growing fiscal problems. As measured by the difference between current government receipts and current expenditures at all government levels, budget deficits became more common than during the 1960s (see Table 2.8). Yet only in Italy were deficits a high proportion of the GDP, averaging 5 percent between 1973 and 1980. Among the six other nations the largest deficits or smallest surpluses were accumulated by the United States, United Kingdom, and Canada—governments in which the welfare state is least developed. Until the early 1980s France, West Germany, and Sweden had budget surpluses. Particularly in Sweden these surpluses amounted to a high proportion of the national income.

Table 2.8

FISCAL SURPLUSES AND DEFICITS AS PERCENTAGES OF GDP

Country	Years	Current Receipts[a]	Current Disbursements	Amount of Surplus or Deficit[b]
Canada	1960-66	27.4%[c]	25.6%	+1.8%
	1967-73	34.3	31.1	+3.2
	1974-80	36.8	36.5	+0.3
France	1960-66	37.0	32.8	+4.2
	1967-73	38.7	34.6	+4.1
	1974-80	42.3	40.4	+1.9
West Germany	1960-66	35.8	29.4	+6.4
	1967-73	38.1	33.1	+5.0
	1974-80	42.4	40.7	+1.7
Italy	1960-66	29.5	27.9	+1.6
	1967-73	30.9	32.0	- 1.1
	1974-80	34.0	39.0	- 5.0
Sweden	1960-66	36.5	28.9	+7.6
	1967-73	46.9	37.5	+9.4
	1974-80	55.0	50.9	+4.1
United Kingdom	1960-66	32.3	30.7	+1.6
	1967-73	38.1	33.6	+4.5
	1974-80	39.7	40.3	- 0.6
United States	1960-66	27.5	26.1	+1.4
	1967-73	30.2	29.5	+0.7
	1974-80	31.9	32.1	- 0.2

Sources: OECD, *OECD Economic Outlook*, no. 31 (July 1982): 148, 150; *National Accounts of OECD Countries, 1963-1980*, vol. 2 (Paris, 1982), table 9 for each country.

[a]Current receipts include taxes, social security contributions, operating surplus, property income receivable, compulsory fees, and employee welfare contributions.

[b]Fiscal surpluses or deficits are current receipts minus current disbursements. A plus sign indicates a surplus; a minus sign indicates a deficit.

[c]Figures are average annual percentages for each seven-year period. They refer to all levels of government.

Marxists, including O'Connor and Gough, mistakenly assume a tradeoff between welfare state expenditures and spending on capital accumulation. Presumably, as social service benefits increase as a share of the total national income, spending declines on gross fixed capital formation (investment in plants, equipment, machinery, buildings, and repair and maintenance of capital stock). Decreasing profits deter capitalists from expanding investment. Between 1955 and 1980 the rate of return on manufacturing investment fell in most Western nations, especially West Germany and the United Kingdom; Canada, Italy, and Sweden showed more modest drops in profits. However, the United States did not experience decreasing rates of return in these years. Manufacturing profits were about as high in 1976 as in 1955. Only during the early 1980s did the rate of return on capital fall. Despite the declining profits for European manufacturers, investment spending from 1960 through 1980 remained about the same in most nations. As shown in Table 2-9, only in Italy, Sweden, and especially West Germany did the share of the GDP allocated to gross fixed capital formation decrease. In Canada, the United Kingdom, and the

Table 2.9

GROSS FIXED CAPITAL FORMATION[a]
(Percentages of GDP)

Country	1960-66	1967-73	1974-80
Canada	22.0%[b]	21.8%	23.0%
France	22.1	23.6	22.5
West Germany	25.5	24.5	21.6
Italy	22.0	20.5	20.0
Sweden	23.7	23.0	20.6
United Kingdom	17.5	18.7	18.6
United States	18.0	18.3	18.3

Source: OECD Economic Outlook, no. 31 (July 1982): 144.

[a]Gross fixed capital formation is a measure of investment. It includes expenditures for plants, equipment, machinery, buildings, and the repair and maintenance of capital stock.

[b]Figures are average annual percentages for each seven-year period.

United States it actually increased somewhat; it was higher during the 1970s than the 1960s, when social service expenditures were lower. Yet the United Kingdom and the United States spent a lower share on capital formation than did the four continental European nations, which had larger expenditures for both investment and social services.[11]

Marxist economists, like some neoclassical theorists, overestimate the severity of the backlash that will strike the welfare state when recession occurs.[12] Of course most citizens in Western societies resent paying higher taxes; regressive taxation particularly afflicts the poor. Most of them oppose granting social service benefits to the "undeserving." High salaries to government bureaucrats also arouse resentment, as do policy measures to secure income equality between "producers" and "nonproducers." Yet such anti-welfare state sentiments attract greatest support in the United States, the United Kingdom, and Canada (especially Alberta province), where governments implement the least generous social service programs. In these countries the ideology of individualism and self-reliance remains strong. A high proportion of their citizens view laziness, thriftlessness, alcoholism, and a failure to take advantage of opportunities as the main reasons for poverty and unemployment. Organizations articulating individualistic attitudes wield extensive political power, as evidenced by the strength of business corporations and right-wing parties (Progressive-Conservatives in Alberta, British Conservatives, U.S. Republicans). Organizations that demonstrate greater support for the welfare state--e.g., centralized industrial unions and cohesive labor or Social Democratic parties--exercise less control over the policy process. In the four other countries collectivist explanations for poverty and unemployment seem more widespread. The French, Germans, Italians, and Swedes blame their personal economic miseries primarily on social injustice, a deprived environment, a lack of education, unfair public policies, misguided political leaders, private corporations, or world economic pressures. Particularly in West Germany and Sweden powerful industrial unions and Social Democratic parties persuade policymakers to implement generous, comprehensive social service programs.

Despite the greater strength of industrial unions, leftist parties, and collectivist attitudes in continental European nations, popular support for the welfare state remains high in nearly every Western country. As expected, voters in France, West Germany, Italy, and especially Sweden enthusiastically back the welfare state. During the late 1970s and early 1980s Swedish citizens generally favored expanding egalitarian social service programs, such as day-care centers, health and dental service, assistance for the elderly, and old-age pensions. Although most Swedes opposed a tax increase, a slight majority also rejected a tax cut that would have reduced government services. West Germans showed the greatest support for government expenditures on old-age pensions, family allowances, medical care, and education. As in Sweden, spending on defense and economic assistance to Third World countries aroused the least enthusiasm. French and Italian voters strongly believe that government assurance of employment and medical care is a basic human right, rather than a privilege granted by the state.

In the tradeoff between higher expenditures and tax reductions, even in the United States and United Kingdom citizens leaned toward higher taxes for social service benefits. In 1980, when Ronald Reagan won the presidential election, only one-quarter of the U.S. public favored reducing government expenditures for social services, especially for Medicare and social security. Most opposed reductions in social security taxes if the reductions caused lower retirement benefits. Around two-thirds favored a comprehensive national health insurance plan and a federal government jobs program for the unemployed. By 1982, when inflation rates had declined but unemployment had increased, over half the U.S. population supported higher federal government expenditures for job training, health care, and education; only 10-20 percent believed that the government should reduce spending on these programs. Most citizens were more eager to maintain these benefits than to cut taxes. Similarly British voters during the early 1980s sought higher expenditures for the National Health Service, education, old-age pensions, and job training for the unemployed—even if higher taxes were needed to finance these policies. Most rejected tax decreases that reduced social services.[13]

EFFECTS OF THE ECONOMIC CRISIS ON ELECTORAL OUTCOMES

If popular attitudes still favor welfare state policies, why did the conservative parties win elections in Canada (1979), West Germany

(1983), Italy (1983), the United Kingdom (1979, 1983), and the United States (1980)? What variables explain the parliamentary victories of leftist parties over incumbent conservative governments in Canada (1980), France (1981), and Sweden (1982)?

Three general reasons explain these electoral outcomes. First, the objective economic situation influences voting behavior. If a nation faces high unemployment rates, high price increases, and low increases in real disposable income, voters may strike out against the incumbent parties that control the government. Both high national rates of unemployment and inflation as well as rapid increases in these rates may displease voters. The economic situation of individuals and families also affects the vote. If they are devastated by unemployment, rising prices, and declining disposable income, they will feel strongly compelled to vote the "rascals" out of office.

Second, voting behavior depends on individual *perceptions* of economic conditions. During times of economic stability, noneconomic issues--e.g., foreign policy, crime, ecology--may have greater importance to the citizenry because neither unemployment rates nor price increases make a great difference to most voters. Moreover, even if unemployment and inflation are salient concerns, people may blame national or personal economic fortunes on sources other than the incumbent government: *fate* ("That's the way things are"); the *individual* (personal laziness causes unemployment; greedy consumption leads to inflation); and *collectivities* (business corporations, labor unions, OPEC, the Japanese, or world economic pressures). Only if voters blame the government will the incumbents lose office. (Of course when several parties form a coalition government, policy responsibilities are dispersed among several agencies, and external events like OPEC price hikes cause economic grief, then citizens will not easily know whom to blame.) Finally, a decision to vote for or against the governing parties depends on individual perceptions about the competence of opposition parties to resolve economic problems that voters regard as important. We assume here that voters have clear perceptions about parties' economic platforms and about past performance of the government in power. If individuals believe that competing parties hold divergent policy preferences, that party control over public policymaking makes a difference, and that changes in party control of government will improve economic conditions, they may vote against the incumbent leaders.

Third, the policy cohesion within the major political parties affects electoral outcomes. During the last two decades policy splits have riven both right- and left-wing parties. On the right "moderate" and "rightist" factions contend for influence within the Conservative, Christian Democratic, and Republican parties. The moderate wing prefers to maintain government social service benefits, cooperate with labor unions, expand public employment, reduce unemployment, grant government subsidies to private businesses threatened with bankruptcy, and ensure that government assumes an active role in managing the economy. The rightist faction wants to reduce welfare benefits, limit trade union power, lower government employment, reduce inflation, deny government assistance to failing private enterprises, and rely on the market and individual initiative for securing a prosperous, efficient economy. On the left "centrist" and "leftist" factions have polarized parties such as the U.S. Democrats, Canadian Liberals, British Labour, and European Social Democrats. Particularly during inflationary times, the "centrists" place their policy priorities on austerity (low increases in the money supply, high interest rates, reduced expenditures for social services), reduced wage increases, rapid economic growth, equality of opportunity, the maintenance of existing defense alliances and weapons, and governance by legislators, cabinet ministers, and civil servants. The "leftists" seek higher government spending for social services, limits on profits rather than on wages, a clean environment, more equal income, nuclear disarmament, and expanded popular control over political decision-making.

In contemporary Western democracies partisan attitudes and identifications shape individual voting behavior and perceptions of economic conditions. For example, Social Democratic voters, compared with Christian Democrats, will more likely believe that an incumbent Social Democratic administration has competently managed the economy. Moreover, past electoral support for a party strongly influences voting behavior. Hence the degree of fragmentation within a party will have a crucial impact on the election. If an incumbent party is highly fragmented, it will face difficulties gaining support from swing voters. When voters with weak partisan loyalties confront too many conflicting policy stimuli, they may switch to an opposition party that more clearly articulates the policy preferences held by many swing voters. Thus if an opposition party achieves greater cohesion, it increases its chances to win an election.[14]

The 1979 victory of the British Conservative party illustrates these three general reasons for electoral outcomes. During the early months of 1979, when the Labour party controlled the government, the inflation rate was over 12 percent; nearly 6 percent of the labor force was jobless. British voters saw inflation, not unemployment, as the most important problem facing their society. Judging that the trade unions had gained too much power, most citizens strongly opposed the strikes that occurred during the winter of 1978-79 and held the Labour party and its union allies responsible for high inflation. Beset by these economic problems, the Labour party failed to agree on a strategy for reducing price increases, lowering unemployment, and increasing growth rates. Some Labour leaders, particularly those in the cabinet, sought greater austerity, especially limits on wage increases. Labourites on the "back bench" preferred to limit profits, expand government ownership of industries, raise social service benefits, and secure greater income equality. By contrast, the Conservative party attained policy cohesion behind the leadership of Margaret Thatcher, who sought to reduce trade union power, limit wage increases, deter strikes, and rely on private enterprise and individual initiative to achieve prosperity. As a result, the Conservatives won the 1979 parliamentary election, gaining over 40 percent of the votes of skilled blue-collar workers—a group that used to vote for the Labour candidates.

During the next four years of Conservative party rule (1979-83) the economic situation scarcely improved. The Thatcher government enacted higher real interest rates, reduced taxes on the wealthy, raised the value-added tax, levied higher taxes on contributions to the National Insurance Fund, increased charges for prescription drugs bought through the National Health Service, raised expenditures for the military and the police, and lowered spending on home help services, job training, public rental housing, public transportation, and education. Partly as a result, unemployment soared to over 13 percent in 1983; workers in the private manufacturing sector were especially hard hit. Many private firms went bankrupt. British corporations continued to face difficulties selling their exports on the world market. Because of the deflationary policies and reduced total demand, the inflation rate fell to only 4 percent.

Despite the continuing economic difficulties, the Conservatives returned to power in 1983 with a greater share of seats in the House of Commons than before (61 percent versus around 53 percent in late 1979). They won 43.5 percent of the British popular vote, compared with only 28 percent for Labour and 26 percent for a Liberal/ Social Democratic alliance.

Why did the Tories emerge victorious in 1983? Even though the inflation rate had dropped, the unemployment rate had doubled under the Conservative administration. Voters perceived that unemployment was a more salient political issue than inflation. Nevertheless, most citizens took a fatalistic view toward unemployment. Only one-fifth believed that the Thatcher government policies had caused the high jobless rates. Few expected unemployment rates to decline quickly, whichever party held government power. Most assumed that lower unemployment would bring back higher inflation. Although only a bare majority expressed satisfaction with Thatcher's leadership, few voters perceived that the Labour party leader, Michael Foot, would make a competent prime minister. Moreover, whereas most Conservatives united behind the Thatcher policies, the opposition parties were highly fragmented. Liberal/Social Democratic party activists disagreed about economic and foreign policy issues. Within the Labour party there was even greater fragmentation. Key leaders campaigned against some major planks in the party manifesto, especially sections dealing with nationalization, wage restraints, defense, and membership in the European Common Market. Because of the fragmentation, only three-fourths of Labour party identifiers—compared with 90 percent of Conservative identifiers—chose a candidate from their party to the House of Commons. Around one-third of trade union members, semi-skilled employees, and unskilled workers supported the Conservatives. Only 33 percent of skilled manual workers voted for Labour. Opposed to the Labour party's backing for wage equality, nationalization, and assistance to ethnic minorities, skilled workers preferred Conservative policies that brought lower mortgage interest rates, tax relief for home buyers, and higher expenditures for pensions.[15]

In West Germany as well, policy fragmentation befell the leftist Social Democratic Party (SPD); hence the conservative Christian Democratic Union (CDU) allied with the Bavarian Christian Social Union (CSU) won the March 1983 elections to the Bundestag, the lower house of the federal parliament. Since 1969 the SPD and Free Democratic Party (FDP) had governed as a coalition administration.

In September 1982, however, that coalition disintegrated. Whereas "liberal" Free Democrats wanted to maintain the alliance with the Social Democrats, "conservative" leaders within the FDP sought an alliance with the CDU. The SPD split between a more youthful "leftist" wing and an older "moderate" faction. The FDP joined the CDU to form a new government, and CDU leader Helmut Kohl became chancellor.

Under the SPD/FDP administration the unemployment rate had grown to nearly 7 percent by 1982—the highest rate since the early 1950s. Consumer prices that year increased about 5 percent—a relatively low rise. Although during past elections voters concerned about unemployment had voted for the SPD, the thirteen years of SPD rule had disillusioned them about the ability of the SPD to reduce the high jobless rates. They perceived that the CDU would be more competent to handle economic issues, especially inflation, the government deficit, unemployment, and vocational training for youths. Thus many former supporters of the SPD deserted to the CDU, which promised greater reliance on private enterprise to reinvigorate the economy.

The fragmentation within the SPD also caused a decline in electoral support. The younger SPD members identified with issues articulated by the Green party: sexual equality, expanded popular political participation, worker involvement in economic management, environmental protection, and nuclear disarmament—i.e., issues that appealed to well-educated urban youth. The older SPD party elite and industrial workers gave higher priority to expanding economic growth, maintaining low inflation, encouraging greater investment by private enterprises, and reducing unemployment. Thus whereas in 1980 the SPD had won 43 percent of the popular vote, in 1983 that figure fell to 38 percent. The CDU/CSU coalition increased their vote by 4 percent. The SPD lost support from both the urban youth, who swung over to the Green party, and industrial workers, who cast their lot with the CDU.[16]

Both economic conditions and party cohesion have shaped electoral outcomes in Italy. Partly because of policy fragmentation among the two major leftist parties—the Partito Comunista Italiano (PCI) and the Partito Socialista Italiano (PSI)—the conservative Christian Democratic party has governed Italy since the end of World War II. However, it has failed to produce impressive economic results. During the late 1970s and early 1980s the unemployment rate remained under 10 percent, but the real hourly compensation of factory workers increased by less than 2 percent annually (compared with nearly 8 percent in the 1960s and early 1970s). Annual consumer price rises surged to double-digit figures—the highest inflation rate among the seven nations in our study. Taking a cynical attitude toward politics, most Italians doubted the ability of any party to markedly improve the economic situation. Thus despite these difficulties, the Christian Democrats won the largest number of votes in the 1979 and 1983 elections to the Chamber of Deputies. Although the PSI and PCI often form coalition governments at the city and regional levels, in the national legislature most PSI leaders have refused to ally with the PCI.

Because of the PCI's factional divisions and its inability to form a coalition with the Christian Democrats, it has failed to gain control of the national government. The national PCI leaders adopted an austerity policy from 1976 through early 1979. They opposed wage increases that exceeded the cost-of-living index, downplayed the need for greater wage equality, promoted more material incentives for skilled workers, and encouraged higher productivity from the workers. Even though the Christian Democrats refused the PCI a place in the government, PCI leaders supported the government on key votes in the parliament. Yet this "historic compromise" failed. PCI activists, both section leaders and particularly party members, rebelled against the compromise strategy. Industrial workers resented the wage restraint policy. Opposed to a bureaucratic state, some radical youth rejected the PCI's support for punitive actions against the Red Brigades, an organization that used violence against state officials. The lack of enthusiasm for its compromise strategy led the PCI back into the opposition in early 1979. In the 1979 parliamentary elections it won only 30 percent of the vote to the Chamber of Deputies—a 4 percent drop from its 1976 record high. In 1983 it managed to hold slightly under 30 percent of the parliamentary vote—mainly by retaining urban working class support.

In the 1983 election the Christian Democrats suffered the greatest losses—from 38 percent of the vote in 1979 to only 33 percent in 1983. Disillusioned by the double-digit inflation and government corruption, many former Christian Democratic voters switched to the Republicans, Liberals, or neo-Fascist candidates of the Movimento Sociale Italiano. The PSI increased its electoral margin from 9.8 to 11.4 percent between 1979 and 1983. Faced with such a setback, the Christian Democrats formed a new coalition government with the PSI, Social Democrats, Republicans, and Liberals and agreed to let PSI leader Bettino Craxi become prime minister.

The PCI faces a dilemma between forming coalitions and mobilizing popular support. On the one hand, if it aligns with the Christian Democrats, backs an economic austerity program, and makes accommodations with the establishment, it loses support from workers, trade unionists, radical youth, and party militants who seek faster transformations of Italian society. On the other hand, if it pursues a more aggressive strategy for gaining political power and stresses the need for fundamental change, it loses support from lower middle-class groups, church-going Catholics, and Southerners.[17]

Although the United States has neither a powerful Socialist nor Communist party, the Democrats seem plagued by similar policy splits that divide the Italian leftists; for this reason, along with a deteriorating economic situation, they lost the 1980 presidential election. During the administration of Jimmy Carter the inflation rate had risen each successive year, reaching 13.5 percent in 1980. The jobless rate fell from 1977 through 1979, but it increased in 1980. The real hourly compensation of employees declined in 1979 and 1980. By 1980 most voters perceived that inflation was the major issue facing the nation. To dampen the inflationary pressures, the Carter administration advocated an austerity program: reduced budget expenditures, higher interest rates, and lower increases in the money supply. Despite this attempt to curb inflation, most people still perceived President Carter as an ineffective leader unable to cope with either inflation or unemployment. According to them, Republican challenger Ronald Reagan, rather than Carter, could provide stronger leadership, control the inflationary surge, and solve national economic problems.

Carter lost crucial support among Democratic voters who felt that their economic position had worsened during the last year. Particularly in northeastern and midwestern cities, workers in the automobile, steel, and construction industries faced high unemployment. Throughout the nation many manual workers, trade unionists, and voters who weakly identified with the Democratic party or who viewed themselves as "independent Democrats" held Carter responsible for the rising prices and jobless rates.

Even some "liberal" Democrats who strongly identified with the party became disillusioned with the Carter economic policies. Perceiving unemployment, not inflation, as the key economic issue, liberal Democratic activists wanted the Carter administration to commit itself more firmly to equality for blacks, women, and the poor. They felt the federal government should expand expenditures for jobs, health care, and education but reduce spending on defense.

The Republican party attained greater policy cohesion than did the Democrats. Most Republicans felt that inflation was the most important problem that government should resolve and thus supported policies to curb rising prices—e.g., reduced government regulation of private businesses, tax cuts for corporations, and lower government expenditures on social services such as job retraining, public education, and especially Medicaid. Even though not all the Reagan supporters preferred these policies as the best way to lower inflation, they perceived him as more competent than Carter to handle economic issues. Because Reagan maintained electoral support among most self-identified Republicans and rallied a large percentage of "weak" and "independent" Democrats to his side, he won the 1980 presidential election.[18]

In Canada as well as the United States voter dissatisfaction with the policy performance of the incumbent federal administration explains the outcomes of the 1979 and 1980 elections, which saw the "out" party emerge victorious. The unemployment rate fell in 1979 (compared with rates in the previous two years), but consumer prices rose each year from 1976 through 1979. Most Canadian voters perceived that strikes and the high cost of living were the most urgent problems facing the nation. Over two-thirds disapproved the Liberal government's handling of inflation, labor relations, and unemployment. As a result, the opposition Progressive-Conservatives attracted some voters worried about inflation. In particular, English-speaking citizens with weak partisan ties switched from the Liberals to the Conservatives. The socialist New Democratic party increased its support among English-speaking people most affected by unemployment. The Liberals won votes from Canadians who favored increased social services, admired the leadership of Prime Minister Pierre Trudeau, and believed that the Liberals could effectively maintain national unity.

The Progressive-Conservatives in May 1979 won a narrow victory, with 48 percent of the seats in the House of Commons. They attracted widespread support from English-speaking Canadians—especially those in Ontario (the most populous province), Prince Edward Island, Nova Scotia, British Columbia, Alberta, Manitoba, and Saskatchewan. However, they gained only two seats in French-speaking Quebec, the second most populous province. Dependent on the votes of the six Social Credit legislators who represented Quebec, the Progressive-Conservatives had to form a minority government.

Seven months after the 1979 election, the Conservatives fell from power when the six Social Credit House members abstained from supporting the government on a crucial budget measure that raised taxes, particularly on gasoline. Inflation and unemployment rates had continued to rise slightly during 1979. In early 1980 voters expressed the greatest concern about inflation, energy prices, and unemployment, and they regarded the Liberals as more competent than the Conservatives to handle all three issues. Throughout 1979 popular support for Prime Minister Joe Clark gradually declined, even in English-speaking Ontario.

By February 1980, when new elections to the House of Commons occurred, popular dissatisfaction with Clark and the Conservative government led to a Liberal party victory. The Liberals gained votes in areas of high unemployment, especially Quebec (where they won an overwhelming victory) and in the Atlantic provinces of New Brunswick, Newfoundland, Prince Edward Island, and Nova Scotia. The New Democratic party increased its electoral margin among the unemployed in Saskatchewan, British Columbia, and Manitoba. Unlike in the 1979 election, the Liberals outpolled the Progressive-Conservatives in Ontario. The victories in Quebec and Ontario enabled the Liberals to return to power with 52 percent of the Commons seats and 44 percent of the national vote.

Significantly, popular opposition to welfare state policies did not explain the 1980 Conservative defeat. Two months before the election, less than one-quarter of Canadians wanted a tax cut if it meant reduced expenditures on health, education, and social services. Over one-third preferred maintaining the existing mix of taxes and expenditures; about 30 percent sought larger social service expenditures even if higher taxes resulted. The Progressive-Conservative party lost the 1980 election mainly because voters dissatisfied with its economic policy performance and personal leadership switched to the Liberals.[19]

Similarly French voters became disenchanted with the conservative government of President Valéry Giscard d'Estaing and in 1981 gave the opposition Socialists control of the presidency and National Assembly. When Giscard became president in 1974, the unemployment rate was slightly under 3 percent; from 1975 it rose successively each year until it reached 7.3 percent in 1981. During the last three years of Giscard's administration, consumer prices increased more than 10 percent annually. Most French voters regarded unemployment a more important problem than inflation. Even though a majority blamed world crises for France's economic difficulties, over one-third believed that ineffective government policies primarily caused the inflation and especially the high joblessness. According to them, the Giscard government unfairly demanded that the poor bear the major sacrifices to bring France out of economic stagnation.

During the 1970s the Communists and Socialists had divided the left-wing opposition to the conservative administrations, but in 1981 the leftists achieved greater unity than the conservative parties. On the right the parties supporting Giscard rallied behind the Union for French Democracy. Another more conservative party—the Rassemblement pour la République (RPR)—battled Giscard and his followers for dominance. Led by Paris mayor and former prime minister Jacques Chirac, the RPR gained 17 percent of the seats to the National Assembly, compared with 13 percent for the Union for French Democracy. During the first round of the presidential elections, Chirac secured 18 percent of the votes; Giscard obtained 28 percent. However, only three-fourths of Chirac's supporters voted for Giscard in the second-round runoff, and Giscard obtained only 48 percent of the vote. The Socialist candidate, François Mitterrand, gained 52 percent and thereby won the presidency. Compared to the conservatives, the leftist parties demonstrated greater unity. During the late 1970s and early 1980s, the Socialists became the dominant party on the left, increasing their support at the expense of the Communists. At the second round of the 1981 election, most Communists voted for Mitterrand. In June 1981 many voters who had formerly supported Communist legislators chose Socialist candidates; thus the Socialists gained 56 percent of the seats to the National Assembly. The high unemployment rates and the perceived inability of the Giscard administration to lower the jobless rates, combined with left-wing unity, led to Socialist victories in 1981.[20]

In Sweden as well, greater cohesion among the Social Democrats led them to defeat the "bourgeois" opposition at the 1982 parliamentary elections. The Social Democratic party had governed Sweden by itself or in a coalition from 1932 through 1976. In 1976 it lost the election to a coalition of Conservatives, People's (Liberal) party, and Center party—which together gained 50.6 percent of the seats in the Riksdag. In 1979 the coalition's support dropped slightly, and it emerged with only a one-seat margin in the Riksdag over the Social Democrats and Communists. Between 1979 and 1982 economic difficulties mounted. Strikes, rising budget deficits, OPEC oil price hikes, trade deficits, and devaluation of the currency all weakened Sweden's economic position. In 1982 the inflation rate dropped below 10 percent, but the jobless rate grew from 2.1 percent in 1979 to nearly 3.5 percent in September 1982 (election time). Most Swedish voters regarded unemployment as the major economic issue; thus the rising jobless rate led to falling support for the governing parties. Moreover, the three non-socialist parties disagreed about the best ways to resolve economic problems. The People's party wanted to maintain generous social service programs. The Center party focused on granting subsidies to farmers and on protecting the environment. The Conservatives preferred tax cuts and some reductions in social service expenditures. Disenchanted with the People's and Center programs, the Conservative party withdrew from the coalition government in 1981. Because of this policy fragmentation on the right, the Social Democrats won 46 percent of the popular vote and 48 percent of the Riksdag seats in 1982. Backed by the small Communist party, which held 20 seats, the Social Democrats could form the parliamentary majority needed to regain control of the government.[21]

In summary, recent electoral returns do not indicate a citizen backlash against social service expenditures. The declining trust in Western governments reflected dissatisfaction with political leaders' performance and policy results rather than discontent with welfare state policies. Voters threw out of office any party, whether rightist or leftist, that failed to reduce unemployment and lower inflation. Particularly when the incumbent parties demonstrated low policy cohesion and the opposition parties achieved greater unity, the "outs" usually emerged victorious. Although the winning parties had a mandate to improve economic performance, voters gave them extensive freedom to devise public policies that would curtail soaring inflation or lower unemployment. As perceived by the citizenry, desirable programs did not involve sizable cutbacks in social service expenditures, especially for pensions, health care, employment training, and education.

ECONOMIC STAGFLATION IN THE WELFARE STATE

If the main problems in Western industrial societies do not stem from threats to individual freedom, oppressive state bureaucracies, falling capital accumulation, or decreased support for social service programs, what then is the current crisis of the welfare state? These societies face a more mundane dilemma: how to cope with the economic stagflation that has plagued the whole world since the mid-1970s. As unemployment grew worse, inflation rose, and growth rates declined, the policy consensus that had prevailed during the robust 1960s evaporated. No policy option seemed likely to bring the best of all possible worlds—low unemployment, low price increases, and high growth. Even though the deteriorating economic situation did not produce the polarization that had plagued political parties from the late nineteenth century through World War II, in many nations parties became more divided in their approaches toward overcoming the economic stagnation. Often poor economic performance led to political stagnation and *immobilisme*, as diverse groups participating in coalition governments failed to agree on the most effective public policies for attaining desired economic goals.

In most Western industrialized countries the unemployment problem became more severe during the late 1970s. Canada, the United States, and Britain faced the highest jobless rates from 1967 through 1980. France, West Germany, and Italy have fared somewhat better, with Sweden maintaining the lowest recent unemployment rate (see Table 2.10 for data on 1960-80). Everywhere the rising jobless rate has especially devastated groups at the bottom of the social ladder—youths under twenty-five years, women, ethnic minorities, migrant workers (in Europe), and unskilled workers in the manufacturing sector (for example, the iron and steel, shipbuilding, and textile industries). By contrast, individuals with greater political power, status, and control over the production process have experienced fewer problems finding or keeping their jobs. Throughout the Western

Table 2.10

UNEMPLOYMENT RATES, 1960-80
(Percentage of Labor Force)

Country	1960-66	1967-73	1974-80	1960-80
Britain	2.4%[a]	3.4%	5.5%	3.8%
Canada	5.0	5.2	7.3	5.8
France	1.4	2.4	4.9	2.9
West Germany	0.5	0.8	3.0	1.5
Italy	2.8	3.1	3.5	3.1
Sweden	1.5	2.2	1.9	1.9
United States	5.3	4.6	6.8	5.6

Source: U.S. Department of Labor, Bureau of Labor Statistics, *Handbook of Labor Statistics*, Bulletin 2175 (December 1983), 419-20.

[a]Figures are average annual percentages for each seven-year period and for 1960-80 era.

world these individuals comprise middle-aged men (thirty to sixty years old), ethnic majorities, and managers and professionals.[22]

During the 1970s citizens in Western societies have faced not only high unemployment but also double-digit inflation. As Table 2.11 shows, the average inflation rate (measured by consumer price increases) rose each successive seven-year period from 1960 through 1980. The British and Italians have suffered the most from escalating inflation, but North Americans and other Europeans (like the French and Swedes) have not escaped the inflationary pressures.

Along with high unemployment and inflation have gone low growth rates. In every nation except the United Kingdom, the real increase in the GDP (controlling for inflation) gradually declined between 1960 and 1980 (see Table 2.12). The growth rates were highest during the early 1960s, descended a bit from 1967 to 1973, and then plummeted in the late 1970s. Throughout the 1960-80 period Canada, France, and Italy attained the highest growth rates, while the United Kingdom's was the slowest. West Germany, Sweden, and the United States showed moderate growth, averaging around 3.5 percent a year between 1960 and 1980; however, they too experienced declines after

Table 2.11

INFLATION RATES, 1960-80
(Percent)

Country	1960-66	1967-73	1974-80	1960-80
Canada	1.9%[a]	4.4%	9.3%	5.2%
France	3.6	5.5	11.1	6.7
West Germany	2.7	3.7	4.7	3.7
Italy	4.2	4.9	16.8	8.6
Sweden	4.1	5.2	10.3	6.5
United Kingdom	3.1	6.4	16.0	8.5
United States	1.6	4.6	9.2	5.1

Source: International Monetary Fund (IMF), *International Financial Statistics Yearbook* (Washington, D.C., 1981), 62-63.

[a]Figures are average annual percentages of increase in consumer prices for each seven-year period and for 1960-80 era.

Table 2.12

GROWTH OF REAL GDP AT MARKET PRICES, 1960-80
(Percent)

Country	1960-66	1967-73	1974-80	1960-80
Canada	5.9%[a]	5.3%	2.8%	4.7%
France	5.6	5.5	2.9	4.7
West Germany	4.5	4.5	2.4	3.8
Italy	5.4	5.3	2.8	4.5
Sweden	4.7	3.6	1.8	3.4
United Kingdom	2.9	3.3	0.9	2.4
United States	4.9	3.5	2.3	3.6

Sources: OECD Economic Outlook, no. 31 (July 1982): 142; OECD Economic Outlook, *Historical Statistics, 1960-1980* (Paris, 1982), 40.

[a]Figures are average annual percentage changes for each seven-year period and for 1960-80 era.

1973. The low growth rates made it difficult to finance government programs and implement policies that provided relief from economic difficulties.

An examination of growth rates since 1870 indicates that the immediate post-World War II era (1950-73) was the greatest boom period. Angus Maddison measured the increase in per capita output (GDP at constant prices) between 1870 and 1979, finding that the yearly average growth rates of the seven countries in our study were 3.5 percent between 1950 and 1973, 2.0 percent from 1973 to 1979, but under 2 percent before 1950. All seven nations had a higher growth rate after World War II than throughout the nineteenth century or the first half of the twentieth. Yet government expenditures as a proportion of national income—especially those for social services—were far greater after the war than before the 1940s.[23]

Several factors explain the economic boom that immediately followed World War II. First, both Western Europe and North America needed to rebuild their economies after a twenty-year period of depressed consumer demand caused initially by the 1930s collapse and then by wartime expenditures. After the war pent-up demand for homes, automobiles, household appliances, and other consumer goods stimulated increased production. Second, technological innovations in the electrical equipment, machinery, scientific instruments, chemicals, communications, space vehicles, and transportation industries caused rapid growth. Third, moderate wage increases and high labor productivity led to low unit labor costs (compensation divided by output per hour), which contributed to high growth. Fourth, the price of oil, a key resource for expanding growth, remained low—under $2.50 a barrel until the early 1970s. Fifth, between 1945 and 1973 favorable economic conditions in the United States helped stimulate high growth rates throughout the world economy. For several reasons the dollar served as a stable medium of foreign exchange. Until the early 1970s the United States held a large supply of gold reserves. Its balance of payments was favorable; before 1971 the dollar value of exports exceeded that of imports. Inflation rates stayed low. Furthermore, the Marshall Plan helped rebuild Western Europe. American diplomats and business executives encouraged free trade (low tariffs and quotas), which expanded markets for goods produced in Western industrialized societies. All these conditions increased total demand, both by business and government. Rapid growth rates resulted.

By the early 1970s, however, most Western economies reached the end of the boom period. European economies had largely recovered from wartime damage. Consumers had partially satisfied their demand for automobiles, homes, and household appliances. The manufacturing sector no longer operated as the locomotive of rapid growth. Some industries—e.g., laser, genetic engineering, electronics, microprocessing, and ophthalmic goods—created employment opportunities for scientists, engineers, technicians, and computer programmers. Yet growing automation threatened jobs of workers in the iron, steel, shipbuilding, garment, textile, and fabricating metals industries. Unskilled employees suffered the most from robotization. The loss of previously existing jobs and a failure to create enough new employment opportunities in high technology led to a lower proportion of jobs in the manufacturing sector, especially in Canada, Sweden, the United Kingdom, and the United States.

When labor productivity declined and wage hikes outstripped price rises after 1973, manufacturing unit labor costs escalated. A large gap arose between rises in hourly compensation and increases in output per hour. As a result, economic growth rates declined. According to the time-series multiple regression analysis in Table 2.13, unit labor costs constituted the most statistically significant variable affecting the growth rate between 1960 and 1980. In every country except Sweden, as manufacturing unit labor costs rose, the growth rate dropped; even in Sweden the two variables showed a fairly high negative relationship.

During the 1970s conditions in the United States no longer played such a dominant role in stimulating worldwide economic growth. The U.S. supply of gold reserves was depleted. Trade deficits grew severe. At the start of the decade the Nixon administration devalued the dollar in an attempt to expand American export sales. The government's commitment to free trade weakened when it enacted protectionist measures such as tariffs, quotas, anti-dumping duties, and subsidized export credits. Consumer prices began to soar. From 1970 to 1980 the dollar was no longer the effective medium of international exchange it had been during the 1950s and 1960s.

The steep rise in OPEC oil prices that occurred first in 1973-74 and again in 1979 also hindered rapid growth rates. Coming at the end of a boom period, the increases caused a supply shock that exacerbated the recession. Consequently growth rates began to plummet

Table 2.13

PREDICTORS OF REAL ECONOMIC GROWTH RATES: TIME-SERIES MULTIPLE REGRESSION, 1960-80

Country	Constant	Unit Labor Costs	Current Government Disbursements	Interest Rate	Defense Expenditures	$\bar{R}^2$ [a]	Durbin-Watson Test [b]	Standard Error of Regression
Canada	17.42[c][d] (3.82)	-.19 (-2.63)	-.19 (-1.74)	-.25 (-2.43)	-1.54 (-2.42)	.69	1.84	1.21
France	9.48 (1.77)	-.29 (-4.88)	-.27 (-2.88)	.42 (2.73)	.81 (1.18)	.77	1.72	.86
West Germany	37.63 (3.36)	-.36 (-2.82)	-.58 (-2.93)	.46 (1.30)	-3.66 (-2.58)	.40	1.45	1.91
Italy	36.43 (2.97)	-.16 (-3.36)	-.67 (-3.63)	.41 (2.28)	-3.79 (-1.43)	.59	1.90	1.65
Sweden	35.25 (1.82)	-.15 (-1.62)	-.34 (-2.58)	.40 (.96)	-5.49 (-1.42)	.40	1.84	1.66
United Kingdom	14.95 (1.95)	-.18 (-3.34)	-.16 (-.95)	.19 (1.25)	-1.29 (-1.67)	.57	1.76	1.40
United States	20.56 (1.54)	-.37 (-2.30)	-.34 (-1.00)	-.06 (-.22)	-.72 (-1.32)	.50	1.76	1.69

[a] Adjusted R^2.

[b] A Durbin-Watson figure around 2 indicates that the error terms corresponding to different time points are not correlated.

[c] Unstandardized regression coefficient based on Cochrane-Orcutt pseudogeneralized least squares.

[d] Figures in parentheses are t-ratios. With fourteen degrees of freedom, any regression coefficient whose t-ratio exceeds 1.76 is statistically significant at the .05 level for a one-tailed test; t-ratios above 2.62 are statistically significant at the .01 level.

after 1973. Unemployment and inflation rose simultaneously—signs that economic stagflation had arrived.[24]

Under these deteriorating economic conditions, increased expenditures by Western governments failed to restore the high aggregate demand that had previously stimulated rapid economic growth. As Table 2.13 indicates, in Canada, France, West Germany, Italy, and Sweden rising current government disbursements went along with falling growth rates. Yet neither social service expenditures nor defense expenditures—the two major categories of government disbursements—showed a significant correlation with decreasing growth. Only in France and Sweden was there a statistically significant negative relationship between social service expenditures and economic growth from 1960 through 1980—that is, as government spending on social services grew, the growth rate fell. Over this twenty-year period Canada and France had the highest growth rates, but the French government spent more on social services than did the Canadian. Although the United Kingdom experienced the lowest growth rate, it spent less on social services than did West Germany, Italy, or Sweden—nations with higher increases in the real GDP. West Germany, Sweden, and the United States showed about the same growth rate. However, Sweden spent over twice as much as the United States on social service programs. In all nations except France defense spending and growth rates showed a negative correlation; as expenditures for defense declined, the growth rate increased. Yet only in Canada and West Germany did this negative correlation attain statistical significance. Thus military investments in technological industries like ordnance, aircraft, space equipment, and guided missiles failed to generate sufficient aggregate demand needed to sustain the economic boom that had brought high growth and low unemployment from the early 1950s through 1973.

National unemployment rates stem from two sources: deficient aggregate demand and technological changes that make certain skills obsolete. Most often demand-deficient unemployment occurs during the downswing of a business cycle. When a bust period occurs, private business firms and consumers decrease their spending. Investment declines, production falls, and more and more people lose their jobs.

If the whole world market faces an economic recession, foreign investment and trade decisions affect a nation's unemployment. Declining aggregate demand leads to falling profits. Small, competitive firms go bankrupt, and thus private enterprises become more concentrated. Because unions exert the greatest power in the more concentrated (oligopolistic) industries, skilled workers' real wages do not fall as rapidly as compensation earned by less skilled workers employed in smaller, non-unionized firms. Hence to recover their profit margins, oligopolistic corporations move to industrializing areas like South Korea, Taiwan, Singapore, Malaysia, Brazil, and Mexico, where weaker unions, lower wages, and higher profits prevail. As a result, higher unemployment emerges in Western Europe and North America. Trade policies also influence demand for particular products, like manufactured goods. By enacting a high foreign exchange rate, policymakers impede the sale of exports on the world market. Currency devaluations in a given country lead to falling import sales. Both falling import sales and a lower demand for exports cause higher unemployment in firms dependent on foreign trade. Increased government expenditures may not prove a powerful enough stimulus to expand total demand and thereby significantly lower the jobless rate.

Technological unemployment occurs when total demand in an economy remains high, but individuals either lack the advanced skills to obtain the available jobs or else can find few jobs that require their particular skills. The former situation appears more common. As new plants, equipment, and machinery facilitate greater increases in production, a mismatch occurs between the level of technological development and workers' skills. Automation, mechanization, and computerization displace unskilled workers and decrease the likelihood of their finding new jobs. As the older manufacturing industries—iron, steel, shipbuilding, textiles—have moved to Latin America and Asia, skilled workers in North America and Western Europe have also become technologically unemployed. Faced with technological changes, governments can try to lower unemployment by providing advanced education in highly demanded specialized skills and by instituting retraining programs for the unskilled.[25]

According to the time-series multiple regression analyses carried out for each nation from 1960 to 1980, current government disbursements and lagged investment, rather than unit labor costs or lagged growth rates, show the stronger association with rising joblessness (see Table 2.14). Although increasing labor costs in the manufacturing sector reduced the growth rate over this period, they had little impact on unemployment. Some neoclassical economists perceive that strong

Table 2.14

PREDICTORS OF UNEMPLOYMENT RATES: TIME-SERIES MULTIPLE REGRESSION, 1960-80

Country	Constant	Current Government Disbursements	Lagged Investment	Lagged Growth	Unit Labor Costs	$\bar{R}^2$[a]	Durbin-Watson Test	Standard Error of Regression
Canada	−9.81[b] (−4.18)[c]	.53 (10.63)	−.09 (−1.13)	.02 (.78)	−.07 (−3.44)	.96	2.17	.28
France	−2.40 (−.51)	.31 (4.04)	−.20 (−1.51)	−.02 (−.51)	.01 (.25)	.97	2.04	.29
West Germany	−6.92 (−3.18)	.31 (7.80)	−.14 (−3.46)	−.05 (−2.30)	.02 (1.67)	.98	1.96	.19
Italy	4.40 (3.76)	.05 (2.96)	−.11 (−3.30)	−.02 (−.90)	−.02 (−2.96)	.86	2.18	.16
Sweden	1.94 (.44)	.01 (.42)	−.01 (−.06)	−.04 (−1.01)	−.03 (−1.47)	.36	1.82	.33
United Kingdom	−.60 (−.14)	.45 (7.29)	−.57 (−2.60)	−.10 (−1.58)	−.03 (−1.37)	.88	1.69	.55
United States	−16.65 (−1.76)	.63 (3.44)	.21 (.56)	−.09 (−1.18)	−.07 (−1.17)	.77	1.51	.66

[a] Adjusted R^2.

[b] Unstandardized regression coefficient based on Cochrane-Orcutt pseudogeneralized least squares.

[c] Figures in parentheses are t-ratios.

unions lead to high wage increases, decreased productivity, and thus rising unit labor costs; as a result, profits fall, capital investment declines, and unemployment rises.[26] However, in all nations except France and West Germany unit labor costs and joblessness were negatively correlated. Only in Canada and Italy did there occur a statistically significant relationship; as manufacturing labor costs in these two countries rose, the unemployment rate declined. Both lagged investment and especially lagged growth had a weaker than expected effect on unemployment. Only in West Germany did a rising growth rate produce lower unemployment a year later. Increased expenditures for gross capital formation led to reduced joblessness only in West Germany, Italy, and the United Kingdom.

The variable most strongly associated with unemployment is current government expenditures. Contrary to Keynesian expectations, higher government disbursements failed to reduce jobless levels between 1960 and 1980. Instead in all countries except Sweden, as expenditures rose, so did unemployment rates. Rather than government spending causing unemployment, the reverse is probably more valid—i.e., higher unemployment led to increased government expenditures. The jobless sought unemployment compensation and public assistance. Workers fearing layoffs retired early and secured their pensions. Despite this linkage between current government disbursements and unemployment, expenditures for social services had a relatively weak impact. Only in Britain, Canada, and West Germany did rising social service expenditures show a statistically significant association with increasing joblessness. In Sweden, the welfare state "leader," no significant relationship emerged between unemployment and government expenditures of any kind. Indeed unemployment rates in Sweden have remained constant over the twenty-year period. Because of this low variance in the dependent variable, all explanatory factors specified in the regression equation lack statistical significance. Instead the low Swedish unemployment stems from policies other than investment levels, growth rates, and current government disbursements.

Although rising unemployment affects the whole world, the major welfare states—Sweden, Norway, Austria, and Luxembourg—have faced the lowest unemployment rates in the capitalist world. In 1981 social service expenditures in these four countries exceeded 27 percent of the GDP, yet unemployment rates were below 3 percent.

Through various public policies that expanded aggregate demand and retrained technologically displaced workers, Swedish officials managed to keep the jobless rate under 3 percent from 1960 through 1981. An investment reserves program encourages private enterprises to deposit part of their pretax profits into a special reserve fund. When a recession occurs, the government releases these funds for capital investment. Travel and subsistence grants enable workers to move from areas of low demand (i.e., northern Sweden) to regions where more employment opportunities prevail (southern Sweden). By authorizing funds to private industries in northern Sweden, the government has tried to promote regional development, thereby lowering unemployment. The Swedish Employment Service provides information, assistance in job placement, and recommendations for job training. The National Labor Market Board (comprised of representatives from government, labor, and business) supervises an extensive vocational training program. Private employers who retrain workers, rather than lay them off during a recession, receive in-plant training subsidies from the government, which also allocates grants to private industries that recruit new workers. Special programs help youths find jobs. School vocational guidance officers transmit information about job placement. Youths who cannot quickly secure employment receive a cash benefit to finance their job search. Numerous public service jobs for both young people and adults give them work in maintenance, repair, conservation, community health, and social service projects. Early retirement and partial pensions for the elderly, lengthier formal schooling for the young, and a shorter work week for employees reduce the labor supply.[27] Through all these policies the Swedish government has aimed to preserve existing jobs, create new ones, train workers in technologically advanced skills, and expand total demand on the downswing of a business cycle. Although economic "fine-tuning" has succeeded in Sweden partly because government officials, Social Democratic party leaders, and labor union heads possessed the power and the will to shape economic developments, in most other market societies government leaders wield less control over the factors that create unemployment.

Inflation poses a similar problem for Western policymakers lacking the power to control all major factors causing high price increases, which erupted after 1972. Economists formulated conflicting models that tried to explain the rapid price rises. Demand-pull, cost-push, monetarist, Keynesian, neo-Keynesian, post-Keynesian, rational expectationist, and Marxist models competed for preeminence. Their exponents not only sought the theoretical explanations for inflation but also offered advice to policymakers about the most effective strategies for curbing the inflationary surge. Conservative policymakers in the United Kingdom and United States leaned toward monetarist remedies. Democratic socialists in France and Sweden showed greater enthusiasm for Keynesian strategies. Taking a pragmatic approach, Canadian Liberals switched back and forth from Keynesian to monetarist models.

The post-Keynesian approach offers the most theoretically insightful and empirically valid explanation for the rapid price increases of the early 1970s. Post-Keynesians consider that prices stem from the level of demand for a good or service, available supplies, average overhead costs for making a product (or rendering a service), and a margin for profits. Where extensive price competition occurs—as in some services and retail trade—prices seem more responsive to changes in supply and demand. When a competitive firm encounters high demand for a product but limited supplies, it can secure a high price for that product as well as a high short-term profit. However, particularly in manufacturing industries and government enterprises, prices respond more to shifts in costs than to changes in demand. Facing little competition from other firms, managers in these sectors set prices that reflect the rising costs of supplies, including labor, land, raw materials (like oil), interest rates, taxes, and the purchase and repair of capital equipment. Because private manufacturers usually achieve high concentration over a product market, their long-term profits are generally higher than those of more competitive firms. Concentrated industries wield the market power to set higher target-return prices— that is, the mark-up over costs to guarantee a certain profit. When demand for their product falls, these industries usually cut production rather than prices. Thus their prices decline less or increase more than prices charged by more competitive firms.

On the downswing of a business cycle, state-owned enterprises also refrain from lowering prices, mainly because powerful unions in the public sector resist wage decreases. As a result, even when costs escalate and demand falls, managers of public corporations maintain fairly stable prices, unless pressured by laissez-faire-oriented government officials to raise prices and increase efficiency.

Inflation arises when certain shocks upset price stability. If an economy operates at low unemployment and full capacity, large increases in expenditures by government, private business, or consumers pose a demand shock that pulls up prices. Supply shocks, like the food and oil shortages that occurred during the early 1970s, also strengthen inflationary pressures. Most important, institutional shocks from government, private business, and labor unions often raise costs. For example, rising interest rates and taxes push up general production costs. Currency devaluations set by government finance ministries and central banks lead to higher prices for imported goods. When public policies index pensions and wages to cost-of-living increases, this indexing helps maintain the inflationary surge. Concentrated industries in the private manufacturing sector often fail to lower prices when demand falls. Powerful in manufacturing industries and state enterprises, labor unions can secure wage increases that exceed the growth in output. Often these wage hikes spread to nonunionized industries. Because labor costs constitute over 70 percent of total production costs in highly industrialized economies, the surge in unit labor costs brings soaring inflation.[28]

From the post-Keynesian perspective, unit labor costs constitute the major reason for contemporary inflation. Basil J. Moore writes:

> For modern post-Keynesians . . . the rate of inflation is determined primarily by the rate of increase of nominal money wages relative to labor productivity. Over wide sectors of the economy, prices are largely cost-determined, based on a mark-up over unit labor costs. . . . To the extent money wages grow more rapidly than the growth of labor productivity, unit labor costs and therefore the price level will rise accordingly.[29]

Manufacturing unit labor costs measure the ratio of hourly wages to output per hour performed by workers. High labor productivity derives from capital-intensive investment, technological innovations, high plant capacity usage, inexpensive energy supplies, managerial effectiveness, and employees' work habits. Managerial decisions, government policies toward wage controls and minimum wages, along with trade union power in an enterprise, together determine compensation. When a nation experiences high demand for labor, low unemployment rates, expectations of rising prices, strong unions, and pro-labor government administrations, workers will effectively realize their claims for higher nominal wages. Except in Italy, over 80 percent of the labor force in each of our seven countries receives wages and salaries; therefore labor costs constitute the largest proportion of production costs. Particularly outside the United States, labor unions organize a large and growing share of the labor force. During the late 1970s, 80 percent of civilian employees belonged to unions in Sweden, over 50 percent in Britain, about 40 percent in Italy, 35 percent in West Germany, 30 percent in Canada, and 24 percent in France, but less than 20 percent in the United States. Unions wield especially strong bargaining power in manufacturing industries and state enterprises; there workers receive higher salaries, more generous fringe benefits, and wage hikes that outpace price increases. Wages drift upward as favorable settlements in the manufacturing sector "spill over" to other sectors. Wage increases represent a rising cost to management but greater spending power (demand) for employees. When gross wages outstrip labor productivity, inflation results.[30]

According to time-series multiple regression analyses for the seven nations, manufacturing unit labor costs most affected consumer price increases (see Table 2.15). In every nation as unit labor costs increased from 1960 through 1980, so did inflation rates. The most rapid rises in labor costs occurred after 1973; as expected, this period also marked the highest inflation rates. Although escalating labor costs often accompanied the consumer price increases, in some nations—e.g., Italy and the United Kingdom—the growth in labor costs preceded the inflationary upsurge during 1974 and 1975. Comparisons across nations show that societies with the highest unit labor costs faced the highest inflation rates (see Table 2.16). Canada, West Germany, and the United States incurred the lowest unit labor costs and experienced the lowest price increases. In North America unions were weaker than in Western Europe. From 1960 through 1981 Canadian and U.S. manufacturing workers received smaller increases in hourly compensation than did their European counterparts. Labor productivity increases were lower. Consequently, yearly labor cost gains remained below those in Europe. By contrast, during the 1970s Italian and British workers won wage hikes that greatly exceeded output per hour, so both nations had to cope with acute inflation. French and Swedish unions have gained moderately high wage increases for manufacturing workers. However, because unit labor costs were lower in France and Sweden than in Italy or the United Kingdom, inflation

Table 2.15

PREDICTORS OF INFLATION RATES: TIME-SERIES MULTIPLE REGRESSION, 1960-80

Country	Constant	Unit Labor Costs	Interest Rate	Lagged Inflation	Lagged Money Supply Increases	$\overline{R}^{2a}$	Durbin-Watson Test	Standard Error of Regression
Canada	3.07[b] (1.17)[c]	.23 (3.20)	.32 (2.03)	-.15 (-.68)	.06 (1.54)	.91	1.54	.98
France	-.24 (-.26)	.32 (4.08)	.48 (3.85)	.24 (2.03)	.02 (.44)	.91	1.70	1.04
West Germany	-1.10 (-1.66)	.16 (3.08)	.28 (2.24)	.65 (6.96)	.07 (1.20)	.80	2.14	.76
Italy	-1.48 (-.60)	.22 (3.48)	.84 (5.19)	.21 (1.39)	.07 (.55)	.91	1.40	1.93
Sweden	-2.19 (-1.95)	.20 (3.35)	.82 (3.76)	.31 (2.16)	.07 (1.26)	.79	1.93	1.49
United Kingdom	.83 (.67)	.45 (6.12)	.03 (.14)	.38 (3.76)	.07 (.52)	.90	2.06	2.02
United States	-.89 (-1.15)	.28 (3.73)	.63 (4.86)	.32 (3.24)	-.04 (-.24)	.95	2.07	.83

[a]Adjusted R^2.
[b]Unstandardized regression coefficient based on Cochrane-Orcutt pseudogeneralized least squares.
[c]Figures in parentheses are t-ratios.

Table 2.16

INFLATION RATES AND UNIT LABOR COSTS
(Percent)

Country	Unit Labor Costs[a]			Inflation Rates[b]		
	1960-66	1967-73	1974-80	1960-66	1967-73	1974-80
Canada	0.2%	2.7%	10.0%	1.9%	4.4%	9.3%
France	3.1	4.4	10.3	3.6	5.5	11.1
West Germany	3.8	4.8	5.2	2.7	3.7	4.7
Italy	3.6	7.8	16.4	4.2	4.9	16.8
Sweden	3.7	4.0	11.4	4.1	5.2	10.3
United Kingdom	2.9	5.5	18.7	3.1	6.4	16.0
United States	0.1	3.2	8.4	1.6	4.6	9.2

Sources: U.S. Department of Labor, Bureau of Labor Statistics, *Handbook of Labor Statistics*, Bulletin 2175 (December 1983), 429; IMF, *International Financial Statistics Yearbook*, 1981, 62-63.

[a]Figures are average annual percentage changes in unit labor costs in national currency in the manufacturing sector for each seven-year period.

[b]Figures are average annual increases in consumer prices for each seven-year period.

posed a less serious economic threat. From 1974 through 1980 West German workers secured comparatively low wage increases but high labor productivity. As a result of low unit labor costs, West Germans experienced the most stable prices during this period.[31]

Compared with changes in the money supply, interest rates have a stronger impact on inflation. From 1960 through 1980 in no country in our study did increases in the money supply (lagged by one year) significantly affect the inflation rate (see Table 2.15). However, in all of them except the United Kingdom escalating interest rates (the discount rates made by central banks to other banks) accompanied soaring consumer prices. As Table 2.17 shows, in each seven-year period average interest rates edged upward and inflation became more severe. Rising interest rates were probably both a response to inflationary pressures stemming from other sources and a cause of the continuing inflation. At least in the short run, they added to costs more than they restrained aggregate demand. As the price of

Table 2.17

INTEREST RATES AND INCREASES IN THE MONEY SUPPLY
(Percent)

Country	Increases in Money Supply[a]			Interest Rates[b]		
	1960-66	1967-73	1974-80	1960-66	1967-73	1974-80
Canada	7.9%	6.7%	6.7%	4.1%	6.2%	10.8%
France	12.9	7.6	10.9	3.6	7.1	9.9
West Germany	8.3	8.3	8.8	3.6	4.8	4.6
Italy	14.0	17.9	18.4	3.5	4.5	11.8
Sweden	8.0	4.5	13.8	4.9	5.7	7.8
United Kingdom	3.2	7.9	12.0	5.6	8.1	12.5
United States	2.7	5.9	5.9	3.6	5.4	8.5

Sources: IMF, *International Financial Statistics Yearbook*, 1981, 56, 58, 59;
OECD, *Main Economic Indicators: Historical Statistics, 1960-1979*
(Paris, 1980), 39, 82, 304, 346, 417, 539, 612.

[a]Money supply refers to M1—currency outside banks and checking accounts
in banks. Figures are average annual increases for each seven-year period.

[b]Interest rates are the central bank discount rates. Figures are annual averages
for each seven-year period.

borrowing money escalated, costs increased for consumers, businesses, and government. During the late 1970s a drastic rise in discount rates imposed by the United States Federal Reserve Board led
to higher inflation in Western Europe. Anxious to attract capital
investment into their countries and to deter European corporations
from investing abroad, European central bankers raised their interest
rates, which aggravated the inflationary situation. Italy, with the
greatest spurt in discount rates between 1967-73 and 1974-80, faced
the highest inflation during the late 1970s. By contrast, West German
central bankers set the lowest interest rates and even decreased them
slightly after 1973 (only in 1979 and 1980 did they rise). Hence West
Germany emerged with the best record of price stability during the
1970s.[32]

Besides high unit labor costs and interest rates, the two OPEC
oil price hikes of the 1970s caused consumer prices to shoot upward
in all seven nations. The five continental European countries import

over 90 percent of their total oil supplies. Although the United States relies more heavily on domestic crude oil, between 1970 and 1979 the oil it imported as a percentage of total supply jumped from 13 to 44 percent. Higher oil prices brought higher production costs, which pushed up the general price level. Because consumers and business executives had to spend more money for oil, they had less disposable income for other goods. This decreased aggregate demand led to economic stagnation—higher unemployment, lower plant capacity usage, and declining growth rates. Hence demand for imported oil declined after 1979. Partly as a result, the inflation rate began to drop in 1981 and 1982 from the high point it had reached in 1980.[33]

Inflationary momentum represents another crucial factor affecting price increases. As Table 2.15 shows, in France, West Germany, Sweden, the United Kingdom, and the United States the inflation rate in one year caused consumer prices to rise a year later. When prices increased in the past, they contributed to escalating prices in the present, probably because government officials, consumers, and business executives expected higher prices and thus adjusted for anticipated inflation. When unit labor costs, interest rates, and oil prices began to decrease in 1981, expectations of future inflation also changed—i.e., decision-makers anticipated lower inflation. Combined with rising unemployment and falling plant capacity use (under 70 percent), these lowered expectations caused downward pressures on general prices.

In sum, during the last decade the major sources behind inflation have been unit labor costs, interest rates, and oil prices; unfortunately Western policymakers have less immediate, direct control over these factors than over taxes and expenditures. Yet according to the time-series multiple regression analyses, total government expenditures, social service spending, levels of taxation, and fiscal deficits bore only a weak statistical relationship to inflation rates between 1960 and 1980. Although government leaders can change tax rates and expenditures, they have less direct authority over unit labor costs, oil price hikes, and interest rates. Of course they have some power to control these variables. For example, they can help reduce unit labor costs in several ways: If unemployment remains high and unions are weak, government officials can pressure business managers to squeeze wages. Temporary wage controls can restrain wage hikes, at least in the short run. Policies that expand capital investment and retrain workers in new technological skills may help increase labor output per hour. Moreover, leaders can encourage oil conservation, which may reduce its price. Central bankers have some authority over interest rates, especially the price that member banks pay to borrow from the central bank.

In most Western economies, however, banks retain some independence from both central bank officials and elected government leaders, such as ministers of finance and treasury department heads. Private banks largely determine interest rates. Particularly when business executives or consumers have a low cash supply, feel optimistic about future economic conditions, become willing to take risks, and are ready to accept higher debt ceilings, the demand for credit increases. If the central bank expands the money supply, interest rates remain low. If private banks seek higher profits, interest rates charged borrowers will rise farther above rates paid savers. National interest rates are also affected by international conditions. Higher discount rates set by the U.S. Federal Reserve Board raise European and Canadian interest rates. During the late 1970s several European nations, particularly Italy and the United Kingdom, incurred trade deficits and balance-of-payments crises. To secure loans from the International Monetary Fund and European banks, which agreed to cover the trade deficits, Italian and British officials had to raise domestic interest rates. Western banks increased their domestic interest rates because of a possibility that governments in the industrializing Third World— e.g., Argentina, Brazil, and Mexico—would default on loans granted them by these banks. The soaring oil prices during the 1970s stimulated the expansion of Eurocurrency to finance imported oil. National central banks, however, had no authority to regulate the interest rates charged by Eurocurrency banks. Hence national government leaders could not easily restrain the inflationary pressures stemming from world financial conditions beyond their direct control.

Oil prices largely depend on international market conditions. OPEC representatives, non-OPEC oil producers (e.g., Norway, Mexico, the USSR), and private multinational oil corporations set crude oil prices, which derive from supply restrictions, the level of demand for oil, and the availability of substitutes. When real interest rates in the United States began to soar during the early 1980s, Europeans had to pay higher prices for oil because world oil prices are pegged to the exchange value of the American dollar.

Political leaders lack the power to control unit labor costs. Business managers and occasionally union leaders decide wages. When the general inflation rate rises, wage hikes may outstrip productivity gains and cost-of-living increases. Government leaders have only limited authority to determine wages and labor productivity.[34] Hence they face difficulties designing public policies that will bring low inflation along with high growth and full employment.

CONCLUSION: THE LIMITS OF ECONOMIC POLICIES AND POLICY ANALYSIS

To citizens like Joe Greenhill suffering from high unemployment, this attention to the limits of public policies implies a resigned, fatalistic attitude toward the status quo. They associate the theoretical analysis of economic outcomes with political paralysis to change existing conditions.

The contemporary stress on policy limitations recalls the famous analogy between navigation and governing. The word government derives from the Latin *gubernare*—to steer, pilot, navigate—which comes from the Greek *kubernan*. For Plato governing involves steering; policymakers act as navigators. Just as the navigator guides a ship and its crew through stormy seas toward a safe port, so the statesman steers government through a conflict-laden society toward certain goals. From the Platonic standpoint, the philosopher has the knowledge, wisdom, and technical skills needed for beneficial rule.[35] According to some modern economists, they among all the social scientists can best supply the policy advice required to govern effectively.

Taking issue with those who postulate an exalted role for economic advisors, Lester Thurow has recently reminded us that the helmsman must often navigate his way through dangerous currents—i.e., intractable economic problems. Political leaders need information to make decisions now and in the future. Yet people's behavior and objective conditions change. Neither government officials nor policy analysts possess perfect knowledge about the causes of economic outcomes. Uncertainty faces those who guide the policy process. Policy analysts can more easily explain historical phenomena than predict future conditions or change the existing world. Only after events have occurred can analysts begin to interpret them. According to Thurow:

For the same reason that economic events are not predictable, they are not completely controllable. At any moment will come unpredicted influences and stochastic shocks as well as policy impacts. . . . Policies exist to influence the economy, but they do not, of course, exist to control the economy.[36]

From Thurow's viewpoint, even if policy analysts cannot change the economic situation, they can describe policy contents, explain policies and their outcomes, and evaluate policy performance according to explicit criteria.

From another perspective, accurate description, valid explanation, and empirical evaluation lay the groundwork for changing public policies. Whatever our attitudes toward specific government policies, only by understanding how and why the policy process operates can we effectively change unfavorable conditions such as high unemployment or soaring inflation. Although political leaders and policy analysts cannot fully control the economy, they can influence its development. Hence theoretical analyses of economic policies serve as a partial guide to political choices as we confront the current crisis of the welfare state.

Chapter 3

THE IMPACT OF EDUCATION POLICIES

As Charles Dickens illustrated in *Hard Times*, an educational system mirrors the national society. Written in the mid-nineteenth century, when England was undergoing rapid industrialization, this novel took place in Coketown, a standardized industrial center dedicated to rapid economic growth and efficiency. Pragmatic usefulness was the town's keynote:

> You saw nothing in Coketown but what was severely workful. . . .
> All the public inscriptions in the town were painted alike, in severe
> characters of black and white. The jail might have been the infir-
> mary, the infirmary might have been the jail, the townhall might
> have been either, or both, or anything else. . . . Fact, fact, fact,
> everywhere in the material aspect of the town; fact, fact, fact,
> everywhere in the immaterial. The McChoakumchild school was all
> fact, and the school of design was all fact, and the relations between
> master and man were all fact, and everything was fact between the
> lying-in hospital and the cemetery, and what you couldn't state in
> figures, or show to be purchasable in the cheapest market and sale-
> able in the dearest, was not, and never should be, world without
> end, Amen.[1]

The McChoakumchild School, established by Mr. Thomas Grad-grind (a retired hardware merchant), taught the facts without any concern for feelings or imagination. From Mr. Gradgrind's perspective, "Facts alone are wanted in life. Plant nothing else, and root out everything else. You can only form the minds of reasoning animals upon Facts: nothing else will ever be of any service to them."[2] He taught these principles to his own children—Louisa, Jane, Thomas, Adam Smith, and Malthus—and he expected Mr. McChoakumchild to place a similar stress on factual learning.

63

Mr. Gradgrind envisioned his school as a model for the emerging capitalist society. He wanted it to embody the values of work, utility, and efficiency and to teach technical information—especially the quantitative facts needed for maximizing rapid economic growth. In school students should learn the skills needed in an industrializing capitalist economy, including the skills practiced by engineers, chemists, economists, land surveyors, clerks, accountants, and manufacturers. In this novel Charles Dickens thus foresaw the mid-twentieth-century stress on skilled labor—"human capital"—as a prime requirement of modern industrial economies. Like physical capital, human beings are now regarded as "factors of production," as facts to be quantified, standardized, and mechanized. According to this contemporary notion, the educational system ought to teach human capital about the most efficient ways to stimulate labor productivity.

Hard Times highlights three basic goals of the school system that policymakers consider important today.[3] First, it should teach the dominant values and norms of the society. For example, in Western societies political values can range from passive civic virtues—national solidarity, political consensus, support for the dominant political institutions—to more activist values: civil liberties, women's equality, and minority rights.

Second, schools must teach cognitive skills for solving problems. Cognitive skills enable individuals to process information in an abstract way—i.e., to ask intelligent questions, gather evidence, analyze information, synthesize data, generalize from evidence, make inferences, evaluate conclusions, and link concrete matters to abstract principles. Since politics deals in part with abstract issues that affect an entire community, a political decision-maker must look beyond personal and immediate interests to the general concerns of society. Moreover, with cognitive skills, the citizen can better understand the public policy process and also play an active part in shaping policies.

Third, schools take responsibility for both economic and political role-training. Not only must they teach specific skills but also instill students with such motives as the need to work hard, defer immediate gratifications, and overcome obstacles; in addition, they must concentrate on normative expectations—the rights and duties associated with diverse roles. In prestigious West European graduate universities like Oxford, Cambridge, the École Nationale d'Administration, and the University of Uppsala, students preparing to enter high-ranking civil service roles learn appropriate styles of language, dress, and social interaction.

Schools prepare students for effective role-performance in the economic arena. Students learn basic subjects in the elementary schools and more specialized skills in secondary schools and universities. As a result of industrialization and expanded opportunities for mass education, youths have greater chances for social mobility than in an agricultural society and more favorable prospects of entering a higher status occupation than their parents hold.

Schools also prepare students to perform political roles. Policymakers' notions about political participation involve two rather divergent role behaviors: active and passive citizenship. Passive citizens grant legitimacy to the political system by displaying love, loyalty, trust, and respect toward it. They pay their taxes on time, vote regularly, and revere national symbols like the flag and anthem. Active citizens play a more participant role in public institutions, including government, political parties, civic associations, and mass movements. Rather than accepting the status quo, participant citizens attempt to change aspects of government and society that they view as operating counter to the public good. Tactics to influence the government often involve less conventional activities than voting, discussing politics with friends, or signing petitions. These activists may also stage demonstrations, occupy buildings, mount rent strikes, and blockade streets.[4] Not surprisingly, in all societies schools place less emphasis on active than on passive citizenship. Even in nations where popular attitudes uphold the need for widespread political participation, obedience toward authority becomes a more important role requirement for the good citizen than political involvement.

In most countries, teachers, administrators, and education policymakers (local school board officials, regional government leaders, ministers of education in national cabinets) give the highest priority to role-training and transmission of societal values. Educational activities attempt to legitimate these values—especially the need for national unity, political harmony, and social order; civil liberties for dissidents assume a much lower priority. Students also learn the skills, information, and normative expectations that will prepare them for some occupational roles in a technologically advanced economy. Few schools place great importance on the cognitive abilities needed for active intellectual inquiry.

IMPACT OF EDUCATION POLICIES

TYPES OF EDUCATIONAL IMPACTS

Before assessing the impact of education policies on values, cognitive skills, and politico-economic role behaviors, we need to distinguish different types of outcomes. One distinction relates to the interaction between education *policies* and educational *experiences*. Education policies involve decisions about the curriculum (course content, textbook materials, instructional methods, testing procedures), administrative organization (degree of centralization, role of public and private schools), enrollment (equality of access to post-elementary education), and expenditures. We assume that policies in these areas shape students' school experiences. However, education policymakers have differential control over these variables. For example, education officials can give priority to certain subjects (mathematics, computer science) at the expense of others (civics and social studies). They can require specific levels of teaching experience and certain degrees, but they have less control over teachers' behavior in classes. Teachers mediate the content of courses. Their behavior inside and outside the classroom may have more profound effects on some children than do variables that are easier to manipulate, like classroom size and number of hours spent each week on civic education.

A second distinction stresses the difference between *individual* and *national* (societal) effects of education policies on values, cognitive achievements, and role behaviors. How does increased education influence an individual's political tolerance for disliked groups? What is the impact of mass education on the degree of civil liberties in several countries? To what extent do more years of formal education expand a person's information about politics and the ability to process political information in abstract ways? Across nations how well do educational systems develop cognitive skills in civic education, mathematics, and science? Although higher education may stimulate greater individual political participation, what impact does education have on national rates of electoral participation and occupational mobility between generations?

Third, not only the school but other agencies—families, peer groups, mass media—shape a person's values, information, and role behaviors; therefore the policy analyst must try to disentangle the separate effects of each agency and discover which exerts the greatest impact. To what extent do the experiences learned in the home and the school strengthen or contradict each other? Although education officials can design the curriculum, select textbooks, and stress particular teaching methods, they have far less power to influence the family, peer group, or mass media. Yet these structures, rather than the school, may wield the strongest effect on student behavior.

Keeping these three distinctions in mind, let us first explore the impact of education policies and the school experience on a crucial political value in Western democratic societies—civil liberties. Then we shall examine the effect of education policies on cognitive achievement and on political and economic role behaviors, specifically political participation and occupational mobility.

IMPACT ON CIVIL LIBERTIES

The freedoms to articulate political views, challenge incumbent leaders, and organize nonviolent opposition against the government gain increasing support as people complete more years of formal education. During the early 1970s the International Association for the Evaluation of Educational Achievement (IEA) conducted a civic education questionnaire at schools in eight Western countries—the United States, Ireland, New Zealand, West Germany, the Netherlands, Sweden, Finland, and Italy. According to this study, students in the last year of secondary school held less authoritarian attitudes than did younger fourteen-year-old children. Where teachers downplayed participation in patriotic rituals, stressed causal analyses, and encouraged free expression of student views in the classroom, support for political dissent seemed most widespread. Such classroom conditions prevailed especially in West German schools, where students gave the highest backing to civil liberties. Compared with West Germans and Swedes, U.S. senior high school students expressed less enthusiasm for granting freedoms to communists and people with views opposed to nationalistic values. The U.S. educational system placed the greatest importance on pledging allegiance to the flag and singing the national anthem—rituals intended to strengthen commitment to national solidarity. Especially during the early 1970s U.S. students expressed stronger support of the national government than did students in the other countries, who took a more skeptical, cynical attitude toward political institutions. Whereas political skepticism correlated with libertarian attitudes, an uncritical loyalty to the national regime weakened commitment to civil liberties.[5]

A college education, rather than a grammar or secondary school curriculum, most strongly leads people to support political freedom for nonconformists. The major chosen by a college student especially influences libertarian attitudes. Those majoring in social sciences and the humanities express the greatest opposition to censorship of political ideas. Business and engineering majors, however, more willingly accept censorship. In Britain, West Germany, and Italy, senior civil servants who majored in the social sciences and the humanities display the greatest political tolerance. By contrast, those who studied engineering, agronomy, or the physical sciences take the least tolerant view of political conflicts among party officials, interest group leaders, and legislators.[6]

Among adults, occupation, age, and education interact to affect an individual's commitment to civil liberties. In most Western nations farmers and unskilled laborers—persons with the least formal education—express the weakest support for civil liberties, while highly educated professionals (lawyers, judges, college professors, teachers, journalists, writers) most strongly hold libertarian values. At each successive stage of education young people show greater enthusiasm for political freedom. Within age groups better educated individuals favor civil liberties to a greater extent than do the less well educated, especially those who finished only elementary school.[7] In short, farmers and unskilled laborers over sixty who have only an elementary education hold the least tolerant views. Young college graduates with a professional job articulate the most libertarian views about criticizing government policies favored by the majority, circulating petitions for government actions, and holding peaceful demonstrations that protest government decisions.

In the Western democracies what variables explain the influence of a college education on attitudes toward civil liberties? Some skeptical commentators suggest that college graduates do not necessarily believe in civil liberties, but that an advanced education merely provides them greater sophistication in supplying the most socially desirable—i.e., libertarian—response to survey questions. Despite such skepticism, high correlations between college education and support for political freedom have appeared in scores of survey studies, however different the phrasing of questions, the samples investigated, and the times of interviewing. Moreover, not everyone in a society agrees on the socially desirable answer to questions about civil liberties. For example, even in groups with the same educational level, whereas some individuals regard the employment of communist teachers as a threat to academic freedom, others view the denial of employment to members of political movements (despite an individual's professional competence) as a threat to civil liberties and therefore undesirable.[8]

Different attitudes toward civil liberties may derive from anticipatory socialization experiences rather than from a college education. At the end of secondary school students who choose to continue their education may hold more libertarian attitudes than those who decide against attending college. Without a panel study that measures political attitudes of the same people over time, we cannot ascertain the direct impact of a university education on students. Ideally researchers should randomly assign a national sample of graduating secondary school students to two groups: an experimental group that attends college for four years and a control group that rejects a post-secondary education. At the beginning and end of the four-year period both groups would answer a questionnaire measuring support for civil liberties. Through this technique investigators could ascertain the attitudinal changes that occurred during the four-year interval and try to estimate the direct impact of higher education, compared with influences emanating from the home environment, peer group associations, and mass media. Because students have the freedom to decide whether or not to seek a university education, this experimental procedure is infeasible. However, a few social scientists, particularly in the United States, have used panel designs to study the same people across time. For example, M. Kent Jennings and Richard G. Niemi supervised the interviews of high school seniors in 1965 and then surveyed nearly 80 percent of these youths in 1973. Over this eight-year period those who attended college showed a greater increase in support for civil liberties than did those who finished their formal education at age eighteen.[9] We need more cross-national research to clarify the precise effects of a post-secondary education on attitudes toward political freedom.

The pre-university curriculum in most nations discourages student involvement with conflict, change, and challenges to the status quo. Teachers emphasize that a "good citizen" obeys the laws, pays taxes, votes, and keeps informed about political events—all consensual values. Neither instructors nor textbooks give much importance to civil liberties and the conflicts that result when people act on their rights to political freedom. However, particularly in the United States and Canada, some teachers influenced by Harvard psychologist Lawrence Kohlberg have presented controversial policy issues in the classroom and encouraged students to make choices among alternative decisions. For example, during the early 1970s some Canadian students explored the conflicts among the Front de Libération du Québec (FLQ), the Quebec government, and the federal government in Ottawa. In 1970 the FLQ kidnapped a British trade commissioner and the Minister of Labor in the Quebec government and demanded the release of FLQ prisoners in exchange for the two men's safe return. The federal government refused to make the exchange, imposed the War Measures Act, and imprisoned over three hundred people without a specific charge, trial, or legal counsel. Students discussed the actions that the Quebec and federal governments should have taken, including the wisdom of making prisoner exchanges, invoking emergency powers, and abrogating individual freedoms. By confronting these conflictual issues, they estimated the consequences of selecting one policy option rather than another. They discussed the policy dilemmas, strove to justify their decisions according to explicit values, and thus gained a greater appreciation of the procedural norms underlying the commitment to civil liberties.

However great the intellectual challenges of Kohlberg's approach, few Canadian schools have incorporated his model of political reasoning into the educational curriculum. Instead most instructors and textbooks focus on nationalism, an idealized interpretation of history, and the formal description of government institutions. As a result, few elementary or secondary students learn to appreciate the importance of civil liberties.

In other countries as well the pre-university social science curriculum exerts little substantial impact on student support for political freedom. One study conducted in the United States, England, Sweden, West Germany, and Italy uncovered no general relationship between the number of civics courses taken in school and tolerance of criticism aimed at the national government. Only in England did students who completed a political science class express a statistically strong commitment to dissent and opposition against the government.[10]

In most elementary and secondary schools the instructional methods used in social studies or civics classes fail to provide experiences that promote the cognitive skills needed to practice civil liberties. The most widely used methods remain textbooks, discussions, and questions that instructors pose to students. Intellectually stimulating methods like student reports, individual conferences, small group interactions, and field trips are rarer. Although French intellectuals stress the virtues of critical thinking and rational inquiry, French teachers transmit knowledge rather than the methods of gaining knowledge. Rote learning and memorization of factual information are more common than oral discussions. As a result, French students gain few opportunities to actively participate in the learning process. Even in Sweden, where education officials seek to expand student participation in the classroom, pupils are reticent to ask questions, initiate discussions, or challenge a teacher's authority. Indeed compared with U.S. or West German teachers, Swedish instructors less often use student reports and discussions in their civic education courses. Hence in nearly all national educational systems, students rarely analyze diverse viewpoints, test hypotheses, critically examine the evidence, and draw conclusions. They do not learn empathy and insight—that is, the ability to take the role of persons different from themselves. Partly because of the inadequate cognitive training, few persons ever fully develop their intellectual abilities. As a result, support for civil liberties remains weak.

The methods of instruction in universities place a greater emphasis on the cognitive skills. Belief in civil liberties implies that people have the intellectual skills to link the abstract principles of freedom to concrete situations and groups; individuals come to realize a cognitive consistency between supporting the general procedural norm of freedom and granting civil liberties to disliked groups. At least in some college courses—mainly those in the humanities and social sciences—students have the opportunity to express diverse opinions, evaluate preferences, and formulate collective rules for settling conflicts. They achieve greater cognitive abilities in applying general rules about civil liberties to unpopular groups and issues.[11]

Even though survey researchers have discovered a fairly strong relationship between advanced formal education and individual support for political freedom, we should not conclude that mass education necessarily strengthens the degree of civil liberties in a nation.

Whereas sample surveys measure attitudes toward political tolerance, national rankings on a civil liberties scale reveal the degree of behavioral freedom to challenge government elites. Rather than mass attitudes, the organizational pluralism in a nation and elite commitments to political freedom primarily affect national ratings on civil liberties. Both democratic and authoritarian leaders are usually highly educated. Although in the aggregate Western political leaders express more tolerant values than do the masses, some segments of the leadership reject political freedom for the opposition. Government policies toward dissidents may also conflict with pro-liberty verbal responses to a questionnaire. Since by definition the elites—the leaders who make the binding decisions for a society—possess the power to quash freedom, they pose a greater danger to the democratic process than do apathetic masses. For example, during the Weimar Republic some pro-Nazi college professors, intellectuals, civil servants, and judges attacked parliamentary democracy; thus they helped undermine the democratic political system and prepared the way for the Nazi rise to power in the early 1930s.

Today among the West German masses both students and adults voice fairly strong support for civil liberties. As we saw, West German students express less authoritarian attitudes than do American youth. During 1977 public opinion polls in Britain, West Germany, France, and Italy asked samples of adults to classify each of several freedoms as either a basic human right or a privilege granted by the state. West Germans most often viewed nearly all the political freedoms—freedom from arbitrary arrest or imprisonment, freedom from censorship of the mass media, freedom to emigrate, and equal legal treatment of racial and national minorities—as human rights. Although the United States has a far higher enrollment at the secondary and university levels, Americans interviewed in sample surveys have expressed lower political tolerance toward atheists, communists, and neo-Nazis than have West Germans. When focusing on groups with the same education, occupation, and age, researchers found that West Germans expressed greater tolerance toward atheists than did Americans, a similar tolerance of communists, and less tolerance of neo-Nazis. Significantly, education had a greater impact on American attitudes toward civil liberties. Americans with the least formal education strongly rejected libertarian values; however, highly educated West Germans and Americans expressed only slightly more political tolerance than did West Germans who had not completed secondary school.

Despite the mass support for political tolerance in West Germany, national rankings on a civil liberties scale indicate that West German elites show a weaker commitment to civil liberties than U.S. officials. From the late 1940s through 1966 West Germany experienced more political coercion than the other six industrialized nations. During the late 1970s West German officials displayed less enthusiasm for civil liberties than did the U.S. leadership. They have felt threatened by the communist-controlled German Democratic Republic, by left-wing terrorists (the Baader-Meinhof band for example), and by youths opposed to nuclear armament and environmental pollution. As a response, city and state (*Länder*) governments required loyalty oaths and security checks for civil servants, including teachers. Länder officials of the ruling Christian Democratic party disbarred members of the German Communist party, the neo-Nazi National Democratic party, and the Socialist German Student League from employment in the civil service or the schools. The Federal Constitutional Court ruled that government employees may not "attack the state." The editor of a book criticizing the prison system was charged with "defaming the state and its officials." The police raided printers, publishing houses, and bookstores. State governments censored television broadcasts. By contrast, particularly between 1974 and 1980, the United States courts affirmed the rights of dissident organizations to express their civil liberties. Neither national nor state government agencies harassed left-wing opposition groups. The media enjoyed freedom of speech.[12]

Elite behavior, not mass attitudes learned at school, thus determines the degree of civil liberties within a nation. To most citizens political freedom for unpopular groups has low priority. Even among well-educated persons it assumes less importance than unemployment, inflation, crime, world peace, and personal freedom to move around, attend church, and choose a desirable job. Government denials of civil liberties to dissidents arouse less opposition than high taxes or nuclear power plants. If elites perceive few threats to national security, accept the general rules of political democracy, and face numerous organized groups that possess independent power from government control, then political leaders will probably refrain from repressing the opposition, whatever the mass attitudes toward civil liberties.

IMPACT ON COGNITIVE PERFORMANCE

Across nations neither the type of secondary school nor post-primary enrollments seem to affect student performance in mathematics and science. During the mid-1960s and early 1970s the IEA administered standardized tests in several nations, including the United States, Sweden, England, France, Italy, and West Germany. At this time over 90 percent of American and Swedish students attended comprehensive secondary schools, where all youths have the opportunity to take similar courses. Education policies in the United States and Sweden encouraged a fairly high proportion of students aged seventeen and eighteen to remain in secondary school. By contrast, in England, Italy, France, and especially West Germany students from different social backgrounds gained divergent educational experiences, usually in a specialized academic or vocational school. Compared with Swedish and American youths, fewer students in these four nations remained in secondary school at seventeen or eighteen. Despite these different policies toward comprehensive secondary schools and student enrollments, the IEA tests uncovered only a weak correlation between education policies and scholastic achievements in the six nations. In mathematics and science examinations for the whole national samples American students received the lowest mean scores. Among the top 4 or 5 percent in each country Swedish and English students earned the highest mathematics and science scores. The top 4 percent of American students had higher math scores than the corresponding West German group; in the science examination they scored the third highest, behind their English and Swedish colleagues but ahead of West Germans, French, and Italians. Hence the more selective European schools in West Germany, France, and Italy did not produce higher cognitive achievements than did the more egalitarian ones in the United States and especially Sweden.

A study conducted among sixth-grade students in several nations during 1983 confirmed the high cognitive performance attained earlier by Swedish and English students. On standardized examinations in science, mathematics, and geography, Swedish youths secured the highest scores, closely followed by the English. Canadian students scored third highest, with U.S. pupils ranking lowest in mathematics and the French doing the worst in geography and science.[13] Yet primary school policies in these five nations scarcely explain the cross-national rankings. Whereas sixth-graders achieved the highest scores in egalitarian Sweden and more elitist England, the worst test performance occurred in France and the United States—nations with divergent educational systems.

Whatever the impact of education policies on national cognitive performance, education does shape an individual's political information and intellectual skills. According to the IEA civic education questionnaire, both grade level and instructional methods influenced students' political knowledge. As children moved from elementary school through early secondary school to the last year of secondary education, they gave increasingly correct answers to questions about the meaning of political democracy, the activities performed by national and local governments, countries with a socialized economy and a single political party, and the best ways to judge the accuracy of sources of political information. If a teacher encouraged students to freely express their opinions in class, placed little emphasis on patriotic rituals, and avoided traditional techniques—printed drills, standardized tests, and rote memorization of facts—then pupils attained higher scores on political information tests.[14]

Higher levels of education not only increase a student's political information but also promote those cognitive skills needed for playing an active role in the political system. Adults who have completed higher educational levels—especially college graduates in professional occupations—know more about politics; they also more actively seek information after finishing their formal education. Compared with the less well educated, they read more books, magazines, and newspapers that focus on political issues. They pay closer attention to politics in the print media. University graduates perceive political events through an abstract ideological prism; they can articulate the meaning of "left" and "right" and use these concepts to evaluate public policies, political leaders, and party stands on issues. Having developed the intellectual skills needed to reason about political matters, these "cognitively mobilized" individuals achieve a greater understanding of political phenomena, particularly abstract issues far removed from their own immediate environment.[15] Instead of remaining politically passive, they actively use their information and cognitive skills to shape the public policy process.

IMPACT ON POLITICAL PARTICIPATION

According to most cross-national investigations of contemporary Western societies, education exerts a weak impact on political interest and trust, two components of passive citizenship. The IEA civic education questionnaire indicated that the school curriculum only weakly influenced political interest. Although teachers who stressed patriotic rituals and encouraged students to express their political opinions in class enlarged students' political interest, variables associated with student interaction with parents and peers more strongly influenced it. Other studies have reached similar conclusions about the moderate effects of school curriculum, instructional methods, and teacher attitudes. For example, in the United States, Canada, West Germany, England, Sweden, and Italy, civic education courses had little or no effect on a variety of political attitudes. In Sweden political education courses at the secondary level decreased rather than strengthened students' political interest. Compared with parents and peers, Swedish teachers wielded less influence on their students' concern for politics.

Why do political education courses fail to measurably increase political interest? Not only in the United States but also abroad education policymakers usually stress passive citizenship at the primary level. Most social studies courses are repetitive, superficial, irrelevant, unrealistic, and boring. For this reason they hardly stimulate an interest in political participation.[16]

Among adults advanced education more strongly influences active political participation than passive trust. Highly educated individuals do not always show greater allegiance to the political system; instead perceptions of systemic performance and personal economic dissatisfaction, not level of education, better explain a citizen's degree of political trust. However, active political participation increases with length of education. In Western democracies today groups with the least formal education generally confine their political participation to passive activities like voting and signing petitions. The more active forms of political participation—campaigning in elections, forming a community organization, holding demonstrations, boycotting a business, and staging a rent strike—involve mainly those with a post-secondary education. Even if the material learned in school does not necessarily directly influence the well-educated to become politically active, their education probably indirectly affects participation. People with the highest education feel more politically efficacious about their ability to shape the policy process. They can more effectively articulate their opinions, have greater access to the communications media, possess more political information, and can better understand the relationship between public issues and personal concerns. Compared with the less formally educated, college graduates conceive of political issues in more abstract terms, pay greater attention to political events in the print media, and participate more actively in voluntary associations. All these educational effects stimulate greater political participation.[17]

Although increased formal education encourages the individual to become more politically active, no strong relationship prevails between education and national voter turnouts. U.S. education policies have promoted mass secondary and college education since World War II. As a result, U.S. residents have completed more years of formal schooling than have Canadians or West Europeans. Yet U.S. citizens have shown the lowest rates of electoral participation. If we compare the number of voters as a proportion of the voting-age population, over 90 percent of Italians, around 87 percent of Swedes, 81 percent of West Germans, 78 percent of French, 76 percent of British, and 67 percent of Canadians voted in parliamentary elections during the early 1980s. However, only 53 percent of voting-age citizens in the United States cast a ballot in the 1980 presidential election. Despite the postwar increase in completed years of formal schooling, voter turnout peaked in the 1960 presidential election but declined thereafter.

Rather than education, other factors more strongly influence national variations in voter turnouts—for example, government encouragement of electoral participation and political mobilization of voters by parties, unions, and churches. In Canada and nearly all West European countries government officials automatically register voters. In Britain and most continental European nations social democratic parties and allied trade unions mobilize the electorate, especially factory workers and low-income citizens. The close linkages between political parties and social groups encourage a high voter turnout. By contrast, in the United States citizens need to register before they can participate in the electoral process. Poorer, less well-educated, and more geographically mobile persons often lack the resources to overcome the registration barrier to voting.* Furthermore, democratic socialist parties and labor unions are weaker in the United States than in Europe. No tight alliances link social groups to political parties; members of the same occupation support both major parties. Except for churches, no strong organizations mobilize poorer citizens. Americans with low socioeconomic status (education, income, occupation) show lower voter turnouts than do Europeans with similar social backgrounds.[18] For these institutional and organizational reasons, the higher levels of completed education in the United States have not led to a more participant citizenry at national elections.

IMPACT ON SOCIAL MOBILITY

Just as education influences the rate of individual (if not national) political participation, so it shapes individual opportunities for social mobility. Upward mobility means that a son or daughter has a higher-status job than does the father. Across several nations a high correlation exists between educational levels and occupational prestige—that is, the longer a person attends school, the higher the status of the occupation he or she enters. In the United States education has the strongest direct impact on occupational status. Family background, as measured by the father's occupational status and education, affects the children's occupational status mainly by providing them the resources to finance the advanced education required for upward mobility. As children become more highly educated, their father's occupational background exerts a weaker effect on their own job status. Individuals from less prestigious backgrounds- mainly blue-collar, farm, and black families—reap the greatest status benefits from a college education, which they need to overcome the disadvantages of their social origins. In Canada, Sweden, and to a lesser extent Britain, post-secondary education enables poorer students to surmount a disadvantageous family position and achieve a higher-status occupation. Education wields a weaker impact on occupational prestige in France and Italy than in the United States, Canada, Sweden,

*When we compare the number of voters as a proportion of the registered population, U.S. citizens attain a larger electoral turnout than the French, British, and Canadians. In the United States the more formally educated individuals show a greater tendency to both register and to vote after becoming registered.

or Britain. Compared with U.S., Canadian, and Swedish youths, French and Italian students enjoy fewer opportunities to gain a post-secondary education. Hence the fathers' occupational prestige more strongly affects the job status of their sons and daughters.[19]

Even when policymakers widen access to higher education and thereby expand the chances for individual upward mobility, they maintain the existing social stratification system. Although Dickens's Gradgrind expected that the school would teach people the skills needed to perform new occupational roles, most individuals learn new skills through on-the-job training, not in a formal educational setting. Even most college graduates acquire advanced occupational skills by informally observing how other employees perform their work. Rather than promoting investment in "human capital," a university education screens individuals, allowing only those with a certain degree, certificate, or examination to obtain a position. A higher degree certifies that a person has taken certain courses and supposedly gained the educational background needed for a prestigious occupation. As John Angle, Steven Steiber, and David Wissmann observe: "Young people coming out of school may be like canned goods; i.e., their contents are unknown and to be guessed at only from their labels—the transcripts and diplomas which are awarded for staying in an institution for a given length of time."[20]

However great the stress placed on equal educational opportunity, all school systems to some extent reinforce the economic role hierarchy. Besides providing certificates of entry into a high-status job, secondary schools and especially colleges offer separate programs that train the masses and the elites and prepare individuals for occupations with divergent wealth, status, and political power.

French educational policies illustrate the elitist relationship between the school curriculum and training for future jobs. At the second cycle of French secondary schools students aged fifteen select a general or technical program or enter a vocational school. Offering a pre-university curriculum, the general education program includes courses in literature, economics, social studies, mathematics, physical sciences, biology, and some modern technological subjects. Generally children from high-status families concentrate on this program. Destined to become France's professionals, managers, executives, and administrators, these students earn the highest grades in class and obtain the best scores on competitive examinations. Lower in the academic hierarchy comes the technical curriculum, which stresses vocational training. Here students secure education and work experience in such fields as health services, computer programming, and drafting. After graduation a few students transfer to more academic programs. Most takes jobs as supervisors, clerks, technicians, and skilled workers. The vocational secondary schools have the lowest prestige; they train children from less advantaged backgrounds to become mechanics, industrial designers, cooks, or secretaries.

The French higher education system is split into three segments. The most prestigious, the *grandes écoles*, serves mainly upper-class students who will secure employment as the highest-ranking civil servants or as managers in private enterprises. Only those who pass a competitive entrance examination gain admission to the grandes écoles. The next level, the French university system, comprises around seventy universities that serve primarily the middle class; they admit all those who have passed the *baccalauréat* examination. In the past these universities trained teachers; however, now the supply of teachers exceeds the demand, so graduates take lower-ranking posts in government and business or else go unemployed. At the bottom of the French higher education totem pole are the Instituts Universitaires de Technologie (IUTs), which resemble American community colleges. Offering a two-year program, the IUTs train technicians for work in business and the services.

During the 1970s Italian leaders managed a less elitist university system than the French, although the specialized upper secondary schools resembled the French pattern. At the bottom of the educational hierarchy, sons of skilled factory workers attended vocational institutes. Normal schools and technical institutes offered an opportunity for children of salaried employees to become elementary school teachers, technicians, and lower-level managers. The most prestigious upper secondary schools—the classical, artistic, and scientific *liceos*—educated mainly those with business, professional, or managerial family status. Until 1969 graduates from the liceos had the best chance to attend a university. After 1969, however, access to a post-secondary education became more widely available. University enrollments at state and private universities escalated. Yet as late as 1980 fewer than 15 percent of graduates from the public University of Milan came from a manual working-class background.[21]

Compared with French and Italian policymakers, West German education officials operate a more elitist system. Even though all West German children attend common primary schools, at the age of eleven or twelve they split into two tracks. According to their academic performance, about 25 percent of the most talented children—mainly from families whose fathers work in the civil service or other high-ranking white-collar jobs—enter a *gymnasium*, where they take college preparatory courses. After graduating from the gymnasium, they attend universities or professional schools. Successful completion of the university-professional curricula will enable them to secure the highest status, best paid white-collar jobs in West Germany. Most of these jobs go to sons of civil servants. Upon graduation from primary school, the majority of students—notably those from less advantaged social backgrounds—take the vocational track, either at the more prestigious technical schools or at the secondary modern schools, which offer a less academic curriculum. Compared with the U.S. and Canadian systems, West German educational practices place more obstacles before students who want to transfer from the vocational to the academic track.[22]

Although the English educational system has become more open during recent years, it too reinforces economic stratification. The independent schools (called "public" by the English) retain the greatest prestige. Even today they stand at the apex of the educational system. Eton, Harrow, Marlborough, Rugby, and Winchester offer the most exclusive education; historically they have trained the civil service elite. Below these schools come the independent schools that receive direct government grants. Among the state schools, the grammar schools have the highest status. Enrolling less than 5 percent of secondary school children, they offer an academic education to students who plan on attending a university. Today over 80 percent of English teenagers go to a comprehensive secondary school. There, as in North American secondary schools, different tracks or "streams" separate vocationally oriented students from those taking academic programs. At the bottom of the educational hierarchy are technical and secondary modern schools, which offer only a specialized vocational curriculum, mainly to working-class youths.

As in most other countries, the higher education system in England reinforces the economic hierarchy. Future managers, administrators, executives, and professionals—themselves sons and daughters of well-educated, high-status families—attend Oxford or Cambridge. Less advantaged students with middle-class backgrounds go to public universities, such as the larger "redbrick" institutions (Birmingham, Durham, Manchester) or the smaller, newer, plate-glass universities (Essex, Kent). Students from lower middle-class and working-class families are most likely to enroll in the rapidly expanding polytechnics—colleges of art, technology, and commerce. The further education colleges and evening institutes provide education to the least wealthy individuals.[23]

Among the seven industrialized nations, U.S., Canadian, and Swedish schools offer the greatest opportunities for upward occupational mobility. Policymakers operate comprehensive schools at the secondary level that all youths can attend. Despite this stress on equalizing educational opportunities, however, elitism still prevails. Often school administrators assign children of different social backgrounds to different tracks. Whereas working-class students usually take the vocational track, middle-class youths choose more academic courses that prepare them for college. At the higher educational level a further occupational sorting takes place. In both Canada and the United States community colleges either train future nurses, computer programmers, office clerks, and skilled craft workers or prepare students to transfer to a state university. State universities usually prepare students for entry into lower-ranking white-collar jobs: accounting, office management, teaching, laboratory work, and so forth. Private schools operated by religious denominations offer a curriculum similar to that of the state universities. At the top of the educational system are the elite private schools (McGill, Carleton, Harvard, Yale, Princeton, Chicago, Stanford) and such public graduate institutions as the University of Toronto, University of Michigan, and University of California at Berkeley. These universities assume the responsibility for educating the future managerial-professional elite.

Like North Americans, Swedish youths secure more equal opportunities at the secondary level than at the universities. Nearly all Swedish students from sixteen to nineteen attend a comprehensive school; there they can specialize in college preparatory, commercial, or technical programs. Swedish policy officials have designed the higher education system to directly serve professional needs. The advanced technical institutions train engineers, business administrators, dentists, librarians, and architects. The universities, such as in

Stockholm, Gothenburg, Uppsala, Umeå, and Lund, prepare students for careers in law, the civil service, scientific research, and academia. Despite the Swedish commitment to expanding the educational opportunities for all individuals, fewer youths from working-class backgrounds than from higher socioeconomic levels gain a university education.[24]

In sum, all educational systems allocate individuals to divergent positions in the economic stratification system. Equal opportunity to gain upward social mobility takes priority over equality of access to higher education for all youths. Although the more egalitarian education policies in the United States, Canada, and Sweden give students from less advantaged families the chance to enter a higher-status occupation than their fathers held, the educational system still enables children of the managerial and professional elite to enter the same prestigious occupations as their parents.[25]

Whatever the impact of higher education on an individual's mobility, the degree of equal educational opportunity within a nation only partially explains national rates of occupational mobility. During the 1970s the United States, Canada, and Sweden offered the most equal access to post-secondary education—that is, a larger percentage of individuals between the ages of twenty and twenty-four attended a higher educational institution in these countries than in France, Italy, West Germany, or Britain.* As expected, citizens in these three nations experienced the greatest upward mobility, measured by the proportion of nonmanual employees who came from manual and farm backgrounds. However, England had the lowest share of youth aged twenty to twenty-four gaining a post-secondary education, but the English experienced higher occupational mobility than did the French, Italians, and especially the West Germans.[26]

The incongruence between access to higher education and national rates of intergenerational mobility partly stems from the supply of high-status occupations in a society. If the number of prestigious jobs exceeds the number of well-educated individuals, expanding the opportunities for post-secondary education will promote upward

---

*According to the *World Development Report 1983* (New York: Oxford University Press, 1983), 197, in 1979 the following percentages of the population aged twenty to twenty-four were enrolled in higher education: 55 percent—United States; 37 percent—Sweden; 36 percent—Canada; 27 percent—Italy; 26 percent—West Germany; 25 percent—France; 20 percent—United Kingdom.

social mobility. However, when the supply of university graduates outstrips the supply of prestigious occupations, increased university enrollments will not lead to greater social mobility. Indeed during the late 1970s and early 1980s graduates outnumbered prestigious jobs when the economic recession brought rising unemployment levels among university graduates. As the possibilities for securing a professional job declined, the educated unemployed became a larger share of the labor force. Swedish policymakers tried to diminish this problem by both expanding the supply of government jobs and restricting access to university majors that held few job prospects. The proportion of the labor force employed by the government rose from 13 percent in 1960 to nearly 31 percent in 1980; over four-fifths of these public employees worked in the health, education, and social service sectors. Although Swedish university students welcomed the more numerous jobs in the public sector, they resented government decisions curtailing their freedom to choose courses that met their needs rather than the needs of government planners.[27] In most Western nations education officials have failed to reconcile the increased demands for access to higher education with the limited supply of prestigious positions in a recessionary economy.

CONCLUSION: THE POLICY IMPACTS REAPPRAISED

What is the general impact of education policies and experiences on values, cognitive achievements, and role behaviors? We distinguished above among three outcomes: policy impacts vs. effects of the educational experience, individual vs. national outcomes of education, and the consequences of the school vs. other socializing agencies like the family, peer group, and mass media. Using these three distinctions, we can draw the following conclusions.

First, educational policies influence a student's behavior only if they shape the school experience. Some of the most important school variables affecting children—especially the interaction between teacher and student—remain beyond the control of education policymakers. Yet everywhere teachers play the key mediating role between the policymakers and students. Teachers' expectations about student performance, their enthusiasm for the course material, their motivation to help students learn, their teaching effectiveness, and students' identification with an instructor's values may have the greatest impact on student behavior.[28]

Second, education policies and the school experience influence individual behavior more than national levels of cognitive achievement, political freedom, electoral participation, or social mobility. As a student moves upward through grade levels, he or she acquires increasingly more political information. Advanced education imparts the cognitive skills needed to process information about the political world. Indirectly these intellectual abilities encourage individuals to actively seek further political knowledge in books, newspapers, and magazines. More educated people, especially college graduates, also place a higher value on civil liberties. Perhaps a university education, particularly in the social sciences and the humanities, provides students with a variety of viewpoints that increase tolerance of diverse groups. The university curriculum may also teach the cognitive skills to link abstract civil liberties to specific situations.

Education also affects an individual's role behavior, especially political participation and occupational mobility. Elementary and secondary schools stress passive rather than active citizen roles. Civics courses uphold the passive virtues of trust, social harmony, political consensus, and allegiance to the political system. As a result, the civics courses taken by pre-university students generally fail to raise their political interest. Yet participation in the most active forms of political behavior—electoral campaigning, forming community organizations to resolve public problems, engaging in nonviolent demonstrations- rises with increasing education. This correlation between active political participation and higher education stems less from the direct effects of the university curriculum than from the tendency of individuals with high formal education to feel more politically efficacious, think more abstractly, and pay greater attention to politics in the mass media. Particularly in the United States, Canada, and Sweden, the policy commitment to expanding equal access to higher education has meant that some individuals from disadvantaged backgrounds have the opportunity to secure a university degree and thereby secure a higher-status job than their fathers held.

Education wields less impact on national (in contrast to individual) indicators of political freedom, voter turnouts, and social mobility. The strength of social pluralism and of elite commitments to civil liberties, rather than mass support for freedom learned in the schools, largely determines a nation's standing on civil liberties scales. High rates of national electoral participation mainly stem from activist organizations that mobilize the vote and from rules that facilitate voting, such as automatic registration of voters by government officials. Years of formal education completed do not explain the cross-national differences in voter turnouts. Similarly the extent of social mobility within various countries depends less on equal access to higher education than on the match between the number of university graduates and the supply of high-status occupations.

Third, other socializing agencies—e.g., the mass media, family, and peer groups—interact with the school to affect political cognition, values, and role behaviors. The influence of each depends on its stimuli, reinforcements, and control over the individual. Radio, television, newspapers, magazines, and books contribute information about the political world. To the extent that this information creates a negative image about politics, people may become more cynical, disillusioned, and alienated toward the government. The legitimacy of officials and policies will decline. Even though education policymakers try to use the school curriculum to inculcate the values of national loyalty, support, and trust, teachers and the civic education curriculum may not exert sufficient power to overcome the delegitimizing effects of the mass media.[29]

In the Western industrial world the family profoundly affects a person's educational, political, and economic behavior. During the pre-university years a student's home background—for example, size of family and parents' socioeconomic status—exerts a strong impact on political interest, discussions about political issues, use of the print media, and the political knowledge learned in school. Children from low-status backgrounds, compared with their higher-status classmates, generally read fewer books, receive less family encouragement to do well in school, have less access to tutors, perform less well on standardized examinations, earn lower grades in school, repeat more grades, participate in fewer extracurricular activities, feel more alienated from school, and drop out of school earlier. As a natural result, they are less likely to attend a university. Their lack of a college education means lower rates of active political participation and less access to prestigious occupations. Children of low-income parents need a post-secondary education to overcome their early home disadvantages. In nations with more closed educational systems, such as

England, France, and Italy, a lower proportion of people between the ages of twenty and twenty-four have the opportunity to attend college. Therefore the family background exerts a stronger influence on the prestige of the first job than in the United States, Canada, and Sweden, where a student's education mainly affects economic achievements. If a Swedish, Canadian, or U.S. father has attained a high education and occupational status, his children will also likely complete college, which will then expand their social mobility. Thus in the more open educational systems family background *indirectly* affects economic success.[30]

Like parents, peers also increase an individual's economic prospects and political participation. Most Western youths rely on personal contacts, particularly friends and relatives, to find employment; newspaper advertisements and job placement agencies hold less importance. By developing peer group friendships, a person can establish the personal ties needed for securing a high-status occupation. Political discussions with friends and family members expand political interest and adult participation in political life. Since friends usually come from the same social background as the students themselves, both families and peer groups reinforce the inequalities of political activity.[31]

Finally, education policies affect political values, information, and role behaviors. Even though a college education exerts a greater impact on political knowledge and support for civil liberties, less orthodox and more democratic methods used to teach a secondary school civics class increase political information and enthusiasm for political freedom. Judith V. Torney, A. N. Oppenheim, and Russell F. Farnen summarize the outcomes of civic education in several Western nations:

> These [IEA] data also lend some comfort to those who for years have advised teachers to step down from their platforms, get away from the flag, throw away their drill sheets and engage students in a discussion of the issues of the day.[32]

A secondary school civics curriculum thus expands students' political information and commitment to civil liberties if teachers downplay the Gradgrind approach to education, as exemplified by rote memorization of facts, classroom rituals, and actions that discourage the free expression of students' ideas about political issues. Even if education policies do not realize the grandiose expectations envisioned by some school advocates, educational institutions still partially shape students' values, information, skills, and role behaviors. From this perspective education does make a difference.

Chapter 4

THE EFFECTIVENESS OF PUBLIC HEALTH POLICIES

During late 1978 Senator Edward Kennedy, who chaired a subcommittee on health and scientific research, held hearings about the quality of health insurance programs in the United States and Canada. To evaluate the two nations' health policies, he heard testimonies from people with similar ages, socioeconomic backgrounds, and illnesses in both countries. For instance, Mrs. Mary Cihak from McGrath, Minnesota, had three sons with cerebral palsy. Because her husband experienced severe headaches, depressions, and high blood pressure, he could secure only temporary jobs. As a result, Mrs. Cihak supplied the family income, yet she earned only $500 a month—hardly enough to pay the more than $20,000 in bills that had accumulated for her family's care. Although the Cihaks applied for private medical insurance, the insurance companies rejected their applications on the grounds that the sons' illness made them poor risks. The only governmental assistance came from a Supplemental Security Income benefit of $189 a month. If Mrs. Cihak's earnings increased, she would lose even that small amount. Without adequate medical care for several years, her sons and husband had grown progressively worse by 1978. In Montreal, Quebec, the Richard Polewzuck family faced similar problems with ill children. Two children were born with spina bifida, which causes paralysis of the spine. One daughter required eight major surgeries, lengthy hospital stays, three sets of lung lead braces, extensive therapy, and twenty-four-hour nursing care in a private room. The Quebec government's health insurance program paid all the expenses—including the hospital care, nursing assistance, braces, and neurosurgical operations at the Royal Victoria Hospital. The Polewzuck family simply received a notice reporting costs of $50,000 incurred by the hospital.

Not only children but also the elderly receive different health care treatment in the United States and Canada. During the 1970s

Mrs. Elizabeth Wolfe, an Ohio resident in her late sixties, experienced a ruptured optical muscle, broken hips, hernia, and gastritis. When the medical problems began, Blue Cross canceled her insurance policies because of excessive claims. Unable to afford the high premiums demanded for a new policy, Mrs. Wolfe relied on social security and Medicare payments, but these failed to cover her medical expenses. When Mrs. Wolfe testified before Senator Kennedy's subcommittee, she had not paid most of her medical bills; collection agencies harassed her to pay the hospital and optician bills. By contrast, the Walter Griffin family of Toronto, Ontario, faced similar medical problems but never went into debt. Mrs. Griffin testified that even though her husband had experienced two heart attacks and a hernia since 1975, he merely received a notice from the hospital that the Ontario Health Insurance Plan (OHIP) had paid the $3325 hospital expenses. Relieved of the financial burdens, Mrs. Griffin regarded the OHIP as "the most wonderful thing that anyone can ever have."[1]

At these hearings people not only described their health care, but also evaluated the public health policies in their countries. I will evaluate health care systems in Canada, the United States, England, West Germany, France, and Sweden according to four criteria: (1) the effectiveness of public health policies in lowering infant mortality rates and raising life expectancy, (2) the equality of health care, (3) the economic efficiency of health programs, and (4) public satisfaction with health care policies. By examining health policy performance, we will see how these countries rank on the four criteria.

Several problems confront the policy analyst who evaluates health care performance. First, the objectives and structures of public health policies reflect a complex pattern. Policymakers aim to fulfill different objectives—equality of access to health care, a high quality of health treatment, economic efficiency, public satisfaction with the policy performance, and general individual well-being. Yet these objectives may come into conflict. Systems that guarantee egalitarian access may sacrifice high quality care. Efficient performance may generate public dissatisfaction with health treatments. Furthermore, many organizations participate in the formulation and especially the implementation of health policies. The central government often has the responsibility to frame general goals, raise revenues, and allocate expenditures. Usually it delegates authority to decentralized agencies— Swedish counties, U.S. states, Canadian provinces, German Länder, and English district health authorities. In France and West Germany semipublic sickness insurance funds review claims and pay benefits. U.S. private insurance companies help administer government health programs such as Medicare and Medicaid. Everywhere in these private enterprise economies doctors retain extensive autonomy. Private medical associations play an active role in the health policy process. Health officials—physicians, nurses, insurance agents, and government leaders at different levels—participate in both preventive and curative medicine.

Second, when making health policies, all these participants face uncertainty about the linkages between policy inputs and health outcomes. To what extent will greater health expenditures, a higher physician/patient ratio, a decentralized administration, or an expanded scope of health care benefits improve the health of a nation's people? Factors other than public policies affecting individual health include environmental conditions—housing, education, the occupational situation—and personal behavior, such as diet, exercise, and hygiene. Particularly in a democratic political system policymakers cannot directly control all the environmental conditions or individual behaviors that produce good health.

Third, although policy evaluation rests on an empirical base, it is also a subjective process that arouses contention among analysts. All investigators do not agree on the specific values that should constitute the evaluative standards. Should quality of health care take priority over equal access to physician treatments? For researchers dedicated to competitive individualism and a free-market economy efficiency is more important than public satisfaction with health programs. Disagreements also arise about the most valid procedures to measure general values like equality, efficiency, and even health. We can verbally define standards, but analysts can less easily find operational indicators that measure them satisfactorily. For example, although the most widely used indicators of "health" refer to infant mortality rates and years of life expectancy, these data reflect death rates, not necessarily the quality of life. People may survive for a long time but be sick during half that period. Yet cross-national information about morbidity is difficult to obtain and interpret. Hence despite the difficulties, infant mortality and life expectancy constitute useful measures of "health"—that is, the ability to perform a role without serious physical or mental impediments.[2]

EFFECTIVENESS OF HEALTH CARE POLICIES IN REDUCING INFANT MORTALITY AND RAISING LIFE EXPECTANCY

Infant mortality and life expectancy rates show an inverse correlation. As Table 4.1 suggests, countries with a low infant death rate (like Sweden) have a high life expectancy. In 1980 only 7 Swedish children out of 1000 live births died during the first year. Average life expectancy at birth was 75 years; throughout the world only the Japanese lived longer than the Swedes. France and Canada also have low infant mortality and high life expectancy. Where more children die during the first year, life expectancy is shorter, as in England and West Germany. Studies of general mortality rates in the six Western industrial nations indicate that the Swedes have the lowest aggregate death rates caused by cancer, coronary heart disease, stroke, and accidents. The West Germans, who have the highest infant mortality and lowest life expectancy, suffer the highest death rates from these four diseases.[3] Using these three indicators, we can rank the six countries in the following order: Sweden, France, Canada, England, the United States, and West Germany.

Table 4.1

INFANT MORTALITY AND LIFE EXPECTANCY, 1980

Country	Infant Mortality (Deaths under One Year per 1000 Live Births)	Life Expectancy at Birth (Years)
Sweden	6.9	75
France	10.0	74
Canada	10.4	74
England and Wales	12.0	73
United States	12.5	74
West Germany	12.6	73

Sources: World Health Organization (WHO), *World Health Statistics Annual*, vol. 1 (Geneva, 1982), 18-20; *OECD Observer*, no. 121 (March 1983): 26; World Bank, *World Development Report, 1982* (New York: Oxford University Press, 1982), 111.

France, Canada, the United States, and England and Wales changed their infant mortality rankings between 1950 and 1980 (see Table 4.2). Whereas France (along with West Germany) had the highest infant death rates during 1950, thirty years later it had the second lowest, next to Sweden. Canada also improved its record over this period. The United States and England, however, performed less impressively in 1980 than in 1950. Five years after World War II ended, the United States had the lowest infant death rate after Sweden. However, by 1980 only West Germany experienced a higher infant mortality rate than did the United States. Similarly in 1950 England suffered about as low an infant mortality rate as the United States; thirty years later it ranked below France and Canada.

Even though infant mortality rates show a more remarkable improvement over time than do life expectancy records, the longevity trends during the 1970s reveal similar cross-national patterns. Women in all six nations lived from six to eight years longer than men. From 1970 to 1980 women in all countries except the United States and England also improved their life expectancy vis-à-vis men—that is, they made greater progress in lengthening the average number of years they remained alive. Life expectancy among men increased the most in the United States and West Germany, the two nations with the lowest records of male life expectancy. By contrast, Swedish men reached a plateau; their life expectancy remained about constant during the 1970s.

To what extent do public health policies account for these cross-national rankings and changes over time? Answers to this question depend on the assumptions about the causes of illness and the impact of health policies on two general causes—individual behavior and environmental conditions. According to the individualist rationale, illness stems from a person's reason, will, and lifestyle. If he or she eats nutritious meals, jogs before dawn, jumps rope at dusk, gets eight hours of sleep a day, avoids stress, maintains personal hygiene, acts without negligence on the job, and refrains from indulging in drugs, cigarets, and alcohol, good health will result—maybe even wealth. Benjamin Franklin, an early advocate of competitive individualism, decreed: "Early to bed and early to rise makes a man healthy, wealthy, and wise." Even James Thurber, who remained skeptical about the favorable outcomes of personal prudence, seemed to feel

Table 4.2

INFANT MORTALITY AND LIFE EXPECTANCY: HISTORICAL TRENDS, 1950-80

Country	Infant Mortality (Deaths under One Year per 1000 Live Births)				Life Expectancy at Birth (Years)					
					Males			Females		
	1950	1960	1970	1980	1970	1975	1980	1970	1975	1980
Sweden	21	16.6	11.0	6.9	72.3	72.2	72.8	77.4	78.1	79.1
France	52	27.4	18.2	10.0	69.1	69.5	70.8	76.7	77.5	79.1
Canada	41	27.3	18.8	10.4	69.3	69.8	71.4	76.2	77.5	78.9
England and Wales	30	21.8	18.2	12.0	68.8	69.7	70.7	75.2	75.9	76.8
United States	29	26.0	19.8	12.5	67.1	68.7	70.1	74.8	76.7	77.8
West Germany	55	33.8	23.6	12.6	67.3	68.1	69.9	73.6	74.7	76.8

Sources: WHO: *Annual Epidemiological and Vital Statistics, 1950, 1960* (Geneva, 1953, 1963), 29-33, 25-28, and *World Health Statistics Annual*, vol. 1 (Geneva, 1970-84); *OECD Observer*, no. 121 (March 1983): 26; U.S. Department of Health, Education, and Welfare, National Center for Health Statistics, *Vital Statistics of the United States, 1970,* vol. 2, *Mortality*, Part A (Washington, D.C.: Government Printing Office, 1974), table 5-3; National Center for Health Statistics, *Monthly Vital Statistics Report* 32 (11 August 1983): 3, 7; Health Division, Vital Statistics and Disease Registries Section, *Life Tables, Canada and Provinces, 1980-1982* (Ottawa: Statistics Canada, 1984), 15.

that individuals have some control over their destinies: "Early to rise and early to bed makes a male healthy and wealthy and dead."[4] Besides the factors that individuals can control, other personal causes of illness stem from inherited genetic complications over which they have little control.

Environmental causes of illness originate in the economy and the political system. Economic changes have accounted for both better health and increased illness. Compared with less developed societies, the more industrialized nations generally experience healthier conditions—more adequate sanitation, less crowded housing, and more nutritious diets. In the most highly industrial countries capital equipment eventually brings shorter working hours, less burdensome work, and fewer accidents. Yet as ecologists recognize, technological "advances" also exert noxious side effects such as air and water pollution, toxic chemical emissions, and various cancer-producing agents (asbestos, bischloromethyl ether, polychlorinated biphenols, trichloroethylene, ionizing radiation, and food additives).[5]

Government policies also represent an environmental cause of health. When government leaders have both the will and the resources, they can devise policies that reduce illness. The will to frame specific public health policies partly depends on the elite's political culture—especially on the way that leaders interpret the causes of illness. Those who stress individual responsibility for personal health may support government measures to encourage healthier lifestyles. Strict controls on the sale of alcohol, severe punishment for drunk driving, requirements for the use of automobile airbags, and media campaigns that promote exercise and nutrition may reduce illness. Yet governments have greater power to issue moral injunctions than to ensure compliance with these edicts. Downgrading the effectiveness of government health programs, Aaron Wildavsky doubts the power of the U.S. government to effectively change personal behavior:

Health policy is pathological because we are neurotic and insist on making our government psychotic. Our neurosis consists in knowing what is required for good health (Mother was right: Eat a good breakfast! Sleep eight hours a day! Don't drink! Don't smoke! Keep clean! *And* don't worry!) but not being willing to do it. Government's ambivalence consists in paying coming and going: once for telling people how to be healthy and once for paying their bills when they disregard this advice. Psychosis appears when government persists in this self-defeating play.[6]

Those who perceive that the primary reasons for good health stem from the environment take a more optimistic view of policy effectiveness. Local community programs may encourage healthful living. Technical expertise can reshape environmental conditions. According to this rationale, government policies have greater power to transform the collective causes of illness than individual behavior. Political leaders can more easily require the pasteurization of milk than ensure that every individual boil raw milk each morning. During the twentieth century governments have formulated various policies intended to promote a healthier environment—for example, fluoridation of water, clearance of mosquitoes from swamps, bans on smoking in public places, elimination of toxic chemicals from work sites, and reduction of overcrowded housing.[7]

The comparative success of national efforts to lower infant mortality and increase life expectancy partly depends on policymakers' conception of the public good, their will to act, and their power vis-à-vis groups resisting government health policies. More than any other country, Sweden has developed public health programs that produce the lowest infant death rates and the highest life expectancy. Most Swedes regard good health care as a public right, not a private privilege. Expressing a voluntaristic ethos, Swedish policymakers believe that government actions can change both personal behavior and environmental conditions. In Sweden, unlike in the United States, private physicians' associations, private hospitals, and private insurance companies lack the political power to obstruct comprehensive public health care programs. The low infant mortality rates stem from the government maternal services available to all Swedish women, regardless of income. Nearly all pregnant women secure prenatal care at a local maternity health center. For the first two years after a child's birth, over 97 percent of all mothers visit a free child health clinic, where pediatric nurses and pediatricians provide physical examinations, diagnostic tests, immunizations, and counseling. Public schools and health agencies make available extensive information about family planning, so that most children are born to women between twenty and thirty-five years old, the period when the fewest infant deaths occur.

Swedes have attained a long life expectancy mainly because their government has designed public programs intended to realize a healthy environment and healthier individual lifestyles. A high degree of income equality, combined with the comprehensive social services available to every citizen, give all Swedes access to health care. Government policies have promoted industrial safety, encouraged hygiene at factories, and reduced industrial pollution. By regulating the sale of alcohol, imposing severe penalties on drunk drivers, and sponsoring anti-smoking campaigns that forbid the advocacy of tobacco use, the government has reduced consumption of alcohol and cigarets. In these ways it has encouraged healthier individual behavior.[8]

Canada represents a nation whose public policies have improved its relative health standing over the past three decades. Whereas in 1950 Canada had the fourth highest infant mortality rate among six countries, by 1980 this rate had fallen to the third lowest after Sweden and France. Life expectancy for men in 1980 was higher than in any other nation except Sweden. Canadian women live nearly as long as Swedish and French women (see Table 4.2). The comprehensive health care programs instituted by the provincial governments after World War II largely explain these longitudinal improvements. In 1957 the federal government implemented the Hospital Insurance and Diagnostic Services Act that provided hospital services for all citizens, regardless of income. Ten years later the federal parliament enacted a medical care act to finance the cost of physicians' care. People of all ages receive inexpensive health benefits under these two programs. Special plans for maternal care have reduced infant mortality. Provincial government health departments sponsor programs for family planning, prenatal care, and nutrition. In local communities public health nurses offer maternal care at child health centers, hospitals, clinics, schools, and homes. Most provincial legislatures require employers to grant mothers a maternity leave both before and after a child's birth; these leaves extend from six to seventeen weeks. According to these laws, no employer can fire a mother for taking her guaranteed maternity leave.[9]

Like Canada, France after World War II made considerable progress lowering infant death rates. Along with the Germans, the French suffered extensive damage from the war. In 1950 both peoples had about the same infant mortality rates; over 50 infants for every 1000 died during the first year of birth. By 1980, however, France's infant mortality ranking had risen from fifth lowest to second highest. As in Sweden and Canada, the maternal care policies implemented by the government partly explain this health progress. All French mothers receive prenatal and postnatal family allowances. To obtain a prenatal grant expectant mothers must take a medical examination. They can get a postnatal allowance for two years if their children have periodic health examinations. Under the national health insurance program mothers receive paid maternity leaves that last between ten and twenty-eight weeks, depending on the mother's health and the number of children living with her.[10]

Despite the rapid economic progress made by West Germany since World War II, improvements in health seem less impressive. At the end of the war West Germany had the highest infant mortality rate of the six Western nations. Thirty years later it still retained that ranking. During the late 1970s West Germans faced higher infant mortality rates than did their East German neighbors, who inhabit a less economically developed country. After the war health policy-makers failed to implement the comprehensive prenatal and post-natal maternal care policies of Sweden, Canada, and France. Like U.S. officials, West German leaders have given less attention to caring for infants than to treating the health problems of the aged. Hence although life expectancy rates remain lower than the average in Western industrial societies, today the typical West German lives to nearly the same age as the average English man and woman.[11]

The infant mortality rankings of England and the United States vis-à-vis other nations have declined. In 1950 England showed a lower infant death rate than all the other countries except Sweden and the United States. Thirty years later, however, England ranked behind not only Sweden but also France and Canada. The United States had the second lowest infant mortality rate in 1950 but the second highest rate in 1980. The structure of the health care systems in the two nations hardly explains the declining performance. Whereas the British government in 1948 instituted a centralized National Health Service (NHS) providing comprehensive benefits to all citizens, U.S. policy-makers have preferred a more decentralized system where nongovern-ment agencies make crucial health decisions. Particularistic programs offer different health care services for divergent groups—the aged, the poor, veterans, and so forth. The U.S. Congress instituted the most significant public program in 1965, when it enacted the Medicare plan for the aged and the Medicaid plan for the poor. Despite the expansion of maternal and infant health programs during the 1960s and the establishment of community health centers, funds for these policies have remained limited. Government programs to provide maternal and child care for low-income mothers have received less support from U.S. officials than have health policies to assist the elderly. As a partial result, infant mortality rates show striking differences according to parental ethnic group and income. For example, in 1980 the death rate of white infants was 11 for every 1000 live births but 21 for black infants. Native American children have infant mortality rates about double the white figure. Poverty influences the probability that an infant will die during the first year. Even if we hold constant the effects of parental education, mother's age, mother's previous pregnancies, birth order of child, infant's weight at birth, possession of health insurance, and location of birth (in or out of a hospital), infants of low-income white mothers suffer 50 percent higher death rates than those of higher income mothers. Significantly, in 1976 only two-thirds of low-income expectant mothers saw a physician during their first three months of pregnancy, compared with 96 percent of high-income mothers. During the 1970s nearly half the states failed to finance prenatal care under the Medicaid program; in 1979 around 40 percent of black mothers, compared with 20 percent of white mothers, had no prenatal health services during the first three months of pregnancy.

Similarly in England infant mortality bears a close relationship with family economic position. During the 1970s infants born to unskilled working class parents had over double the mortality rate of infants whose parents worked in professional occupations. Compared with other mothers, unskilled working class mothers make the least use of child health services. When they do seek medical care, they visit a less trained general practitioner with access to poorer facilities. English policymakers have given less attention than Swedish health officials to providing specialized child care services. There are fewer child health centers in England than in Sweden; during the first year of life fewer English children visit a physician or a public health nurse. As a consequence, a higher proportion of English than Swedish children die during the first year. The comparative scarcity of specialized child health care services particularly endangers low-income English children.[12]

In sum, throughout the Western world public policies have achieved greater success in lowering infant mortality rates than in raising life expectancy. Particularly if governments promote prenatal and postnatal care for all mothers, the overall infant death rate should decline. Public programs to increase life expectancy, however, involve greater control over individual lifestyles and environmental conditions. In every industrial nation the wealthier are healthier. People at the top of the social stratification system—those who have a college education, hold professional and managerial jobs, and earn more than twice the national median income—achieve a longer life expectancy and fall less prey to cancer, tuberculosis, pneumonia, or illness stemming from violence and accidents. These people experience greater physical fitness, shorter illnesses, and briefer absences from work. By contrast, primary school educated persons, unskilled manual workers, and people earning less than the median income live a shorter life and show a greater likelihood of dying from cancer, tuberculosis, bronchitis, pneumonia, violence, and accidents suffered on both the job and the highway. The low-status people also suffer from poorer physical fitness, lengthier disabilities, and longer absences from their jobs.[13] Illness stems from both individual and environmental causes. People from higher socioeconomic backgrounds can more effectively surmount the individual obstacles to a healthy lifestyle. Because they live in a healthier, safer environment, they also experience better personal health. To the extent that public policies can help overcome the individual and environmental causes of illness, they will narrow the socioeconomic differences in life expectancy.

Certain aspects of individual behavior cause groups at the bottom of the social stratification system to face lower life expectancy. For example, people from unskilled working class backgrounds consume more cigarets than do professional employees. Cigaret consumption leads to greater risk of death from lung cancer. Moreover, unskilled manual workers usually have less formal education and thus lower personal efficacy. More resigned to their situation, they feel less optimistic about the prospects of improving their health. When interacting with a physician, they ask him fewer questions about their illness, provide less information, converse for a shorter time, and achieve less rapport with both doctor and nurse. From a cognitive perspective individuals with little formal education know less about the causes and cures of illness, have less information about specific techniques for good health, can less easily understand complex advice given by a physician, and experience greater difficulty appraising the long-range consequences of their behavior on personal health.[14] By promoting mass education programs for all citizens, public policymakers can help such people learn the cognitive skills needed to maintain a healthy lifestyle and extend their life expectancy.

Environmental sources affect the health status of different social groups because people from lower socioeconomic backgrounds work in a less safe environment, live in more dilapidated housing, eat less nutritious food, and have less access to health care services. Hence they die younger. The work experience particularly affects life expectancy. Compared with managerial, professional, and white-collar employees, manual workers become more exposed to toxic chemicals, defective machinery, radioactive wastes, dirt, heat, noise, contaminated water, and polluted air. Their jobs involve more repetitive, boring tasks. As a result, they suffer more from industrial accidents, skin cancer, radiation diseases, and other industrial injuries. Along with unsafe, unhealthy working conditions go problems associated with poverty. Lower-income individuals have less money and thus fewer resources to purchase nutritious food. Plagued by higher rates of unemployment, they face more malnutrition, stress, and depression. Whether employed or not, manual workers live in more overcrowded, substandard housing that lacks adequate sanitation.

Compared with U.S. leaders, Swedish officials have implemented more effective policies to improve industrial working conditions and upgrade housing for all economic classes. Sweden has one-half the number of annual industrial injuries for each worker than does the United States. In 1974 the Swedish parliament enacted a law that established a health and safety committee in every large plant with over fifty workers. Comprising a working class majority, these health committees can stop dangerous industrial operations, inspect medical records and work conditions, supervise each enterprise's occupational health service, appoint physicians and sanitary engineers, and veto plans for new machines that injure workers' health. Within a factory safety stewards have the authority to suspend production if they perceive dangers to health. Representatives from Swedish government agencies like the National Board of Occupational Health and Safety, the Joint Health and Safety Council, and local inspectorate councils prescribe national health standards, inspect factories to ensure compliance with these standards, and provide information to factories about safe new technical innovations that promote industrial health. By contrast, the U.S. government has experienced difficulty promoting healthier conditions in factories. Opposed by Republican government officials and business executives, the Occupational Safety and Health Administration remains underfunded and understaffed. Few inspectors are available to guarantee compliance with standards for health and safety. (For every 100,000 workers, Sweden has approximately four times the number of inspectors as the United States.) Employers found guilty of violating health regulations incur low fines. Less than 10 percent of U.S. factories have health and safety committees. Managers, rather than workers, dominate these committees, which possess only limited authority to veto injurious work practices and remove defective machinery. As a consequence, U.S. workers face greater health hazards on the job than do Swedes. Similarly, the U.S. government has shown only a weak commitment to expanding safe public housing for the poor because the housing market is dominated by private banks, realtors, and home builders. By contrast, the Swedish government has authorized the construction of extensive public housing; in 1975 municipal nonprofit housing companies and cooperatives owned about 35 percent of all housing units. By granting housing allowances to residents and disbursing loans to local government agencies, cooperatives, and nonprofit housing associations, the central government has promoted more equal access to adequate housing for all citizens. Through these job safety and housing policies Swedish officials have helped raise life expectancy rates to the highest of the six countries.[15]

EQUALITY OF HEALTH CARE

The equality of health services—a standard closely related to social group differences in life expectancy and infant mortality rates— refers to several dimensions. At the least stringent level it means access or availability—i.e., all groups, regardless of education, income, or occupation, have the same access to physicians, dentists, hospitals, and other medical facilities. A second dimension involves equal use of health services vis-à-vis individual need. All people with the same disabilities and chronic limitations make the same number of visits to a physician's office, clinic, or hospital. Third, equality can mean equal health care. All individuals with the same physical-mental needs receive the same quality of medical treatment, as measured by (1) the competence of physicians (particularly their education, training, and skill), (2) the adequacy of hospital facilities, medical equipment, and health supplies, and (3) the availability of effective drugs and medicines.[16] Health policymakers can more easily guarantee equal access than equal use of health benefits or particularly the same quality health care for everybody.

Although the establishment of the NHS in 1948 brought more equal access to health care in Britain, striking group differences still mark the use of its health programs. The poor now receive lower quality, less available care, especially from a trained specialist. Semi-skilled workers, unskilled manual workers, and domestic service workers gain the fewest benefits from the NHS. Generally areas with high concentrations of unskilled factory workers, especially in northern England, secure the lowest number of physicians, the fewest health clinics, and the fewest expenditures. Middle and upper class individuals (professionals, managers, administrators) have greater access to a general practitioner and hospital specialist; they receive a higher ratio of NHS expenditures for every person who reports ill to a general practitioner or who goes to a hospital.

Relative to their physical-mental needs, British upper class groups make greater use of health care services. In particular, middle and upper class mothers use preventive health services before and after birth to a greater extent than do working class mothers. What variables explain the differential use of health services? Individuals from professional and managerial families have more time to visit a doctor. Wealthy enough to afford a telephone and car, they can phone for a medical appointment and drive to the doctor's office in their own automobile. Usually they have medical facilities near their homes. Since they earn a monthly salary, they can more easily take the time off from employment to visit a physician. By contrast, unskilled working class persons often lack their own telephone and hence cannot phone for a doctor's appointment. They must use public transportation, rather than their own car. Fewer medical facilities are located near their residences. Paid in wages by the hour or day, working class employees suffer greater economic losses when taking time off from their jobs to secure medical treatments.

Individuals from the British middle and upper classes also gain higher quality health care. Administered by middle class professionals, the NHS provides the best services to people with the same prestigious social background. Compared with working class patients, middle and upper class people secure access to physicians who not only have greater professional training but also show greater interest in their patients. Doctors consult with an upper class patient for a longer time. They know more about the home situation of upper status persons, who gain more information about their case as well as a faster response to their complaints. By contrast, working class patients have less ready access to a technically trained physician. Feeling less rapport with their doctor, they perceive him as more uncommunicative, indifferent, uncaring, and unhelpful. Particularly in the poorest areas of London, general practitioners serving low-income people are older and less qualified than physicians treating wealthier persons.[17]

In the United States too, socioeconomic status affects an individual's contact with health care services. True, the 1965 Medicare and Medicaid laws made health services more available to the poor. In 1976 the differential access rates between high- and low-income individuals were narrower than in 1970. All economic groups now make about equal use of a physician relative to their health needs. Regardless of this progress, the poor still remain disadvantaged by certain aspects of the health care system. Lower-income groups have less access to health services, particularly those provided by their own physician. Relative to their physical-mental needs, the rural poor, compared with wealthy urban residents, visit a doctor less often. As expected, the poorest persons, especially those who live in rural regions and central cities, receive the lowest quality medical care.

The young, the nonwhite poor, rural low-income citizens, and Southerners have gained the fewest benefits from the Medicaid legislation. Fewer than 40 percent of those below the poverty line legally qualify for Medicaid benefits. Individuals who fail to receive Medicaid transfers include unemployed fathers and medically needy indigent children. Youths receive only one-fifth the Medicaid benefits obtained by the elderly. As a result, low-income children under fifteen years old are least likely to see a doctor, even when they suffer from a disability. Because the Medicaid program does not pay for dental care, a lower proportion of poor persons than wealthier individuals visit a dentist at least once a year. Higher-income people can afford to purchase private insurance policies that include dental care.

Poorer Americans remain least satisfied with the quality of medical care they obtain, especially the services dispensed in a hospital emergency room or public health clinic. The shortage of private physicians in poor areas means that public hospitals primarily serve low-income citizens, people with no private insurance, the unemployed, part-time employed workers, and Medicaid recipients rejected by private for-profit hospitals and private physicians. These public hospitals lack adequate revenue, staff, and medical equipment. Because neither Medicare nor Medicaid reimburses public hospitals for all their costs, expenses usually exceed revenues. Hence they cannot provide the higher quality medical treatments supplied by the private, profit-oriented hospitals serving wealthy suburban residents.[18]

In West Germany as well, the health care system fails to allocate equal benefits to rich and poor. The Federal Constitutional Court ruled that no sickness insurance funding agency has the constitutional right to designate geographic areas where physicians must practice; after this ruling, fewer doctors located in the countryside. The low physician-patient ratio in rural areas, the scarcity of physicians' services at factories, and the limited health services provided outside a hospital or doctor's office impede poor people from gaining equal access to health care services.

Although Canadian, French, and Swedish health policies provide more equal access to health care than do the U.S. or West German systems, low-income persons, unskilled workers, and the unemployed still receive less adequate care. For example, in Montreal, the Quebec provincial government in 1970 implemented a comprehensive public health program that financed all physicians' costs. Before 1970 wealthier people made more yearly visits to their doctor; after that date, physician visits became more equalized among income groups, especially those with similar health status. However, the poor secured primary care in hospital clinics and emergency rooms rather than at a doctor's office or private clinic. Because the public health insurance program did not finance dental care costs, higher-income individuals obtained more dental treatments each year than did the poor. In other provinces user fees for hospital stays, extra-billing for physicians' fees (charges that exceed the fee schedules approved by provincial health ministries and medical associations), and monthly premiums that

105

help finance provincial health care services hurt young mothers, the poor, and the elderly. In France low-income groups—workers, service personnel, farm laborers, and the unemployed—showed the greatest tendency to use public hospitals during the early 1970s. Although the French government has recently attempted to upgrade the medical equipment and personnel in the public hospitals, until the 1970s the private *cliniques* (for-profit hospitals) maintained fewer beds and better equipment. Hence those in upper-status occupations—professionals, administrators, managers, and highly paid salaried employees— frequented the cliniques. Like their West German colleagues, French physicians have resisted government policies that deny them the right to practice where they choose. Specialists in particular remain less available to France's rural population. Thus the poorer citizens use specialized medical services less frequently than do higher-income groups. In Sweden as well, residents outside the cities have more limited access to a doctor. Government officials have attempted to remedy these shortages by granting monetary incentives to persuade recent medical school graduates to set up practice in rural areas. They have also encouraged young physicians to carry out their internship training in sparsely populated regions. Certain areas are designated as closed to new practices, thereby directing doctors to underserved areas. Nevertheless, despite these policy efforts to equalize access to medical care, poorer areas like the north remain underserved by physicians. Throughout the country unemployed workers have less access to a physician than do professionals, who receive medical care from occupational health centers.[19] In short, although Canadian, French, and Swedish public health policies have secured more equal access to health services, geographical and occupational inequalities still mark the health care delivery system.

EFFICIENCY OF HEALTH CARE PROGRAMS

During the last two decades as health benefits became more accessible to a larger share of the population, public policymakers showed a greater concern for economic efficiency; this criterion for evaluating public health programs bases assessments on cost-benefit ratios. It assumes that policymakers, hospital staff, and physicians should provide the highest quality health benefits at the lowest possible costs.[20] Two indicators of the least-cost dimensions of economic efficiency are (1) the annual rise in total health care expenditures and (2) yearly administrative costs as a percentage of total expenditures for health programs. By comparing the costs and benefits of six national health systems, we can gain insights into their relative economic efficiencies.

Between 1965 and 1975 total public and private health care expenditures as a percentage of the GNP rose in all six Western industrial nations (see Table 4.3). Increases ranged from 1.5 percent in Canada to over 8.5 percent in West Germany, with the other countries averaging a 4-5 percent rise each year. During this period the yearly increase in health care expenditures exceeded the annual general rise of the consumer price index. Hospital expenses, which constitute the largest share of total health care expenditures, have shown the fastest

Table 4.3

COSTS OF HEALTH CARE BENEFITS, 1965-75

Country	Total Public and Private Expenditures on Health Care as Percentage of GNP		Rise in Total Expenditures	Administrative Costs as Percentage of Total Health Care Expenditures	
	1965	1975	1965-75		
West Germany	5.2%	9.7%	86.5%	5.0%	(1974)[a]
Sweden	5.8	8.7	50	7.6	(1972)
United States	5.9	8.5	44	5.3	(1971)
France	5.9	8.1	37	10.8	(1974)
Canada	6.1	7.1	16.4	2.5	(1973)
United Kingdom	3.9	5.6	43.6	2.6	(1975)

Sources: Joseph G. Simanis and John R. Coleman, "Health Care Expenditures in Nine Industrialized Countries, 1960-1976," *Social Security Bulletin* 43 (January 1980): 5; Robert J. Maxwell, *Health and Wealth: An International Study of Health-Care Spending* (Lexington, Mass.: D. C. Heath, 1981), 83; *Public Expenditure on Health: OECD Studies in Resource Allocation*, no. 4 (Paris, 1977), 23.

[a]Figures in parentheses are dates.

acceleration; physicians' salaries have risen less rapidly. Other basic expenses include those for medicines and for administration of the health care programs—specifically the costs of raising revenues and processing the claims made by physicians, hospitals, insurance funds, insurance companies, and patients.

Health policymakers can secure greater efficiency by either reducing benefits or by maintaining benefits while trying to curb costs. Because most Western publics support an expansion of health care benefits to include medicines and dental care, government officials have shown little enthusiasm about reducing benefits. Instead they have tried to lower costs by regulating physicians' fees, limiting hospital expenditures, placing price controls on drugs, and curtailing administrative expenses.[21]

Among the six industrial nations, Canada has achieved the most efficient health care system. As Table 4.3 indicates, in 1975 total Canadian expenditures on health benefits amounted to just over 7 percent of the GNP—the lowest figure except that in the United Kingdom. Between 1965 and 1975 health care expenses rose less than 2 percent a year; from 1975 to 1980 health expenditures as a share of the GNP remained about 7 percent. During the early 1970s administrative costs accounted for only 2.5 percent of total health care expenditures. Relative to these low costs, the quality of health services has been high, as indicated by availability of trained physicians, excellent hospital care, needed medicines, and advanced medical equipment.

By contrast with the Canadian plans, the U.S. health programs operate less efficiently. True, U.S. physicians and hospitals provide high quality benefits; the U.S. medical system has pioneered in advanced technological equipment and competent professional treatment by well-trained physicians. Yet the costs of health care are greater than in Canada. U.S. residents spend a higher proportion of their national income on health care than do Canadians. Between 1960 and 1980 health care expenses rose at a faster rate in the United States—from 5.3 percent of the GNP in 1960 to 9.5 percent twenty years later, compared with a rise of 5.5 percent (1960) to 7.1 percent (1980) in Canada. U.S. administrative costs are double the Canadian rate.

Why has the Canadian health program attained greater economic efficiency than the U.S. plans? The Canadian provincial governments, which operate the health care system, have secured tighter controls over physicians' salaries. The ministry of health in most provincial governments negotiates fee schedules with the provincial medical association. These negotiations have restrained the rapid rise in physicians' salaries that occurred in the United States. In 1967 Canadian governments enacted the Medicare program to pay for physicians' fees. Although doctors' real income nearly doubled between 1962 and 1971, from 1971 through 1978 their income rose at a slower rate than that of other professionals such as dentists, lawyers, engineers, architects, and self-employed accountants. During the early 1980s most fee increases for physicians averaged between 4 and 5 percent a year—a lower rise than the general inflation rate.

Provincial public health officials have devised several techniques for restraining physicians' fees. For example, to help limit fraud the health insurance program in each province prepares a statistical outline of the services performed by all physicians, their number of patients, the number of services for each patient, and the payments received by the doctor. Then for each specialty and community size a physician's fees can be compared with those of his peers. The Ontario Health Insurance Plan (OHIP) conducts sample surveys among randomly selected subscribers to verify that a doctor actually did provide the health benefits paid by the OHIP. Unlike their U.S. counterparts, Canadian doctors face fewer malpractice suits. The provincial government, not the patient, pays most medical expenses. Canadian judges show little sympathy toward defendants who file malpractice suits. For clients to win their case they must prove that the physician acted negligently. Thus the financing of the health care system, along with the court procedures, deter patients from charging their physician with malpractice. As a result, doctors need not purchase expensive insurance that raises physicians' fees.[22]

Physicians have enjoyed a more advantageous economic position in the United States than in Canada, partly because the U.S. public health programs have increased, not restricted, physicians' salaries. Between 1950 and 1965, the year Congress enacted the Medicare and Medicaid plans, doctors' fees rose about 3 percent a year. From 1966 to 1975, however, their fees showed an annual 7 percent increase, due partly to inflation but also to public policies. In 1965 government expenditures accounted for 6 percent of physicians' incomes, but ten years later funds from public programs like Medicare and Medicaid contributed 27 percent of doctors' incomes. Private insurance plans also added a growing share to doctors' revenues. By 1977 U.S. physicians on the average earned more than 33 percent higher incomes than did Canadian doctors, even though physicians in both nations worked about the same number of hours and saw an equal number of patients each week.

Two reasons explain the income differentials of Canadian and U.S. physicians. First, despite the American Medical Association's commitment to the "free market," U.S. physicans hardly engage in pure competition. Through their control over medical education and licensing, state medical associations discourage competition from paramedical health personnel. By opposing advertising by physicians, these medical associations deter patients from gaining full information about doctors' fees. Hence the consumer can scarcely make a rational price choice on the medical market. Second, U.S. government officials have placed fewer restrictions on physicians' salaries. Some Canadian provincial governments, such as those controlled by the Progressive-Conservative party in Alberta, Ontario, Nova Scotia, and Prince Edward Island, have allowed doctors to "opt out" of the provincial health program or else to "extra bill." However, except in Alberta, Nova Scotia, and Ontario, physicians have largely accepted the negotiated fee schedules. By contrast, in the United States before 1984 neither the Medicare nor the Medicaid plan restrained doctors' escalating fees. Under the Medicare program the insurance plan pays 80 percent of the "reasonable" charges levied by a physician; however, these charges usually exceeded the Medicare-approved fees. Unlike the Canadian situation, in the United States no medical association negotiates with public health officials about "reasonable" fee schedules. Refusing to accept the Medicare or Medicaid rates for specific services, many doctors have charged higher fees than recommended by health care administrators. The patient and private health insurance companies pay the excess charges. Hence even though the government finances over one-quarter of physicians' incomes, they largely retain the power to set their own fees.[23]

Neither the Canadian nor the U.S. government has effectively curtailed the rapid rise in hospital expenses. From 1960 through 1975 hospital expenditures rose at a slightly higher rate in Canada than the United States. The Canadian provincial governments have tried to reduce hospital costs by curbing hospital construction and using their authority to veto certain expensive parts of hospital budgets. However, they have shown less enthusiasm about limiting wage increases to hospital employees. Canadian hospital workers are more highly unionized than their U.S. colleagues, and this union power has led to favorable wage settlements. In the United States the actions of hospital workers' unions do not explain the escalating costs. Unions exert little power. From 1955 through 1975 labor costs as a proportion of total hospital expenses actually fell; hospital labor costs increased more slowly than did non-labor costs. The decisions taken by private insurance executives and government officials better account for the rising hospital expenditures. Private health insurance plans have pushed up hospital expenses. Most private programs reimburse patients who receive hospital treatments but not patients treated outside the hospital. By encouraging increased hospitalization, the private insurance companies bring financial gains to the hospitals and thereby raise hospital costs. Under the Medicare program government payments for hospital expenses used to depend on "allowable" and "reasonable" charges; thus higher costs brought greater reimbursements. Only in 1983 did Congress pass a law that placed limits on soaring hospital charges. According to the new system, which resembles a program adopted by the Ontario provincial government's Ministry of Health in 1982, the U.S. federal government sets yearly rates for health treatments in specific "diagnosis-related groups." Hospitals that can provide the service at less cost than the official federal rate receive the whole fixed fee and thereby enlarge their revenues. Government officials intend for this new reimbursement plan to give hospitals an incentive to maximize efficient administration.[24]

Due to the power of the U.S. pharmaceutical industry, drug expenses have pushed up health care costs faster in the United States than in Canada. The United States has a more concentrated drug industry; the major drug manufacturers control a larger share of the pharmaceutical market. As a result, less price competition occurs; drug prices and profits are higher. The U.S. drug industry now earns higher profits than any other manufacturers. From 1977 through 1982 the after-tax profits of U.S. drug companies ranged between 11¢ and 15¢ for every dollar of sales, compared with the general manufacturing average of 4-6¢. Canadian drug costs have remained lower. The federal and provincial governments amended patent laws to encourage more firms to manufacture, import, and sell prescription drugs. Hence each Canadian drug manufacturer exercises less market power than U.S. manufacturers. More price competition ensues, leading to cheaper drug prices.[25]

Compared with the United States, Canada also allocates a lower proportion of total health care expenditures for administrative costs. In Canada one agency reimburses physicians and hospitals. The patient receives no bills for medical expenses from physicians in the provincial health plan. Since Canadians have a comprehensive program providing health benefits to all, the government does not have to finance the costs of checking a person's eligibility for services. Physicians no longer must spend money trying to collect unpaid medical bills. The provincial governments administer the program; thus they need not negotiate with insurance companies about acceptable administrative expenses. The U.S. private insurance companies spend a higher share of their revenues on administrative costs than do Canadian provincial governments. Unlike Canadian physicians, U.S. doctors must cope with complex insurance forms. To handle this administrative paperwork each U.S. physician employs about two staff persons, compared with one for the typical Canadian doctor. In short, the pluralistic U.S. system of providing health services, processing claims, and reimbursing expenses produces higher administrative costs than the more streamlined Canadian program. By fragmenting administration among different government and private agencies, U.S. health policies have brought lucrative financial rewards to private insurance companies, private for-profit hospitals, and private physicians but have incurred economic inefficiencies.[26]

The same reasons that explain the efficiency of the Canadian public health program also account for the lower costs associated with the British than the West German health plans. As Table 4.3 indicates, between 1965 and 1975 total public and private health care expenditures as a proportion of the GNP increased twice as fast in West Germany as in the United Kingdom. During the mid-1970s German administrative expenses amounted to double the British rate. British policymakers achieved greater economic efficiency mainly because their more unified health program established tighter controls over physicians' fees, hospital expenditures, drug expenses, and administrative costs.

Within the European Community, British physicians earn the lowest salaries—about one-half the income of West German physicians. Relative to the average income of the nation's labor force, West German doctors make higher salaries than do their British colleagues. In Britain general practitioners receive a basic practice allowance and a payment for the number of patients listed on their registry. Hospital specialists receive a salary. By contrast, West German office physicians, like North American doctors, secure a fee for their services. Local medical associations and sickness insurance funds negotiate these fee schedules without tight control by either the federal or Länder governments. Because of the power wielded by associations of health insurance doctors, the sickness funds cannot monitor physicians' salaries. This system tends to protect the private physicians' economic position.

The West German federal government has also confronted greater difficulties than the British government in limiting the rapid rise of hospital expenses. From 1960 through 1975 German hospital costs increased faster than the salaries of office physicians and dentists. Pressured by the powerful *Land* hospital associations, the federal parliament refused to enact legislation that would have required the hospitals to finance more of their current expenditures, now funded largely by state and federal grants. By contrast, British health officials spent little money on building new hospitals and purchasing advanced medical technology. Instead most funds for hospital care went to nurses and ancillary staff. Although still low, their average earnings during the early 1970s increased faster than the wages received by manual workers. The considerable power exerted by British hospital unions, especially the Confederation of Health Service Employees, the National Union of Public Employees, and the Royal College of Nursing, largely explains these wage hikes. Even though hospital wages have risen, the physical plant in most British hospitals has deteriorated; the hospital facilities are antiquated, unsafe, and poorly equipped. Particularly in some inner-city areas, hospital care for the mentally ill and the aged is inadequate. In short, monetary savings and cost reductions have occurred, but the quality of hospital care has declined.

As a proportion of total expenditures for health care, drug costs are nearly twice as high in West Germany as in Britain. The British Department of Health and Social Security (DHSS) negotiates wholesale prices of medicines with the Central National Health Service (Chemist Contractors) Committee, the agency representing the nation's pharmacists. If the DHSS believes that pharmaceutical industries earn "excessive" profits, it can levy price controls on drugs. West Germany, however, lacks price controls on medicines, even though government regulations limit the mark-up of drug prices paid by the consumer. Pharmaceutical firms engage in little price competition. As a result, German pharmaceutical manufacturers, like those in the United States, have earned high profits.

Administrative costs are higher in West Germany than in the United Kingdom. West Germans have established a complex system of 1200 sickness insurance funds that need numerous personnel to process claims and make payments. Physicians employed by the associations of insurance doctors monitor medical care to ascertain the correspondence between one doctor's claims and group averages for performing the same services. Yet the administration of this eco-economic review costs ten times more than the money saved from the monitoring. By contrast, the British government, rather than nongovernment agencies, manages the NHS. Administering a simpler, more unified system, it spends little money on processing claims or monitoring doctors' treatments. Instead its main administrative activities revolve around raising revenues, paying physicians, and financing hospital care.[27]

Compared with British and Canadian policymakers, Swedish and French officials have incurred higher costs operating their health care systems. Sweden has secured greater efficiencies than France. As recipients of fees for their services, French doctors earn high incomes; during the mid-1970s they made seven times the income received by the typical manufacturing worker—a higher ratio than in any other Western industrial nation. Through their medical associations French physicians negotiate a fee schedule with national officials who work for the various social security plans, including the Caisse Nationale d'Assurance Maladie des Travailleurs Salariés (CNAMTS)—the national health insurance fund for salaried workers, a nongovernmental organization covering three-fourths of the French people. Even though nearly all French physicians have accepted the national fee schedule for health treatments, they can charge higher fees for extensive services to patients. Medical specialists and doctors who have earned certain university degrees or won special honors also have the right to charge higher prices than allowed in the fee schedule. French physicians have thus secured lucrative financial rewards from the national health insurance system. In Sweden as well, physicians earn a higher income than most other professional groups. Yet unlike French doctors, who receive a fee for their services, nearly all Swedish physicians earn a government salary, usually paid by the county government. The Swedish Medical Association (SMA) lacks the political power wielded by French medical groups like the Confédération des Syndicats Médicaux Français and the Fédération des Médecins de France. Strong labor unions and a powerful Social Democratic party wield countervailing influence against the SMA. Committed to income equality, Social Democrats at both the central and county government levels have restrained physician demands for higher salaries. Hence during the mid-1970s Swedish doctors earned 3.5 times the income received by a typical manufacturing worker, compared to a ratio of 7.0 in France.

In both Sweden and France hospital costs have shown a rapid rise. The Swedish county governments own and operate most hospitals. Under pressure from hospital physicians and local residents, elected county councillors have supported increased revenues for hospital care financed through a proportional income tax levied by the council. As a result, the Swedish system provides outstanding hospital facilities, high quality hospital surgery, and modern medical equipment. In France private companies control around one-fifth the total number of hospital beds. Usually owned by private physicians, the profit-oriented hospitals (cliniques) earn high profits, mainly because they provide maternity care and routine surgery in wealthy areas and leave the more serious, expensive medical treatments to the public hospitals. Through their reimbursement policies, the Ministry of Finance and CNAMTS have favored the private cliniques by granting them more investment funds and higher fees than the public hospitals. Although the Ministry of Health prescribes the fees for public hospitals, the CNAMTS negotiates clinique fees with powerful hospital associations, which receive generous reimbursements. Hence general hospital expenses soared from 1950 through 1980.

Compared with Swedish policymakers, French officials have less effectively restrained drug prices. Even though the French government has controlled drug prices since 1941, the cost of medicines has risen sharply so that pharmaceutical expenses now comprise about 20 percent of total health care expenditures. Although most Swedish pharmaceutical companies remain under private ownership, over half the drugs are imported; this price competition helps keep down the costs. During the early 1970s the government nationalized all privately owned pharmacies and reorganized them into a nonprofit corporation. This policy also helped restrain rising drug prices.

Because civil servants and professionals make key public policies in both France and Sweden, administrative costs comprise a relatively large share of total health care expenditures in both nations. Among the six Western nations, France incurred the highest administrative expenses (see Table 4.3). Managing the complex structures involved in health care—the central government, communal governments, national health office, regional health insurance offices, primary health insurance offices, private health insurance companies, public hospitals, private voluntary hospitals, private, profit-oriented hospitals—involves sizable administrative expenses. With a simpler structural system comprising the central government, county governments, local social insurance offices, and public hospitals, Swedish health policymakers more successfully limited administrative costs than did French officials.[28]

In summary, the more public and unified health care programs secure the greatest efficiencies. For each one of the three pairs—Canada and the United States, Britain and West Germany, Sweden and France—where nongovernment agencies (medical associations, private health insurance companies, sickness insurance funds, private hospital associations, private pharmaceutical industries) wield the greatest power over the health policy process, the society bears the highest costs, especially for administrative expenses. Thus the United States has higher costs than Canada. West German officials spend more on health care than do the British. Although both the French and Swedish policymakers manage expensive health care systems, the French allocate a higher share of total health expenditures to administration. Rather than saving funds, the dispersion of power among several different agencies seems to expand costs.* Particularly when the central government exerts only limited control over the prices of medical goods and services, policy fragmentation may bring greater economic inefficiencies than a simpler, more streamlined system.[29]

---

*According to Wildavsky, "Doing Better and Feeling Worse," *Daedalus* 106 (Winter 1977): 120-21, public health care systems have the lowest per capita costs, private systems cost the next most, and mixed public and private systems will likely show the highest per capita costs. Under the mixed systems private

POPULAR SATISFACTION WITH PUBLIC HEALTH POLICIES

The degree of satisfaction with a health care system presumably depends on health costs, ease of access to health personnel, and quality of medical treatment. Citizens express the greatest satisfaction if they secure low-cost care from qualified health providers who are accessible to everyone.

According to sample surveys conducted in Western nations during the 1970s and early 1980s, public attitudes toward health care systems appear relatively favorable. For instance, over two-thirds of the French and West German publics expressed satisfaction with their health programs. Over 80 percent of British and Canadians supported the existing health care systems. In the United States as well, around four-fifths of citizens voiced general satisfaction with the medical care that they personally received. Yet in 1984 around half the U.S. population saw a need for "fundamental changes" in the national health care system, one-fifth desired "minor changes," and one-fourth sought a complete restructuring. During the 1970s people in the United States, England, and West Germany regarded health care as a very important issue for which government should take responsibility. Most of them favorably assessed government health policy performance, although U.S. citizens voiced greater dissatisfaction with public health policies than did the British or West Germans.[30]

The primary sources of dissatisfaction with health care systems evolve around the costs, the treatment in hospitals, and the difficulty establishing rapport with a physician. Except for U.S. residents, people in Western nations voice little discontent with the costs of health services. During the mid-1970s the Gallup Poll International asked West Europeans and North Americans this question: "Have there been times during the last year when you did not have money enough to pay for medical or health care?" Whereas only 5 percent of West Europeans cited a lack of money, over 15 percent of U.S.

health agencies competing with government health plans claim to offer "higher quality" health benefits. To satisfy their customers government health officials must match the benefits provided by private plans. Thus the costs escalate. Usually the private health agencies receive government subsidies. In a pluralistic society where private groups retain extensive independence from government control, public officials cannot easily limit these subsidies.

citizens complained about high medical costs. Nearly half the U.S. public expressed dissatisfaction with the rising costs of health services, especially the expensive hospital care and the failure of health insurance plans to make sufficient payments to cover the costs of physician and hospital care.

Although faced with growing health care expenses, citizens in all Western nations support larger government expenditures for health services, even if higher taxes result. In 1975 a majority of French, West Germans, and British preferred improving health programs despite the increased taxes and wage deductions required to finance these improvements. Even during the severe economic stagnation that plagued Britain in the late 1970s and early 1980s, few British citizens supported the Conservative government's plans to decrease expenditures for the NHS. Over two-thirds regarded the NHS general practitioner and hospital services as a "good value." Between 60 and 70 percent wanted higher expenditures for the NHS; only 5 percent supported spending reductions. In 1980 Swedes expressed the least enthusiasm for reducing government spending on health care; the largest percentage of citizens sought increased expenditures for health services. In 1981 half the Canadians favored extending local government services to the sick and disabled, even if increased expenditures brought higher taxes; only 10 percent preferred both lower taxes and reduced expenditures. In the United States, where opposition to social service programs remains higher than in Canada or West Europe, most people rank health care as a primary government priority; they either want to maintain existing expenditures or else favor higher spending on medical care. Of the two major health programs, Medicare grants to the elderly arouse greater enthusiasm than do Medicaid benefits to the poor. During the Reagan administration, over half the U.S. population preferred increased expenditures for health care; other than job training programs, no other domestic public policy attracted such widespread support.

The main nonfinancial reasons for discontent focus on individuals' treatment in physicians' offices and hospitals. West Germans remain most dissatisfied with the lengthy waiting period in their doctors' offices. Canadians also complain about the long waits in physicians' offices and the short time that their doctors spend treating them. According to sample surveys, British patients feel that their doctors spend too little time with them and use such technical jargon that communication between patient and physician becomes difficult. Even though most English citizens are satisfied with their hospital care, many dislike the hospital food and the early awakening time—before 6 a.m. They voice only limited dissatisfaction with the waiting period before admission to a hospital. During the late 1970s about one-half of patients were admitted to a hospital within one month; 14 percent had to wait more than six months. British citizens show greater concern about lengthy waits to see a hospital specialist treating outpatients. Under the British system a general practitioner must refer patients to a hospital specialist. Sixty percent gained an outpatient appointment within three weeks; however, nearly one-fifth waited over six weeks. By contrast, most patients in the United States can see a physician or enter a hospital after only a short delay. Nearly two-thirds visit a doctor's office within two days after making an appointment. However, U.S. patients voice greater dissatisfaction with the long waiting time in a physician's office and with the scarcity of family doctors in a patient's neighborhood. Thus compared with the English, who perceive that they enjoy ready access to a doctor, people in the United States feel slightly more deprived of equal access to health care.[31]

In both West Europe and the United States attitudes toward public health care policies depend on individuals' positions in the social stratification system as well as their political party and ideological identifications. As expected, low-income individuals working at less prestigious jobs express the greatest support for expanded public health benefits. Party identification has a greater impact on attitudes toward public health policies than does social group membership. For instance, in 1975 citizens who identified with the rightist parties in West Germany, England, and France—the German Christian Democrats, English Conservatives, and French Gaullists—most preferred to reduce health benefits and taxes. The leftist partisans—German Social Democrats, British Labourites, French Socialists, but *not* French Communists—expressed greater opposition to reducing health care benefits, even if tax rates declined. In the United States as well, the leftist identifiers—Jews, self-styled "liberals," and citizens who feel strongly attached to the Democratic party—give the greatest support to a government-financed comprehensive health care program. Self-styled "conservatives" and those who strongly identify with the Republican party tend to reject any federal government program that finances low-cost health care for all people.[32]

CONCLUSION: HEALTH POLICIES AND SOCIAL STRATIFICATION

This evaluation of national health care programs has shown that the policy benefits received by social groups mainly depend on their political power, wealth, and prestige. Groups at the top of the social stratification system usually obtain the best quality care. Despite the growth of comprehensive programs that have widened access to health care, groups with high socioeconomic status and political power still find health services most accessible, particularly from technically trained specialists. Everywhere rural residents, low-income citizens, and ethnic minorities—migrant workers in Europe, Canadian Indians and Eskimos, U.S. blacks, Latinos, and native Americans—receive the fewest benefits relative to their health needs. From the perspective of economic efficiency, the high administrative expenditures in France, Sweden, West Germany, and the United States primarily reward middle and upper class individuals who manage these health programs. Private pharmaceutical industries realize sizable profits in both West Germany and the United States. French, West German, and U.S. private health insurance companies operate profitable enterprises. Everywhere physicians rank among the nation's highest paid groups. Finally, social stratification conditions the degree of satisfaction with the health care system. Wealthy persons employed at managerial or professional jobs voice the greatest approval. Low-income unskilled workers who face dangers of unemployment remain most discontent. Experiencing the highest infant mortality rates, the greatest incidence of disabling diseases, and the lowest life expectancy, these social groups perceive that they gain the fewest benefits relative to their physical-mental needs. As Edward Kennedy observed in the Senate hearings, the inequalities in a society shape the allocation of health policy services.

Chapter 5

AN OVERVIEW OF POLICY PERFORMANCE

As Chapter 1 indicated, comparative policy analysis describes, explains, and evaluates. This chapter, which surveys policy performance in seven Western industrial societies, first describes economic, education, and health policy trends by exploring structural administration, expenditures and financing of programs, and the scope of policy benefits. Assuming that the policy variations in different industrialized societies reflect the interaction between the power of key political actors and their policy preferences, I next examine the power and beliefs of the electorate, political parties, business organizations, labor unions, and government agencies. Finally, I evaluate economic, education, and health policy performance in light of four standards: institutional goal attainment, equality, economic efficiency, and popular satisfaction with the programs.

DESCRIPTION OF POLICY TRENDS

During the last three hundred years Western industrial societies have seen a changing conception of political authority. Throughout this period most people have faced unemployment, inflation, low growth rates, inadequate education, and poor health. Political leaders have had to choose the most appropriate agencies that would help resolve these problems. To what extent do political agencies take the primary responsibility? How do society's key leaders define the scope of political activity?

Originally the family and church, not the government, handled economic, education, and health issues. Some families worked their own land; others raised crops on land owned by feudal lords or the Roman Catholic Church. The father and local priest offered the children an education, including information about proper health care.

Later the local government and private organizations assumed the primary responsibility for social problems. Local government leaders and private businessmen allocated expenditures for education, health, and services to the poor and unemployed. Private charities along with village or city governments provided some assistance to the poor. Until the twentieth century more European children went to private than public schools. Local officials also viewed health care as an essentially private activity.

Only during the twentieth century have most central governments taken a positive role to supply social services. More and more problems now come under the scope of political authority. As a result, governments formulate comprehensive economic, education, and health policies. Particularly in Canada and Western Europe, professional civil servants, rather than family members, clergy, or private entrepreneurs, implement these policies.

In short, over the last three hundred years the following trends have occurred in the policy process: More centralized implementation has supplanted decentralized administration. Private control has yielded to greater public control. Governments have enacted higher expenditures and taxes. Public programs now provide more extensive coverage and comprehensive benefits.

Among the seven Western industrialized societies, Sweden and the United States reveal the sharpest contrast in policy performance. The Swedish government has most fully enacted the above-mentioned changes. Administration of economic decision-making is fairly centralized; civil servants from the national government play a crucial role in framing and implementing policies. County and city governments exert less policy influence than does the national Cabinet or the Riksdag. Nevertheless, county and municipal governments have asserted their autonomy from central government directives over financial policy. Local governments collect a larger share of total tax receipts in Sweden than in any other country among these seven except Canada, and proportional local income taxes finance expenditures made by county and city governments.

Local governments in Sweden retain autonomy over education policy. The local income tax funds around one-half the educational expenditures. The National Board of Education plans and coordinates the operation of public schools, but the county school board appoints teachers, inspects schools, and authorizes school construction. Elected local boards of education operate the municipal schools; primary and secondary school teachers work as city employees, not as civil servants accountable to the National Board of Education. During the last two decades the higher education system has become more decentralized as the major universities established regional branches and as city/county governments instituted specialized colleges for training teachers, librarians, nurses, technicians, and farmers.

Swedish officials also operate a decentralized health care system. The central government's National Board of Health and Welfare supervises the general system. It formulates general health plans, grants subsidies to county governments, authorizes the construction of new hospitals, allocates health personnel, and reviews medical care performance. Despite these important central government powers, elected county councils, as well as three municipal councils in Malmö, Gothenburg, and Gotland, play the decisive policy role. Advised by county medical care and hospital boards, county officials administer health services, operate most hospitals, employ over three-fourths of Sweden's physicians, and finance around 60 percent of health care costs. The county councils retain the independent authority to allocate expenditures for health services; these expenditures comprise the major spending programs enacted by local governments.

Compared with the other six nations, Sweden spends the highest percentage of its GDP on total government outlays; taxes also comprise the largest share of the national income. During the 1970s the Swedish government spent the most for social services. Government expenditures for health care represented the highest proportion of the GDP; over 90 percent of health care revenues came from public sources, including general taxation and public insurance. In the late 1970s the Swedish government allocated a higher share of the GDP to education than did any other Western government.

Swedish social service benefits—health care, pensions, family allowances, and public assistance—are the most generous in the industrialized democratic world. All Swedes participate in the public health program, which provides comprehensive benefits. Nearly all secondary students attend comprehensive schools; in 1979 nearly 40 percent of individuals between twenty and twenty-four years old were enrolled in higher education—a higher percentage than in any other country except the United States.

Particularly in the education and health policy arenas, public institutions remain dominant. The central government owns all pharmacies. Few private hospitals now function. Only around a tenth of Swedish citizens have purchased private health insurance. About 5 percent of physicians remain in private practice. Less than one percent of students attend private elementary schools. Although 90 percent of Swedish industries are privately owned, in 1980 31 percent of the labor force worked in general government agencies; public corporations employed an additional 8 percent.[1] In short, compared with other Western political leaders, Swedish officials have expressed the strongest commitment to an activist government. For them public agencies take the primary responsibility for tackling social problems.

By contrast, leaders in the United States prefer a less public route to attain economic, education, and health objectives. Government plays a more limited role; private organizations help formulate and implement public policies. Private businesses often administer public programs, such as job training. Government officials grant subsidies to private enterprises for teaching unemployed persons marketable skills. During the last decade government employment as a percentage of total nonfarm employment fell from 19 percent in 1975 to under 18 percent in the early 1980s—a lower proportion than in most other Western nations. Public corporations employ only 1.5 percent of the labor force. Among the seven industrial societies, the United States also has the fewest government-owned industries. Although a semigovernmental corporation, the U.S. Postal Service, dominates the handling of mail, it must compete with a private agency, the United Parcel Service, which delivers more parcels than does the Postal Service. Besides the postal service, only railroads and electricity fall under partial government ownership; here, however, the private sector dominates. Federal and state agencies regulate many privately owned large industries, but since the late 1970s the federal government has moved to deregulate the airline, rail, trucking, television, radio, telephone, oil, and banking industries.

Compared with other Western democracies, the United States has accorded the greatest autonomy to private health care organizations like nursing homes, pharmaceutical companies, hospitals, physicians' associations, and insurance firms. These institutions not only offer private health care benefits to individuals but also become actively involved in the public health policy process. Although the

Social Security Administration supervises the Medicare program for the aged and the national government raises the revenues for its operation, private insurance companies review claims for benefits and issue payments. In some areas a commercial insurance company serves as the intermediary. In other regions two nonprofit health insurance corporations—Blue Cross for hospital care and Blue Shield for physicians' treatments—help implement the Medicare program. During the early 1980s private organizations owned over 70 percent of community hospitals; 15 percent operated for profit. The investor-owned chains—American Medical International, Hospital Corporation of America, National Medical Enterprises, Humana, Inc.—constituted the fastest growing segment of the hospital industry. These chains own a rising share of hospital beds and increasingly manage public hospitals. For example, in California even though the county governments retain ownership of hospitals, some have turned to private management firms like Western Hospital Corporation, National Medical Enterprises, and National Affiliates International to process information, prepare cost reports for Medicare/Medicaid, and collect hospital fees. Federal government health policies have favored the for-profit hospitals over the public hospitals. Reduced expenditures for Medicare and Medicaid, combined with local property tax reductions, have caused several urban hospitals to close. The Medicare program grants profit-oriented hospitals extra reimbursements for returns on equity linked to interest rates—payments denied to nonprofit hospitals. Private nursing homes have also benefited from government policies. Around 80 percent of all nursing homes operate for-profit businesses, yet in 1975 nearly 60 percent of their funds came from government sources. Most drugs are produced by private pharmaceutical companies, which secure the highest profits of any manufacturing corporation.

Of all the private groups, physicians play the most decisive role in the health care field. Doctors prescribe drugs manufactured by private pharmaceutical industries. They administer hospitals, both private and public. The American Medical Association sponsored the Blue Shield plan for physicians' services. State boards dominated by private physicians administer medical schools, license doctors, and accredit hospitals. As professionals, private physicians have demanded and secured extensive autonomy from government control, even though the growing strength of investor-owned hospital chains threatens their formerly unchallenged independence. According to the Professional Standards Review program approved by Congress in 1972, physicians have the right to regulate themselves. This peer review process not only ensures that physicians retain the independence to govern their own practices, but also gives them control over the purchase of government-funded health care services. Because U.S. physicians charge a fee for their services, they receive higher government payments for providing more health care treatments.

Despite the early establishment of a mass public education system, U.S. private schools are still important. Among these seven industrial countries, only France has a higher proportion of primary school children attending private schools; the private share in the United States has grown during the last century. Whereas in 1900 only 7 percent of all U.S. grammar school children went to a private school, by 1980 that figure had reached 12 percent.

U.S. fiscal policies also reflect a commitment to private responsibility as the best way to satisfy human needs. Compared with Canadian and European governments, U.S. government expenditures at all levels amount to the lowest share of the GDP. Public expenditures for health care, sickness benefits, family allowances, and unemployment compensation are especially low. From 1950 through 1977 the United States showed the lowest annual increase in government transfers, mainly income-maintenance benefits. In the 1970s total government spending on social insurance, public assistance, health programs, and education as a proportion of the GNP peaked in 1976, declined during the next three years, and rose again in 1980. More than any other Western citizenry, people in the United States must rely on private resources to finance health care costs. For example, in 1982 federal, state, and local governments funded 42 percent of total costs; private health insurance companies financed 30 percent. Patients themselves had to pay the remaining 28 percent, especially the expenses for nursing homes, dental care, and drugs. In Canada and Western Europe individuals rarely pay more than one-fifth of their health care costs; either general taxation or public insurance covers over 75 percent of these expenditures.

Besides its reliance on private responsibility, the U.S. policy process features extensive political decentralization, fragmented decision-making, and overlapping jurisdictions. During the last decade state governments assumed increased responsibility over industrial investment, housing, environmental regulation, health care, and education. To carry out these growing activities, both the executive and legislative branches have become more professionalized; career governors and legislative staffs prevail in most states. Under the revenue-sharing process, Congress allocates most funds to the state governments, which then distribute them to municipalities. State governments administer most national social service programs, including food stamps, Medicaid, Aid to Families with Dependent Children, and Supplemental Security Income.

Whereas in the past U.S. local school boards made key education policies, now state governments have assumed the primary responsibility for public education. Local school boards still appoint teachers, principals, and superintendents, but the state governments have come to formulate decisions about curriculum, textbooks, methods of instruction, and financing. Before World War II state governments financed around 30 percent of school expenditures, local property taxes contributed over two-thirds of the revenues, and the federal government allocated less than two percent. By the late 1970s, however, the state governments' share of public education receipts rose to 50 percent; local agencies financed 38 percent, and the federal government 12 percent. Several factors have increased the states' control over education policymaking, including the drive for greater equality among schools, a concern to standardize the curriculum, pressures from the federal Department of Education, collective bargaining movements by teachers, and taxpayer resistance to paying local property taxes that used to finance education.

Of the three levels of government, the state governments wield the greatest influence over U.S. health policy; yet even their authority is restricted by other government agencies and private organizations. The federal government contributes around 60 percent of the funds needed to operate the Medicaid program for the poor, blind, and disabled. The state governments contribute the remaining finances. They determine eligibility, specific benefits, and scope of health services. Representatives from the state governments must negotiate with federal officials about health program details. Since hospitals and private physicians provide health services under the Medicaid program, they have some veto power over its implementation. State governments operate medical schools, but state medical societies dominated by private physicians actually manage these institutions.

Even though the state governments have the authority to license a doctor, they delegate this right to state medical boards, which private physicians also control. Formal control over private insurance companies resides in the state governments; however, few of them regulate either the premium rates or the types of benefits offered by commercial insurance companies. In short, both the federal and state governments have seen their authority over health policies limited by private organizations, especially physicians' associations, hospital chains, and insurance corporations.

The power of private organizations in the U.S. policy process has deterred the establishment of comprehensive public policies. Most programs serve only part of the population. For example, family allowances benefit low-income women with dependent children rather than all parents as in Canada and Western Europe. Public health policies serve mainly the elderly, the poor, veterans, and native Americans. Others must rely on private insurance or their own resources to finance health care costs; yet among those under the age of sixty-five, 25 percent lack private insurance plans. These include mainly children, young adults (aged nineteen to twenty-four), blacks, Hispanics, rural residents, and low-income workers employed on farms or in small, non-unionized firms. Unlike income maintenance or health policies, U.S. public education programs have provided more comprehensive coverage. Nearly all secondary students attend comprehensive high schools. During 1979 over 50 percent of youths aged twenty to twenty-four went to some post-secondary educational institution, such as a vocational institute, community college, four-year college, or graduate university. Thus U.S. policymakers have shown the strongest commitment to educational opportunities for all citizens; public health programs and public income maintenance policies, except for the elderly, take lower priority.[2]

In Canada leaders have chosen a more political route to the solution of social problems; yet as in the United States, the policy process remains highly decentralized. The provincial governments dominate decision-making. Since Canada gained independence from Britain in 1867, they have gained increasing power to determine public policies. Today they assume major responsibility for education, health care, most social services, and the development of natural resources like oil. Provincial crown corporations operate such public enterprises as financial institutions, automobile insurance agencies, housing projects, industrial development corporations, mines, power utilities, shipyards, steel firms, communications facilities, and transportation systems.

Although the least wealthy provinces—New Brunswick, Nova Scotia, Newfoundland, and Prince Edward Island—depend on federal transfers, wealthier provinces—especially Ontario, Alberta, British Columbia, and Quebec—wield extensive political autonomy from federal directives. Ontario's power rests on its political, economic, and cultural assets. As the most populous province, Ontario elects the most members to the central House of Commons; hence a party must gain a majority of seats in Ontario to control the House. Economically Ontario has a large market and diversified manufacturing sector. The cultural center of English Canada, Ontario sets the pace for the other eight English-speaking provinces. The only province where a majority of citizens speak French, Quebec has always practiced extensive cultural autonomy. Since the Parti Québécois gained control of the provincial government in 1976, it has campaigned for greater political independence and increased French-speaking control over the provincial economy. Impressed by Quebec's efforts to assert its political autonomy, leaders from the Western provinces have also sought more authority over economic matters. Alberta has vast oil deposits. Controlled by the Progressive-Conservative party, the Alberta government has demanded the right to develop oil resources, set oil prices, tax profits, and export oil on the world market free from federal government interference.

Despite these decentralizing trends, the Canadian federal government still wields extensive economic authority, including the right to formulate broad economic guidelines, raise taxes, levy wage and price controls, and operate enterprises such as railroads, airlines, steamship lines, seaways, a television network, radio stations, pharmaceuticals, power commissions, oil industries, and chemical plants. All these publicly owned firms represent a larger share of all enterprises than found in the United States. Over 4 percent of the Canadian labor force works for public corporations, compared with under 2 percent in the United States. Total public sector employment includes nearly a quarter of the workforce.

Canada's education policies also reveal a commitment to public but decentralized authority. Few students attend private schools; in 1977-78 only 3 percent of all elementary pupils and 5 percent of secondary students were enrolled in a private educational institution. Political leaders have placed primary decision-making authority for education issues in the provincial governments. Canada represents one of the few Western nations with no ministry of education in the central cabinet. Provincial ministers of education supervise teacher training, approve textbook selection, prepare guidelines for the curriculum, and authorize school construction projects. Local school boards manage schools in a district, hire teachers and administrators, decide specific courses of study, authorize construction of new buildings, and raise funds for education. During the 1980-81 academic year, local taxes, usually levied on property, accounted for 20 percent of public education expenditures. Provincial governments supplied 71 percent, while the federal government provided only 9 percent.

Similarly Canada has decentralized health policymaking to the provincial governments; they, rather than the federal government or private organizations, formulate and implement crucial decisions. The federal Department of National Health and Welfare mainly coordinates provincial services, offers technical advice, and prescribes uniform standards for health and hospital care. The provincial governments must abide by following federal guidelines: (1) comprehensive coverage for all medically required services; (2) universal coverage to nearly all residents, at least 95 percent of a province's population; (3) continuation of coverage when a person moves to a new residence or changes jobs; (4) administration of the program by a non-profit, public agency. Under the fourth guideline, private insurance companies lost the right to administer the comprehensive hospital and medical insurance programs, which provincial government agencies— the department of health, the ministry of health, or the commission of health services—now implement. These provincial agencies carry out a wide range of responsibilities. They bargain with physicians' associations about fees for doctors' services, pay physicians' bills, approve hospital expenditures, authorize hospital construction, negotiate hospital employees' salaries, and purchase medical equipment. Owing to a bill passed by the federal House of Commons in 1977, the provincial governments gained even greater autonomy in managing their health programs. Under this law the federal government decreased expenditures for health care. Now the provincial governments contribute over half the revenues for health care. Provincial officials also won more discretion over allocating federal block funds for medical insurance, hospital expenses, and post-secondary medical education. As federal control lessened, physicians' associations secured greater influence over health policymaking, especially in Ontario and Alberta.

Even though physicians' associations help shape Canadian health policies, neither they nor other private organizations have the extensive control exerted by private health care institutions in the United States. Most Canadian hospitals operate under public or non-profit private ownership. Usually community boards made up of consumers, business executives, and trade unionists manage the local public hospitals, which the provincial governments finance. Unlike in the United States, in Canada most finances for health services come from public sources, such as federal grants, provincial taxes, and provincial health premiums; private insurance companies pay less than 3 percent of total expenses. No private insurance company can legally offer the same benefits covered under public health plans. Instead private health insurance programs provide supplemental services—for example, ambulance services, private nursing home care, certain prescribed drugs, dental care, eyeglasses, and hearing aids.

Dedicated to public provision of social services, Canadian policymakers provide comprehensive benefits. For example, all Canadians receive hospital services, physicians' care, and treatment by a dental surgeon operating in a hospital. Most provincial governments also offer dental services for children and prescription drugs for the elderly. Family allowances go to all parents. During the late 1970s public education expenditures as a percentage of the GNP were higher than in any other country except Sweden. Nearly all high school youth attend comprehensive secondary schools. Along with Swedes, Canadians enjoy more extensive opportunities to gain a post-secondary education than do youths in any other Western nation except the United States.[3] Despite their commitment to decentralized authority, Canadian government leaders have relied on public institutions as a crucial means to fulfill popular demands for social services.

Among the three federal systems (Canada, United States, West Germany), the Federal Republic of Germany operates the most centralized government; nevertheless, regional dispersion of power has long characterized German policymaking, except during the Nazi Third Reich. The national bureaucracy specifies uniform administrative standards for all the Länder (states); it supervises local administrative practices and regulates the training of Länder civil servants. Under the West German revenue-sharing procedures, the federal government in Bonn allocates receipts from individual income taxes, corporate income taxes, and value-added taxes to the Länder and cities. Because the Länder governments remain economically dependent on the national government for around 25 percent of their revenues, the Bonn officials can influence social service programs and economic development policies.

Although West German state government officials implement policies formulated at the national level, they still retain considerable authority over some economic decision-making. The Länder supervise radio and television, collect most taxes, and negotiate with Bonn leaders about ways to promote regional economic growth. The upper house of the federal parliament—the Bundesrat—represents state government interests; the legislature in each Land selects members to the Bundesrat and directs their voting on specific issues. Unlike in the U.S. Senate, within the Bundesrat all delegates from a specific Land must vote as a single unit; the political party controlling the state legislature dictates its preferences to the Bundesrat representatives. Even though the lower house of parliament—the Bundestag—plays the dominant policymaking role, the Bundesrat has the authority to delay laws passed by the Bundestag and to seek amendments in them. During the 1970s the Christian Democrats controlled the Bundesrat, but the Social Democrats held a plurality in the Bundestag and governed in coalition with the Free Democrats. Control of the federal upper house by the opposition party thus gave the states increased leverage to press their policy preferences on Cabinet officials. Not only the state governments but also city governments check the power exercised by the federal government. Municipal governments own several key economic sectors, including savings banks, housing projects, local transportation systems (buses, trains), water facilities, and cultural centers like operas, museums, and theaters. Local control over these enterprises, along with Länder ownership of banks, transportation networks (airports, canals, ports), and gas/electric plants, illustrates the historic German commitment to a decentralized federal system.

West German education policymaking also reveals extensive decentralization. True, even though each Land wields decisive authority over education policies, national standards provide considerable uniformity. For example, ministers of education in all eleven states have agreed that their schools will follow similar policies toward certification of teachers, academic standards, the content of some courses, times for offering instruction in a second and third language, and even the format of students' exercise-writing books. Several interstate education agencies help enforce the uniform standards. Despite these centralizing tendencies, state and municipal governments determine most education policies. Ministries of education within the Länder develop the curriculum, select the textbooks, set qualifications for teachers, recruit and pay teachers, supervise teacher training programs, and determine the schools' organizational structure. State governments finance nearly 70 percent of all public education expenditures, including 63 percent of revenues for primary and secondary schools. Municipal authorities fund around 30 percent. The federal government, which supports public universities and research activities, provides little revenue to primary schools except through indirect fiscal equalization grants to the least wealthy Länder. Like the federal government, local school authorities in the cities wield limited influence over education; they hire administrative staff, maintain buildings, and provide educational materials to the schools.

Similarly the key decision-making powers over health policy reside in the Länder governments. The federal Minister of Labor and Social Affairs mainly supervises the performance of public health insurance programs. He tries to ensure that the states, local governments, sickness insurance funds, and commercial insurance funds adhere to federal regulations. State governments oversee sickness insurance funds, authorize hospital construction, determine the types of services offered by hospitals, formulate programs for upgrading environmental health, and allocate positions for new health personnel. Working with federal government leaders on federal-state councils, the Länder officials also help shape national health policies. Local governments, mainly municipal, own slightly over 50 percent of total hospital beds; voluntary nonprofit organizations, usually churches and foundations, control 35 percent of beds, and private commercial firms manage the remaining 10 percent.

In the German Federal Republic private organizations as well as local government agencies play a key role in policy implementation, particularly in the economic and health policy arenas. German leaders rely on public institutions to carry out education activities; less than one percent of primary students and under 10 percent of secondary students attend a private school. Most enterprises are owned by private firms or by the Länder and municipalities. The federal government owns the postal service, telephone and telegraph systems, and the railways. It also holds minority shares in such industries as coal, raw steel, primary aluminum, petroleum, and electric power. In 1980 public corporations at the federal, state, and local levels employed nearly 8 percent of the work force—a slightly lower share than in Sweden and the United Kingdom. The proportion of the labor force working for general government agencies at all levels totaled about 15 percent, a lower percentage than in most other Western industrialized nations.

Private agencies, particularly physicians' associations and sickness insurance funds, administer public health policies. Several private medical associations coordinate physicians' activities. At the federal and Land levels physicians' chambers license new doctors, register them, certify their right to practice new specialties, and regulate their professional conduct. The Association of German Physicians articulates the interests of doctors who remain committed to the present fee-for-service system. The Marburgerbund represents physicians who work in hospitals. At the county, state, and federal levels associations of insurance doctors negotiate physicians' fee schedules with the sickness insurance funds. The Federal Committee of Physician and Sickness Funds formulates financial health policies for the nation. Then the Land associations of insurance doctors bargain with insurance funds to adapt general guidelines to regional situations. Around 1200 semipublic sickness insurance funding agencies implement health insurance for 93 percent of German citizens. Half the members belong to local or Land sickness funds. The other half enroll in occupational funds for white-collar employees, miners, sailors, factory workers, farmers, and business people. These agencies carry out comprehensive activities. They collect premiums through payroll taxes, negotiate with local physicians' associations to provide health services, pay the doctors, and finance hospital stays for their members. Operating according to a quasi-market model, these nonprofit sickness funds compete with each other and with private, profit-oriented insurance companies for members. Today in West Germany 7 percent of the population, mainly civil servants and self-employed business executives, remain outside the public health insurance program; they have purchased private commercial insurance policies. Nearly one-fifth of those who belong to a sickness insurance fund also hold private insurance. In 1975 private insurance financed over 5 percent of total health care expenditures; only the United States exceeded this figure. Public revenues, including general taxes (15 percent) and public health insurance (63 percent), paid for most of these expenditures; payments from individuals and employers financed the remaining costs.

Compared with the U.S. and Canadian governments, the West German government provides more comprehensive benefits to the citizenry. During the early 1980s total spending on social services was higher than in any other nation among the seven except Sweden. Most sickness insurance funds offer extensive benefits, including hospital care, physicians' treatments, prescription drugs, medical supplies, surgical appliances, and dental care. German youths, however, have fared less well from public policies. They have fewer opportunities to secure a post-secondary education than do most North Americans and West Europeans.[4]

In contrast to the three federal governments, the unitary states of France, Italy, and Britain practice more centralized policymaking. The national bureaucracy not only implements public policies but also formulates policy options; senior civil servants act as close advisors to Cabinet ministers, who assume major policy responsibilities. Moreover, unlike in the United States and West Germany, where the upper houses of the national parliaments represent regional interests, the three unitary states provide no legislative mechanisms that uphold subnational policy preferences. In France and Italy the upper houses, the Senates, play a subordinate role to the lower houses, the National Assembly and Chamber of Deputies respectively. Similarly over the last fifty years in Britain the House of Lords has lost the little power it used to wield at the turn of the century. Today as before, the House of Commons embodies sovereign authority. Finally, the fiscal policies enacted by these states illustrate a more centralized pattern than in the federal systems. For example, during 1980 expenditures by regional and local governments as a percentage of disbursements by all governmental levels totaled 34 percent in the United States, 40 percent in West Germany, and 56 percent in Canada. By contrast, local governments spent 13 percent in France, 25 percent in Italy, and 28 percent in the United Kingdom. Tax data and educational financing show a similar pattern: Subnational governments collect a larger share of tax revenues in the federal nations than in the unitary states; central government revenues finance over 60 percent of total public education expenditures in the United Kingdom, over 70 percent in France, and more than 80 percent in Italy.[5]

Despite these centralizing tendencies, unitary states still delegate important policy responsibilities to local governments. National bureaucrats rely on local leaders for information on which to base a policy. Because local officials carry out central directives, they have the power to amend national decisions to suit particular conditions; often they can thwart the implementation of a policy chosen by national politicians. For example, even in France, the most centralized state of these seven nations, urban mayors, councillors in the *départements*, and regional assemblypeople share policymaking authority with national civil servants. Particularly under President Mitterrand's commitment to deconcentration, the communal (town, city), département, and regional governments secured greater authority over economic decision-making, especially public investment, transportation, and professional training. Regional governments take charge of economic planning. The départements administer social service programs, such as allocation of housing grants. Headed by powerful mayors, the *communes* also distribute national social service benefits, plan public housing projects, and regulate the local environment. All these decentralizing reforms have reduced the controlling power of the national bureaucracy and expanded the influence wielded by elected officials in the communes, départements, and regions. National civil servants—the *commissaires de la République*—now advise elected local officials, coordinate the implementation of central government services, administer local policies, and act as intermediaries between national ministers and subnational government leaders.

French health and education policymaking also blends centralized with more localized control. The National Health Office within the Ministry of Health coordinates the activities performed by regional and primary health insurance offices. It prescribes uniform health standards for the nation, finances most construction costs of public hospitals, and distributes funds to regional health insurance offices, which supervise the programs prescribed by the Ministry of Health. Within each département primary health insurance offices provide basic health services to citizens. Organized primarily by geographic area, the over one hundred primary health insurance offices regulate contributions to the insurance fund and oversee payments to ill persons. They also support the national government's preventive health care programs, provide maternity care benefits, and partially finance hospital construction. Even though the French national government operates a more centralized educational system than do most other Western nations, policymakers during the last decade have decentralized the administration of primary and secondary schools. The national Minister of Education and his staff still dominate the education policy process. The ministry establishes a national school curriculum, recommends teaching methods, and decrees the guidelines for recruiting teachers, who work as state civil servants. It selects rectors, who supervise education activities within twenty-three academies, each of which includes several départements. Even though the rector, a national civil servant, appoints elementary school teachers, département leaders have recently gained greater authority to manage primary education; they have the right to raise local school taxes. Despite the formal bureaucratic control wielded by educational inspectors-general, who represent the Ministry of Education, local school personnel still retain extensive influence. Teachers have the freedom to choose teaching methods, topics for emphasis, and the sequence to present topics. Elementary school teachers also select the textbooks they want, free of approval by the Ministry of Education.

Like the French, Italians have recently experienced a trend toward more decentralized policymaking. Historically the Italian state bureaucracy, compared with the French civil service, has shown less cohesion, greater corruption, and less power. As a result, it faces difficulties carrying out the policies of the central government in Rome. Discouraged about the limited capability of the national government to overcome economic stagnation, regional government leaders during the 1970s gained greater authority over urban planning, territorial economic development, light industry, and such agricultural policies as farm modernization and managerial training. Particularly over education decision-making, the twenty regional governments have increased their influence. The central government still establishes new schools, recruits teachers, prepares the curriculum, selects textbooks, and contributes most finances. Nevertheless, since 1972 regional government leaders have participated more actively in school construction, transportation, textbook distribution, and ways to finance school building. At the local level the communal governments assume the major responsibility for primary education. The regional leaders have delegated to them the authority for implementing such activities as school construction and maintenance, provision of teaching equipment, and the recruitment of some personnel.

The British government operates a more decentralized system than do the French or Italians. True, the House of Commons exercises sovereign authority throughout the United Kingdom; local authorities mainly apply rules made by members of Parliament in London. Elected leaders of the local authorities depend on property taxes or "rates" to finance their expenditures. Yet these regressive property taxes raise insufficient revenue; thus local officials remain dependent on Parliament for supplying rate support grants for financing local projects, such as land use planning, housing, environmental protection, garbage collection, road construction, and education. Viewing local government as inefficient and wasteful, the Conservative government recently moved to curtail the authority of local councils to increase public expenditures and raise property taxes.

Despite the drive toward greater central control over economic policymaking, decentralized authority still prevails in the British education and health policy arenas. Wales and especially Scotland maintain autonomy from London. The Secretary of State for Education and Science in England dominates national education policymaking. He sets the qualifications for teachers, makes recommendations about teachers' salaries, and places limits on expenditures for local school buildings. Through Her Majesty's Inspectorate, he supervises school operations. Despite the considerable national potential to shape education policies, local education authorities and head teachers actually retain the dominant influence. The local education authorities manage primary and secondary schools, hire teachers, and decide how to spend the rate support grants supplied by the central government. Although local education authorities appoint the teaching staff, they have little authority over the curriculum. The national Department of Education and Science distributes syllabi and teaching handbooks; however, teachers have no obligation to follow these guidelines. They need no approval from a government agency to select their textbooks. Within each school the head teachers generally control curriculum and organizational issues. The Scots operate an independent school system governed by the Scottish Education Department (SED). Although the formal structure resembles the English pattern, the SED and local education authorities make the crucial decisions about the curriculum, teaching staff, and school organization.

Throughout Britain health policymakers practice decentralized administration. England, Wales, and Scotland reveal somewhat dissimilar features. Whereas family practitioner committees function in England and Wales, none exists in Scotland. District health authorities recently strengthened their power in England but were abolished in Wales and Scotland. English officials eliminated the area health authorities; in Wales and Scotland, however, they continue to exert the dominant influence at the local level. Whereas England has regional health authorities, these do not operate in Wales or Scotland.

Within England the London government administers a fairly centralized health system. Under the law establishing the National Health Service (NHS) in 1948, the central government assumed ownership of nearly all hospitals; prior to that time county governments and voluntary associations, including churches, owned the hospitals. A reorganization of the NHS in 1974 further centralized administration. Local governments yielded their authority to implement health policies and provide school health services in the counties and districts. The contemporary structure allocates responsibilities for health care among the Department of Health and Social Security (DHSS) in London, regional health authorities, and district health authorities. The Secretary of State for Social Services, who governs the DHSS, makes the crucial decisions about the distribution of resources, including money, physical equipment, and even personnel. Taxes collected by the central government finance most health care services. The DHSS allocates health expenditures, oversees physicians' performance, and accredits hospitals. Other agencies lower in the hierarchy exert less influence than does the DHSS. As in all other countries, the major localized control over the health policy process emanates from the physicians, both general practitioners and hospital specialists.

State-owned enterprises dominate the "commanding heights of industry" in Britain, Italy, and especially France. Under President Mitterand the French government has nationalized most private banks, other financial institutions, and such basic industries as electricity, aluminum, electronics, chemicals, and industrial engineering. The state also gained a majority share in the iron, steel, and armaments industries. As a result, it now owns about 40 percent of manufacturing industries—a larger public share than in any other Western

139

industrial democracy. Deposits in the public banks total 74 percent of all deposits. Nevertheless, private enterprises, mainly small and medium-size firms owned and operated by families, still dominate the service, retail trade, light industry, and farm sectors. The government depends on them to promote economic development plans.

Similarly in Italy powerful public agencies shape economic policies. These include the Bank of Italy and numerous state holding companies. The Bank of Italy controls the financial system. Although government officials appoint members to the boards that direct state holding companies, these companies, like the Istituto per la Ricostruzione Industriale (IRI) and Ente Nazionale Idrocarburi (ENI), retain extensive managerial independence. The IRI and ENI operate a vast array of industries: iron, steel, machinery, telephone, airline, broadcasting, oil, natural gas, textile, nuclear energy, engineering, and petrochemicals. Despite this large public sector, managers of state holding companies make their decisions based on market considerations, not on decrees from the national government's civil service or elected politicians.

British public corporations also retain extensive autonomy. They control crucial industries like oil, gas, electricity, coal, railways, some airlines, the post office, and telecommunications. The British public corporations employ over 8 percent of the labor force—a higher proportion than in any other country except Sweden. When the Conservative government came into power in 1979, it stressed the need to strengthen private enterprise, extend competition, and reduce the power of the public corporations. To accomplish these aims it denationalized a few industries, sold some shares of the public corporations to private shareholders, and deregulated such industries as aviation, telecommunications, postal services, bus transportation, gas, and electricity. Through these economic policies the Tory government has tried to enlarge the influence of private enterprises over economic decision-making.

Private institutions play an important educational role in Italy, Britain, and France. Italian private schools enroll around 7 percent of primary school students; about the same percentage of British youths attend independent and assisted schools. In France enrollments at private (mainly Catholic) elementary schools total 15 percent—the highest proportion in any of the seven Western nations. In Paris approximately one-fifth of primary school students go to private schools, which mainly serve children whose parents are industrialists, large-scale business executives, professionals, and senior civil servants. Since 1959 private French schools have received government subsidies to finance teachers' salaries and nearly 50 percent of operating expenses. Strong opposition by the private schools and the Roman Catholic Church forced the Mitterand administration in 1984 to abandon a plan to give private school teachers civil servant status and to require state approval of teachers hired by Catholic schools.

In Britain and especially France private agencies, along with government institutions, help satisfy health care needs. In Britain neither private hospitals nor private insurance companies wield such extensive power as in France. Fewer than 10 percent of British people have purchased private insurance plans, mainly from the Private Patients Plan, the Western Provident Association, and particularly the British United Provident Association (BUPA), which enrolls over 70 percent of private insurance subscribers. These private policies supplement the services of the NHS by securing private nursing homes, private hospital rooms, and speedier treatment by surgeons, gynecologists, and anesthetists. Yet private insurance premiums comprise under 2 percent of total health care expenditures; general taxes that finance the NHS provide nearly 90 percent of health revenues. Private hospital beds constitute only 2 percent of the total; the BUPA operates most British private hospitals. However, the Thatcher government has encouraged the construction of small private hospitals. During the early 1980s four large U.S. corporations—American Medical International, Hospital Corporation of America, Humana Inc., and Community Psychiatric Centers—built several new private hospitals, and these corporations now own nearly one-half the beds in all private British hospitals.

In the French health care system government organizations collaborate with private agencies. They jointly make crucial decisions. At each governmental level representatives from physicians' associations and health insurance offices determine health policy. National government officials from the ministries of Health, Finance, and Education formulate general health plans, specify standards, contribute funds, and approve decisions made by nongovernmental agencies. For example, the National Health Office coordinates the activities of regional and primary health insurance offices. It approves the salary schedules negotiated between the National Health Insurance Fund (CNMATS) and the physicians' associations, such as the Federation of French

Doctors and the Confederation·of Medical Associations. The social insurance funding agencies at the national and local levels function as legally independent organizations, neither wholly "public" nor entirely "private" but rather "semipublic." Under government supervision the CNMATS receives public funds from social security payroll taxes paid by employer and employee. During 1976 these taxes financed about 71 percent of all health care expenditures; direct payments and private insurance premiums contributed nearly a quarter of these expenses. Private insurance companies and private hospitals play an influential part in the French health care system. Privately owned hospitals manage about 35 percent of the total hospital beds; over one-half of these are in private for-profit cliniques, usually owned by groups of physicians. Recently, as in Britain, American Medical International has built private hospitals in France. Over 60 percent of the French population has purchased private insurance from either mutual aid societies or commercial insurance companies. Because the French sickness insurance fund pays only between 70 and 80 percent of medical expenses for physicians, dentists, prescription drugs, and hospital care, citizens need private health insurance to provide supplemental benefits. During the late 1970s private insurance premiums paid for around 4 percent of all health care expenses; individuals' direct payments financed around 20 percent.

France and Italy generally provide more comprehensive benefits than does Britain. From 1954 through the late 1970s government expenditures for old-age pensions and health care as a share of the GDP increased more rapidly in France and Italy than in the United Kingdom. The French government supplied generous pensions, family allowances, and financial assistance for maternal care. In Britain, however, total social service spending during the late 1970s amounted to only slightly more than in the United States and Canada. British pension benefits were especially low. France, Italy, and Britain did not enact programs that brought equal opportunities for a higher education. Compared with Swedish, Canadian, and U.S. youths, students in these three countries had fewer prospects of attending a post-secondary educational institution. Britain had the lowest proportion of people aged twenty to twenty-four enrolled in higher education.[6] Hence these three unitary states combined comprehensive health and income maintenance services with more restricted access to post-secondary public education.

In summary, this description of policy contents has revealed divergent patterns among the seven industrial nations. Whereas U.S. leaders have enacted limited, particularistic social service programs, especially for health care and family allowances, Swedish officials provide the most generous, comprehensive benefits. To finance these benefits, Swedish tax receipts total nearly double the U.S. rates. Government-owned enterprises are more prevalent in France and Italy than in the United States. Some governments like the French operate a centralized educational system; others such as the Canadian and German decentralize education policymaking to regional governments. Canadian policymakers have chosen a decentralized but public route to satisfy health care needs; however, U.S. policymakers have opted for a decentralized private system. Although British and Swedish health policies depend on public revenues to finance health care programs, French officials place greater stress on the need for private insurance companies and private individuals to pay health costs. In the following section we shall analyze the variables that explain these differences in policy contents.

EXPLANATIONS OF PUBLIC POLICIES

Explanations of the diverse public policies center on the interaction between the power of influential organizations and their policy preferences. In contemporary capitalist societies with a democratic political system, the major structures shaping the policy process include the electorate, political parties, business organizations, labor unions, and government. Analyzing the power of each structure, I focus on three dimensions: resources (finances, information, staff, numbers of members), organizational cohesion, and access to key policymakers—the Cabinet in parliamentary systems, the presidency and Cabinet in France, and the White House and Congress in the United States. Despite the crucial importance of power as the means to enact binding government decisions, an organization's impact on public policies also depends on its policy preferences and the degree of attitudinal unity among its members. Explicit preferences supply the *will* to frame certain policies; power represents the *way* to overcome opposition, mobilize the apathetic, and coordinate resources—tasks required for effective policy performance.

POWER OF THE ELECTORATE

Despite the populist cries of "power to the people," rank-and-file citizens exert little influence over the major decisions taken by economic, educational, and health institutions; instead managers, administrators, and professionals make the basic policies. Whether in a private corporation or a state enterprise, workers rarely control the investment of money and capital, the use of machinery, or the performance of the labor force. Except in Sweden and to a lesser extent in West Germany, where trade unionists share some responsibilities with management, workers' representatives generally lack the power to mount effective challenges against mangerial prerogatives. Similarly lay people wield only limited influence over decisions made by local boards of education and school councils. Parent organizations merely legitimate the policies already reached by these boards and councils, which defer to the expertise of education administrators—school superintendents, principals, and head teachers.

Populist practices seldom shape the policy process in health care institutions. Although political leaders have tried to organize decentralized mechanisms that make health care providers accountable to the public, these structures for mass control remain relatively powerless. For example, the U.S. neighborhood health centers, established during the 1960s under the Office of Economic Opportunity, tried to promote citizen control over the delivery of health services. Yet when the Nixon administration transferred management of these centers to the Department of Health, Education, and Welfare, government officials insisted that the health centers conform to cost-efficient norms, managerial competence, and hierarchical procedures. As expected, citizens no longer controlled the neighborhood centers' decisions. Although intended to promote consumer participation in health care planning, the health systems agencies established in 1974 came under the dominant influence of hospital administrators and physicians, not consumers such as low-income persons, disabled individuals, labor union heads, or even business executives. Rather than expanding consumer power, the health systems agencies mainly transmitted information from health professionals to citizens. In Quebec the powerful Federation of General Practitioners blocked the efforts of local health and social service centers *(centres locals de services communautaires)* to provide health care and educate citizens about poverty, environmental pollution, and occupational safety. The British community health councils supposedly offer the public opportunities to influence health policies formulated by health authorities. However, these councils lack the resources (staff, information, money, time) to wield effective managerial power; instead they inspect health facilities, occasionally protest against inadequate NHS care, and provide information about the needs of pregnant women, the elderly, disabled persons, and the handicapped. French and West German health insurance funds have organized local governing boards composed of employers and employees; in France but not West Germany physicians sit on these boards. Yet professionals still dominate health policymaking. Elected representatives lack specialized information and the time required for learning about an insurance fund's operations. Physicians, full-time insurance administrators, hospital staff, and government officials working for the health ministries formulate and implement health policies; the boards then endorse and thus legitimize these administrative decisions.[7]

Citizens also have limited opportunities to shape public policies through the electoral process. Most Western democracies except Switzerland hold few national referenda on policy issues; in the United States all referenda and initiatives occur at the state and local rather than the federal level. Elections better enable voters to choose candidates than to force their policy preferences on their representatives. The mandate theory of representation has only partial validity in Western nations. Specifically this theory makes the following five assumptions: (1) Candidates running for election clearly articulate their policy preferences and take different stands on issues. (2) Voters possess accurate information about the candidates' policy views. (3) The electorate bases its choices primarily on the candidates' policy stands. Oriented to the salience of public policies, voters blame government leaders and their policies for personal problems— high prices, unemployment, inadequate education, and ill health. (4) Programs formulated by a winning candidate correspond to the views of the voters, which may comprise a majority of the total electorate, those who favored the winning candidate, or the legislator's partisan supporters. (5) Clear accountability prevails in the government. The winning parties and candidates have not only the power but also the obligation to implement the policies desired by the voters.[8] As the following discussion indicates, these five assumptions exaggerate the power of the electorate to mandate its policy preferences.

First, during many elections issue stands often remain fuzzy. True, most candidates articulate divergent positions on at least some issues, mainly those involving domestic economic policies about equalitarian government policies, the decision-making authority of private enterprises, and trade union influence. Despite the tendency for candidates to express opposed ideological viewpoints, some candidates never clarify their positions toward specific issues. Rather they promise to eliminate corruption, protect family values, uphold national defense, reduce inflation, curtail unemployment, increase the growth rate, expand educational opportunities, and promote individual freedom.

Second, even when candidates do take divergent stands on particular issues, many voters remain uninformed about these positions. Candidates often fail to stress their policy preferences. Neither the mass media nor local party organizations provide detailed information to the electorate. Some voters find particular issues either unimportant or incomprehensible, particularly the esoteric details of monetary, fiscal, and foreign trade policies.

Third, the correspondence between citizens' ideological stands on issues and a candidate's policy positions only weakly explains voting behavior; instead party identifications, images of the candidates, and evaluations of the incumbent government's performance represent more important reasons for electoral choices. Often voters blame fate, themselves, or world conditions, not government leaders and public policies, for personal problems. Some voters may find a candidate's policy positions irrelevant to their personal lives; instead they base their vote on a general assessment of national conditions. Elections give a citizen the chance to reward incumbent leaders with "good" performance, however defined, and to punish them for "bad" conditions like high inflation, high unemployment, and declining educational standards. Yet voters may choose to "throw the rascals out" without really understanding a challenger's specific policy proposals to resolve these problems.

Fourth, even if voters choose a victorious candidate, they may not necessarily agree with the policies that the winning party enacts. During the last decade most citizens in the Western democracies have opposed expenditure cuts in pensions, health care, and public education; however, the austerity programs implemented by governments of varying ideological hues have brought spending reductions. Voters show greater support for imposing price controls than do government leaders, who generally regard these controls as an ineffective long-range solution to inflation. Because the public holds divergent, vague, and contradictory policy preferences, an election rarely produces a clear policy mandate. M. Stephen Weatherford points out: "No electoral mandate provides authorities with specific advice about policy choices. Public opinion, as V. O. Key emphasized, maps only the broad channels within which policymakers must set a course."[9] Electoral returns indicate the proportion of voters selecting a candidate, not their policy preferences and particularly not the intensities of these preferences. Thus winning candidates and parties enjoy broad discretion to frame policies that will handle such salient issues as unemployment, inflation, low-quality education, and deteriorating public health. Most often the policies chosen follow the mandates of the victorious partisan activists more than the preferences of a national majority or even all the candidates' supporters.

Fifth, particularly in systems that disperse power among different governing parties, voters cannot hold one party accountable for public policies, their social impacts, and the problems plaguing society. Most continental European parliamentary regimes, such as Sweden, West Germany, and Italy, feature multiparty governments; several political parties, not just two, hold seats in the lower house of parliament. Because one party rarely secures 51 percent of seats, the leading parties must form a coalition government. Through bargaining with each other, party leaders eventually reach a decision about which of them will become prime minister and cabinet ministers. Thus the legislators, not the voters, select the government. A party may lose executive power because its leaders cannot form a coaltion with other parties, not necessarily because of popular opposition to it or its policies. For example, in the 1976 Swedish election the Social Democratic party won nearly 44 percent of the parliamentary seats, the highest percentage of all parties. In the past the Social Democrats had often organized a coalition government with the Center party. During 1976, however, such an alliance was infeasible. Unable to coalesce with any other party except the Communists, who held 5 percent of the seats, the Social Democrats lost government office. The three "bourgeois" parties—Conservatives, Liberals, and Centrists—

formed a coalition government with a combined total of 51 percent of the seats. Similarly in West Germany delicate processes of coalition formation better explain recruitment to government office than do electoral returns. The governing Social Democrats in 1980 won only 44 percent of the total seats in the Bundestag, the lower house of parliament; the Christian Democratic Union/Christian Social Union (CDU/CSU) gained 45.5 percent. Yet the CDU/CSU failed to assume government power, mainly because the Social Democrats were able to continue their coalition with the Free Democrats (FDP), who secured nearly 11 percent. Two years later, however, the alliance between the Social Democrats and the FDP disintegrated; the FDP joined the CDU to form a new government. The Social Democrats fell from power when they could no longer maintain their coalition.

In a two-party system such as in the United States political accountability appears more direct. If most voters oppose the leadership or policies of the majority party in Congress, they can choose the opposition party as the majority party. The voters, not the legislators, select the president, who governs the executive branch. Yet if different parties control the legislature and presidency, the electorate cannot hold only one party responsible for any perceived policy failures. Particularly since World War II a Republican president has often governed with a Democratic Congress, thereby fragmenting policy accountability.

Under the Fifth Republic the French system locates responsibility in the president, who represents sovereign authority. Since 1958 the same party has controlled both the presidency and the National Assembly. The Gaullists ruled from 1958 through 1981; that year the Socialists took power. Because the policy process falls under unified control, the voters know whom to blame for bad policy performance. Yet according to the constitutional provisions of the Fifth Republic, elections for president and the National Assembly occur at different times; although the president serves a seven-year term, the legislators hold office for only five years. Thus a situation could arise whereby the National Assembly comes under the control of parties opposed to the president. This situation would fragment the policy process and diffuse policy accountability.

The electoral procedures of the Western democracies cannot easily reconcile the dilemma between accountability to the voters and representation of their policy views. The proportional representation

(PR) system used in West Germany, Italy, and Sweden brings a close correspondence between the percentage of votes won by a party and the percentage of seats it takes in the legislature (see Table 5.1). However, the PR system produces multiparty governments; hence voters cannot hold one party responsible for policy performance. Under the first-past-the-post system of Britain, Canada, and the United States, the legislative candidate who wins a plurality gets elected. From 1945 through 1980 one party secured sufficient seats in the U.S. Congress to comprise a governing majority. Except in 1974 and 1976-79, one party gained a majority of seats in the British House of Commons to form the ruling Cabinet during the post-World War II period. Yet this electoral system demolishes the parliamentary power of third parties, which may gain a fairly high share of the popular vote but few legislative seats. For example, in the 1983 elections to the House of Commons, the Conservative party won only 42.4 percent of the United Kingdom vote but 61 percent of Commons seats. The Labour party secured 27.6 percent of the vote and gained 32 percent of the seats. The Liberal/Social Democratic alliance obtained almost as large a percentage of votes—25.4 percent—as did the Labourites; yet it wound up with only 3.5 percent of the seats. Similarly since the early 1960s the Canadian New Democratic party, the third largest party, has won between 10 and 20 percent of the popular vote; yet it has rarely secured more than 10 percent of the House of Commons seats. In short, plurality electoral procedures produce high accountability but underrepresent voters who choose third-party candidates. Although the PR system achieves a similarity between popular votes and legislative seats, it diffuses policy accountability.[10]

POWER OF POLITICAL PARTIES

To what extent do political parties make a difference in the policies implemented by Western democratic governments? Although ideological party activists take divergent stands on domestic policy issues, the economic, education, and health policies enacted by diverse governing parties show greater similarities than the activists' ideological manifestos. The commitment to a coherent ideological program depends on a person's degree of party activism. Passive party

Table 5.1

ELECTORAL AND LEGISLATIVE STRENGTH OF POLITICAL PARTIES, 1960-80

Country	Political Parties	Percentage of Popular Votes in Legislature[a]			Percentage of Seats Held in Legislature[b]		
		1960-66	1967-73	1974-80	1960-66	1967-73	1974-80
Canada	Progressive-Conservative	39.3%	32.1%	35.1%	49.3%	30.5%	38.5%
	Liberal	38.5	43.7	42.2	38.6	54.9	49.6
	New Democratic	12.8	17.2	16.7	5.8	8.7	8.1
France	Gaullist	29.5	43.6	30.8	46.4	67.8	44.2
	Independent Republican, MRP, Radical, reformist, center	25.3	12.8	17.3	27.8	7.0	15.7
	Socialist	21.5	17.9	23.2	19.4	15.2	21.3
	Communist	20.7	20.5	21.0	6.0	9.3	16.0
West Germany	Christian Democrat and CSU	47.0	46.6	47.0	50.3	48.6	47.5
	Free Democrat	10.9	7.8	8.1	11.4	8.0	8.1
	Social Democrat	35.4	41.7	44.0	37.3	43.4	44.5
Italy	Christian Democrat	40.0	38.9	38.6	43.2	42.1	41.9
	Liberal and Republican	6.9	7.6	5.2	5.8	5.6	4.0
	Socialist and Social Democrat	19.4	18.4	14.2	18.4	17.1	12.7
	Communist	24.2	26.8	31.2	25.1	27.9	32.7
Sweden	Conservative	16.2	12.5	15.7	16.3	12.5	16.0
	Center and Liberal	30.8	32.7	34.0	31.8	33.5	34.6
	Social Democrat	47.4	47.2	43.2	48.8	49.1	44.1
	Communist	4.5	4.4	5.1	2.5	3.4	5.2
United Kingdom	Conservative	47.5	44.5	38.4	54.0	47.2	46.9
	Liberal	7.0	7.9	17.3	1.2	1.4	1.9
	Labour	44.4	45.2	38.3	44.7	50.9	47.5
United States	Republican	47.5	44.5	53.4	36.5	42.8	36.4
	Democrat	51.9	47.2	44.7	63.5	57.1	63.6

Source: Thomas Mackie and Richard Rose, *The International Almanac of Electoral History* (London: Macmillan, 1974); September issues of *European Journal of Political Research, 1974-81.*

[a] For all countries except the United States these percentages indicate the mean proportion of popular votes won by parties in elections to the lower house of the legislature during the three periods indicated. In the United States the percentages show the mean votes for the presidential candidates.

[b] For all countries except the United States these percentages indicate the mean proportion of seats held by parties in the lower house of the legislature during the three periods indicated. In the United States the percentages show the seats held by Democrats and Republicans in both the Senate and House of Representatives.

supporters—either voters or psychological identifiers—rarely hold coherent policy positions. Voters with different party attachments often share similar views. By contrast, party activists express more coherent, consistent ideological principles. Compared with passive supporters, they have attained more formal education and can interpret political events in terms of a comprehensive set of ideological principles--liberalism, conservatism, democratic socialism, Marxism-- that systematically relate various issues. Activists not only think more abstractly, but also voice more polarized stands than do passive supporters.

Since World War II the main policy issues dividing political partisan activists have revolved around government promotion of social equality, public control of private enterprise, and the rights of trade unions. Generally left-wing activists more strongly support egalitarian social service programs, government control over private enterprise, and expanded trade union rights. Right-wing activists express greater opposition to comprehensive, egalitarian income maintenance, education, and health policies. They seek more government assistance to private health plans and private schools. Rejecting the extension of government-owned enterprises, they prefer to denationalize and deregulate the public sector so that private managers gain autonomy from both government officials and trade union leaders.[11]

In the United States Democratic party leaders have stressed government policies that expand social equality. For example, they show more enthusiasm for a government-administered national health insurance program, increased spending on public schools, a higher tax on oil companies' "excess" profits, and policies that guarantee employment and a minimal standard of living. By contrast, Republican party leaders prefer to cut spending on public health and education programs. They oppose government payments for abortion and support tuition tax credits for parents with children in private schools.[12]

On the role of government in society the British Conservative and Labour activists take more polarized positions than do the two major U.S. parties. The 1983 election manifestos revealed sharp policy differences. The Conservatives defended government grants to independent (private) schools, supported the growth in private health insurance, opposed a government wage or price freeze, favored the sale of shares in publicly owned industries to private enterprises, and sought greater competition in the gas and electricity industries. The

Labourites sought higher spending on public education, the NHS, child benefits, pensions, unemployment benefits, and cash grants for the disabled. Opposed to a government wage restraint, the Labour activists supported price controls. From their perspective the government should eliminate grants to private schools, end private practice in the NHS, and establish more publicly owned firms in the pharmaceutical, electronics, and health equipment industries, as well as the banking sector.[13]

Although the major Swedish parties have achieved a greater policy consensus than have the two largest British parties, during the early 1980s the partisan activists on the left (Social Democrats) and right (Conservatives) became more polarized. Of the five largest Swedish parties the Conservatives express the least support for government policies that would expand income equality, raise income taxes on the wealthy, increase the government-owned sector, and strengthen trade union authority. They want to decrease income taxes, promote private schools, introduce private competition in the health care sector, and reduce trade union power to manage private enterprises and to share in the profits. By contrast, the Social Democratic leaders strongly support egalitarian policy programs toward wages, taxes, and expenditures for health, education, pensions, childcare allowances, and unemployment benefits. They show less concern about expanded government involvement in the economy. According to them, government and unions should cooperate with private corporations to increase employment opportunities, promote investment, plan for the public good, and control externalities such as air pollution. Backed by the Swedish Federation of Trade Unions, the Social Democratic party during the 1982 election campaigned for a wage-earners' fund, a program strongly opposed by the Conservative party and the private business sector. According to this program, the central Cabinet determines general economic policies, five regional wage-earners' funds decide the best strategies for investing capital, and employees within a firm choose the company board. Through this program Social Democratic leaders hope to realize greater economic democracy—that is, enhanced employee participation at the workplace.[14]

Despite the ideological polarization splitting party activists, the policies implemented by diverse governing parties show only modest differences. Cross-national studies of policy performance during the

1970s indicated that in countries where right-wing parties maintained a strong majority in government for a lengthy period, expenditures for social services were lower as a percentage of the GDP. Where Social Democrats controlled the government, they gave stronger support to these programs, including public education, income maintenance, and especially public health care. The Social Democrats, compared with right-wing parties, also enacted revenue measures that collected a higher share of tax receipts as a proportion of the GDP. Nevertheless, political parties by themselves did not produce these variations in tax and expenditure policies. Social Democrats wielded a strong policy impact, as in Sweden, only when the conservative party opposition was fragmented, unions held considerable strength, labor leaders and business executives retained cooperative relationships, and the dominant political leaders expressed a commitment to solidaristic, egalitarian values.[15]

Government officials usually share greater policy consensus than do party activists. For example, in the United States from 1941 through 1976, changing party control of Congress and the presidency led to only minor variations in the level of expenditures and types of funded programs. The major difference was that the Democrats spent less money on agriculture than did the Republicans. Since World War II both parties have pursued a counter-cyclical fiscal policy. During peacetime contractionary periods government spending increased more than during an economic expansion; the rate of expenditure growth in the bust period of the business cycle was about the same during the Carter and Eisenhower presidencies. Federal social service expenditures as a percentage of the GNP peaked in 1976 under the Republican Ford administration rather than in 1977-79 under the Democratic Carter presidency. In the Nixon and Ford administrations federal government expenditures for social programs (pensions, Medicare, Medicaid, child nutrition, unemployment insurance, veterans' compensation, Aid to Families with Dependent Children [AFDC], food stamps, education, student loans) showed an average yearly real increase of 10 percent, compared with 8 percent during the Democratic Kennedy and Johnson presidencies, 4 percent during the Carter years, and 1.5 percent during President Reagan's first term (1981-84). Johnson and Nixon implemented more activist health policies than did Carter. The Johnson administration and Democratic Congress enacted the Medicare and Medicaid programs in 1965. During the early 1970s the Nixon administration, along with the Democratic-controlled Congress, reduced defense expenditures, increased spending for social security, and approved legislation that regulated the environment, expanded government health programs, and promoted factory safety through the Occupational Safety and Health Administration (OSHA). The Carter administration, however, gave little backing to a new comprehensive national health insurance plan.[16]

In Canada, Britain, Sweden, Italy, and West Germany as well, different parties controlling the government either implement rather similar public policies or else enact policies that diverge from their rhetoric. As expected, the Progressive-Conservative government in Alberta imposed a user fee on most hospital patients—a policy opposed by federal Liberal officials. After winning the 1983 election in British Columbia against the socialist New Democratic party, the Social Credit government reduced spending for health care, public universities, and public assistance but raised taxes on low-income citizens. Less expected, however, were the Parti Québécois provincial government actions that in 1983 levied low taxes on business profits, placed few restrictions on foreign capital investment, reduced social service expenditures, limited civil servants' wage hikes, curtailed their right to strike, and laid off teachers. Ironically this self-styled "social democratic" party had won strong support from teachers at the provincial elections.

At least until the Conservative Thatcher government took power in Britain in 1979, the two major parties' spending priorities showed only slight differences. Between 1950 and 1976 the Labour governments gave priority to expenditures for employment services and comprehensive schools, while the Conservative governments allocated more funds for housing, research, and the environment. Both parties supported the NHS. Although the expansion of comprehensive schools proceeded most rapidly when the Labour party controlled the national government and local government councils, influential Conservative officials showed a pragmatic flexibility about extending the number of comprehensive schools; they just wanted to proceed at a slower pace than did most Labourites.

The Swedish Social Democratic party and the three main "bourgeois" parties—Conservative, Liberal (People's), Center—share a policy consensus about most education, health, and economic issues. All parties stress equality of educational opportunity, support comprehensive schools, and prefer rather similar public health programs. When the three nonsocialist parties formed a coalition government in 1976, they increased the state-owned share of the economy. Trying to rescue some private firms from bankruptcy, the government partially or fully nationalized the shipbuilding, steel, computer, and textile industries. Social service spending remained high. After the Social Democrats regained power in 1982, they sold some shares of state-owned firms to the private sector.

Both the West German Social Democrats and Italian Socialists have implemented austerity policies. Dominating the West German federal government between late 1969 and 1982, the Social Democrats initially extended unemployment compensation, raised family allowances, and encouraged greater union/worker participation in firms. After the 1974 recession, however, they switched to a pro-business economic policy that favored large corporations, export firms, and banks. Along with their junior partners, the FDP, they enacted programs that promoted private capital investment, rapid growth, and collaboration among government, business, and unions. Opposing greater income equality, Chancellor Helmut Schmidt even implemented a program in 1981-82 that reduced real wages and limited expenditures for pensions and health care (but not for unemployment benefits or sick pay). In Italy Socialist Prime Minister Bettino Craxi, allied with the Christian Democrats, enacted a program that reduced wages, pensions, and health care benefits.[17]

The most striking departures from past public policies have occurred under the Reagan Republican administration, the Thatcher Conservative government, and the Mitterrand Socialist presidency. Both the U.S. Republicans and the British Conservatives reduced taxes on business corporations and the wealthy, increased poor people's taxes, raised expenditures for the military and police, and lowered spending on social programs: job training, unemployment benefits, public housing, public transportation, school meals, and public education. Particularly in the Reagan administration, egalitarian health programs came under attack. The administration reduced expenditures for Medicaid, maternal and child health services, public health clinics, community health centers, and programs to help the handicapped. Compared with the Carter administration, the Reagan presidency decreased the power of OSHA and the Environmental Protection Agency (EPA). Fewer OSHA workplace inspections and fewer serious citations occurred under Reagan. The EPA conducted less research into the effects of environmental pollutants on health. Medicare users had to pay higher hospital deductibles and higher premiums for physicians' services. Although spending for the British NHS increased under the Thatcher government, the Conservatives stressed the need for a more privatized health care system, including more private hospitals, the preparation of NHS hospital meals by private firms, tax deductions for private health insurance, and higher user fees for prescription drugs, dental services, and eye examinations. Committed to a laissez-faire economic approach, both the Reagan and Thatcher policymakers favored a restricted growth in the money supply, rejected wage and price controls, and promoted deregulation of large corporations such as railways, airlines, telecommunications, and natural gas.

Departing from the consensus politics followed by their predecessors—Republican president Richard Nixon and Conservative prime minister Harold Macmillan—Reagan and Thatcher stood behind more programmatic policies based on conservative ideological principles. The ideas of Milton Friedman arouse widespread enthusiasm from the Republican conservatives, who since the early 1970s have steadily increased their influence within state party organizations and the national party headquarters. The dominant wing of the Conservative party leans toward the policy preferences of Friedrich Hayek.

Despite this movement away from consensus politics, both conservative governments continue some policy emphases of previous opponent administrations (British Labourites and U.S. Democrats). Under the Thatcher government British public expenditures as a proportion of the GDP increased by 3 percent between 1979 and 1983; total tax revenues as a share of the GDP also grew. Between 1975 and 1983 both Labour and Conservative administrations reduced spending on public housing and education. Moreover, under Tory rule two institutions established mainly by Labour governments—the NHS and comprehensive schools—continued operating as before. In the United States both Congressional Democrats and Republicans have favored lower taxes on business, deregulation of major corporations, limits on social security benefits, and restrictions in the growth of money. Even though congressional Democratic leaders rejected President Reagan's programs that reduced expenditures on social programs for the poor, they supported some tax reductions and defense spending increases.

Under the Reagan administration total federal expenditures as a percentage of the GNP increased from 22.9 percent in 1980 to 24.8 percent in 1983; during the same period receipts declined from 20.6 to 19.4 percent. Labeled "supply-side" economics by Reagan Cabinet officials, the policies that cut taxes and raised defense expenditures actually resemble some features of the Keynesian demand-expansion programs pursued by Democratic administrations during the 1960s, even though the Republican fiscal policies produced far more inequality.[18]

Although the Mitterrand administration implemented far-ranging policy changes during its first year in office, the severe economic problems plaguing France in 1982 led Mitterand to enact policies that resembled those of his Gaullist predecessors. From June 1981 through June 1982 the government expanded social service benefits, such as family allowances, pensions, and grants for the handicapped. Its health policies canceled supplementary medical fees. Workers gained a higher minimum wage, longer vacations, and a reduced work week. Even if the Socialist administration refrained from establishing *autogestion* (workers' self-management) in the factories, it increased trade union power by expanding collective bargaining procedures, strengthening works' committees, and restricting employers' rights to discipline workers. Attempting to promote capital investment, modernize industry, and enlarge the sale of French exports, the Mitterand administration nationalized the largest private banks and large-scale industries. Egalitarian fiscal policies levied higher taxes on the wealthy and lower taxes on the poor. By lowering the eligibility age for full pensions, increasing cash transfers to the poor, and creating new public sector jobs, Socialist policymakers hoped to reduce the unemployment rate. Yet these expectations proved futile. By mid-1982 France faced a slightly higher jobless rate, lower investment by domestic and foreign capitalists, a severe trade deficit, and a higher inflation rate. From June 1982 the Mitterrand presidency switched tactics toward an austerity program. To discourage import purchases, expand export sales, and preserve the value of the franc, the government imposed higher taxes on income, gas, liquor, and tobacco. It also limited wage increases, instituted price controls, and set higher prices for electricity, gas, and travel—services provided by state-owned industries. All these deflationary policies marked a retreat backward toward some policies pursued by Gaullist Prime Minister Raymond Barre.[19]

Several factors explain the gap between party rhetoric and actual policy performance. First, nearly every Western political party experiences policy factionalism. Rarely does one party have a united, coherent stand toward pressing issues. Ideological policy fragmentation necessitates compromise among the diverse factions. One reason that the Reagan and Thatcher administrations were able to implement new policies stems from the greater policy cohesion reached by Republican and Conservative parties compared with their Democratic and Labour oppositions.

Second, a change in party control of government produces policy changes only when the major parties hold divergent policy preferences; however, the period from 1950 through the mid-1970s saw a waning ideological polarization among rival parties. This era showed rapid economic growth and declining class tensions. Conservative, Christian Democratic, liberal, socialist, and communist parties all supported, though in varying degrees, expanded social services, government planning, and government aid to private schools. As the economic recession grew worse during the late 1970s, ideological polarization became more acute, especially in Britain and the United States. Yet most Western political parties remain less divided on policy issues today than before World War II.

Third, although political parties do shape the policy preferences of legislators and Cabinet ministers, party activists wield only limited structural control over government officials. Particularly when a party holds executive power, government leaders dominate the party, rather than vice-versa. They retain discretion to mold public policies free from direct pressures by partisan activists. Government officials usually share a greater policy consensus than do rival party leaders. Ideological desirability often yields to the demands of political expediency when elected leaders bargain with other organizations involved in the policy formulation process.

Fourth, one party rarely governs alone; it must share power with other parties and government institutions controlled by opposition parties. Most Western governments comprise a coalition of parties. The need for compromises among parties impedes any drastic change in policies from one administration to another. During the postwar years, a multiparty coalition has governed the West German federal republic. Under the SPD-FDP coalition that lasted from 1969 through late 1982, an FDP member usually held the Economics Ministry. The head of the FDP, the SPD chancellor, the SPD finance minister, the FDP economics minister, the labor minister, and the president of the Bundesbank decided key economic issues. Control by the opposition CDU/CSU over the Bundesrat, Länder governments, and urban governments also limited the SPD's power to implement the economic policies it preferred. Some SPD officials wanted to establish more comprehensive schools; however, opposition by the CDU education ministers from the Länder led the SPD to deemphasize secondary school reform and concentrate instead on economic and foreign policy issues. Similarly the U.S. federal system divides decision-making authority among national, state, and local institutions. Although a Republican president often controls the executive branch, the Democrats usually hold a majority in Congress. Both Republican and Democratic governors may reject the policy positions taken by their own party's president in the White House. Around three-fourths of all school boards hold nonpartisan elections. Because no single party controls all government agencies, officials from the two parties must bargain over policies.

Fifth, agencies other than parties and elected government leaderships shape the content of public policies. The actions taken by the U.S. and USSR governments constrain European policy choices. During the late 1970s and early 1980s the growing military capabilities of the Soviet Union led to a rise in defense expenditures as a percentage of the GDP in France, Italy, and especially Britain. At that time higher interest rates imposed by U.S. financial institutions caused European bankers to raise their interest rates in an attempt to halt capital outflow. Multinational institutions like the IMF and World Bank have financed trade deficits faced by Britain and Italy. Under pressure from IMF officials and multinational bankers, who supplied loans to cover these deficits, British and Italian leaders had to impose an austerity program that curbed import purchases. Domestic private businesses and multinational industrial corporations provide investment funds as well as employment; hence government officials often refrain from enacting policies that would threaten "business confidence." Particularly in Sweden labor union leaders participate with business executives in making economic policies. Most Swedish decision-makers have hesitated to place excessive restraints on wage increases or trade union authority. In Sweden, France, and other European states civil servants have exerted a decisive influence over the content of public policies. Whereas party politicians take ideological stands toward the left or right, civil servants assume more centrist, pragmatic positions. Rather than desiring drastic changes in society, they seek greater continuity. Oriented toward prudence, the civil service brings moderation to the policy process.[20]

POWER OF GOVERNMENT, BUSINESS ORGANIZATIONS, AND LABOR UNIONS

In contemporary Western industrial societies government officials, business executives, and trade union leaders shape public policies. Government officials have the main legal responsibility for making and implementing binding decisions for a society; thus their policy role becomes crucial although often underestimated. In private enterprise market economies business managers invest capital, produce consumer goods, decide the prices for products and services, and set the wages and fringe benefits of employees. Because all these activities affect the well-being of people both within a nation and overseas, business entrepreneurs wield extensive influence over public policies. They advise elected officials, take appointed positions in the government, contribute money to parties and candidates, and communicate their policy preferences through mass media advertising. According to Charles Lindblom:

> In all market-oriented societies, the great organizing and coordinating tasks are placed in the hands of two groups of responsible persons, functionaries, or leaders. One group consists of government officials at sufficiently high levels. The other group consists of business people. The tasks assigned to business people are of no less importance than those assigned to government officials. . . . None of the market-oriented polyarchies has ever practiced pluralism without the lopsided participation of businessmen in their double role as leaders of enterprises and as members of disproportionately strong electoral and interest-groups.[21]

Although generally not as powerful as business organizations, labor unions organize part of the work force, provide information about employment opportunities, press for higher wages and fringe benefits, influence workers' productivity, demand improved working conditions, and ally with political parties to transform their policy preferences into binding government decisions. These activities enable trade unions to wield some influence over public policymaking.

As indicated, the power of government, business, and labor varies in different Western nations. To explain the power of these agencies over policy contents, I will use three models: the market model, democratic corporatism, and state planning.

Market Model. Of the three, the market model features the weakest role for the government in the public policy process. Central government officials possess only limited power to impose their policy preferences on other participants. Decentralized government prevails; often regional and local governments wield considerable influence over the formulation and especially implementation of public policies. Rather than defining the general interest for society, the government establishes the institutions and laws that enable social groups to reconcile their interests, negotiate political bargains, and accommodate differences. Embodying the ideals of representative democracy, the legislature plays a crucial role in making public policy. Territorial representation focuses on elections to the parliament. Just as diverse interest groups compete in the economic market, so different political parties compete on the political market. At election time voters choose party candidates; the winners become legislators, who try to satisfy constituent interests for greater concrete benefits like increased business subsidies, more generous tax credits, higher wages, larger fringe benefits, higher old-age pensions, expanded educational opportunities, and less expensive health care services.

Under the market model social groups like business firms and trade unions retain extensive autonomy from the central government. Civil society prevails over the state. Government officials depend on business support for policy success. Because the business sector hires workers, sets prices, and invests capital, it has the power to affect public policies designed to lower unemployment, restrain prices and expand economic growth. Despite their power, private firms in a competitive market economy hardly form a united, highly coordinated interest group. Divergent ideological, economic, and regional interests fragment business organizations, hindering their ability to dominate the policy process. Similarly labor unions operate incohesive organizations. Professional staffs remain limited. Unions lack the finances needed for lobbying activities and recruitment drives. Several unions compete for workers' support, often in the same industry. Rather than allying with a single political party, union officials align with diverse parties. Yet while labor unions exert less political power than the business sector, they have some influence over government decision-making. Their right to strike and their ties with a governing political party may give them at least veto power over certain public policies. Although rivals in the policy process, union officials and business executives share a commitment to voluntarism. Seeking autonomy from state control, they prefer that collective bargaining occur with little government interference.[22]

The U.S. and Canadian policy processes best embody the market model's assumptions. In these two federal systems strong regional governments limit national control over the formulation and implementation of economic, education, and health policies. Government officials play a more active role in Canada than in the United States. At both the federal and regional (state and provincial) levels Canadian civil servants and legislators more strongly support government expenditures for social services than do their U.S. counterparts. Whereas in the United States private organizations—commercial insurance corporations, profit-oriented hospital chains, physicians' associations—have dominated the health policy arena, in Canada federal government officials initiated Medicare legislation in 1966. Liberal party legislators sought to reduce health costs, standardize health care throughout the nation, and win greater electoral popularity. Although labor union heads also wanted a national health insurance plan, they exerted only weak pressure on the government. Private life insurance companies mounted the strongest opposition, but other corporate enterprises expressed muted antagonism to the Medicare program. Thus federal officials played the decisive role in gaining House of Commons approval of this policy.[23]

In the United States and Canada the business sector plays a similar role in the policy process. The two nations are geographically large and culturally diverse. No single business group can represent all business people. Both the U.S. and Canadian Chambers of Commerce operate as decentralized organizations. Although organizing local support for legislation and candidates that favor small business, they have little power to shape national economic policy. Moreover, Canadian as well as U.S. businessmen have ready access to legislative and executive institutions. For example, in both nations most members of the federal cabinets are either lawyers or business executives. Whether liberals or conservatives, they support policies that will maintain a strong private-enterprise economy. Moderate welfare services, restraints on wage hikes, low business taxes, and government subsidies to corporations are preferred by both major parties. Professionals and managers dominate local public school boards; business executives wield the greatest influence on the governing boards that oversee publicly funded community hospitals. Like U.S. executives, Canadian corporate leaders face no major challenge from a powerful labor movement or socialist political party.[24]

Despite these similarities, the U.S. economic elite exerts stronger power than does the Canadian. Throughout the history of the United States few other organizations have wielded the power to rival business dominance. In Europe the landed aristocracy, established church hierarchy, professionalized civil service, and socialist political parties helped govern the state; but in the United States these organizations remained weaker. As a result, government leaders usually enacted policies that favored business interests – for example, low increases in the money supply, low taxes, and minimal government expenditures, especially for social services, transfer payments, and a national public health care system. Business lobbyists also prevented the establishment of government economic planning, publicly owned industries, and an incomes policy matching wage hikes with gains in labor productivity.

However great the power wielded by business organizations, from the end of the Civil War through the 1980s their effectiveness in shaping public policies varied from period to period. Business enjoyed its greatest policy successes between 1870 and 1930, during the 1950s, and from 1977 through the 1980s. At brief interludes, however, organizations less supportive of business interests gained a greater leverage – for example, in the 1930s New Deal era and from 1965 through 1977. Demoralized by the 1929 depression, the capitalist class became weakened during the early 1930s. The president, federal civil servants, and liberal Democrats gained the initiative to formulate policies intended to bring the nation out of the most severe depression in its history. Labor unions gained legal recognition from the Wagner Act, the right to bargain collectively with management, and great influence within the Democratic party. National government officials, Democratic party activists, and trade unionists retained some independence to deal with the economic crisis. Between 1965 and 1977 business groups once again lost some power to organizations representing consumers, environmentalists, and civil rights' advocates. At this juncture liberal Democrats increased their influence in Congress. Congress passed the Medicare-Medicaid legislation, expanded federal financial grants to public schools, and strove to integrate the schools. New federal laws regulated automobile emissions, air pollution, factory safety, consumer products, and the environment. By the end of the 1970s, however, business organizations regained their dominance over the policy process. Both Democrats and Republicans in Congress supported deregulation, tax cuts for business, government subsidies to promote capital investment, and higher expenditures on defense projects that benefit arms contractors. Under a pro-business Republican president, the federal civil service and the legislature responded sympathetically to business claims. In 1984 a survey of 1500 U.S. "opinion makers" rated large business the second most influential institution behind the White House. Specific business organizations ranking in the ten most powerful agencies included television, banks, the oil industry, and Wall Street investment houses.[25]

The power of business over the U.S. policy process largely stems from its considerable resources, concentration, and access to government officials. Compared with European and Canadian industries, U.S. industries earn higher profits on their investments. From 1955 through 1980 U.S. manufacturing firms secured a larger rate of return on capital than did similar industries in Canada, West Germany, Italy, Sweden, or the United Kingdom. These returns enabled U.S. businesses to finance activities intended to translate their policy preferences into binding government decisions. Business executives promote their policy beliefs in the mass media, universities, research institutes (the American Enterprise Institute for Public Policy Research, Heritage Foundation, Hoover Institution, American Council for Capital Formation, Institute for Contemporary Studies), Business Roundtable, Business Council, Committee for Economic Development, and political action committees. All these organizations help set the political agenda—both general policy objectives and specific issues that government officials should tackle through public policies. Then Congress and the Presidency determine the means—the organizational mechanisms, expenditures, and finances—for achieving these policy goals.[26]

The growing concentration of business firms has given large industries the power to shape the economic policy process. Compared with Europeans, fewer U.S. citizens work in small firms. For example, in 1980 employers, self-employed persons, and workers in family-owned enterprises comprised 29 percent of the civilian labor force in Italy, 17 percent in France, 14 percent in West Germany, 10 percent in Canada, 8 percent in Sweden and the United Kingdom, but under 7 percent in the United States.[27] Although today U.S. industries probably remain less concentrated than those in Canada, Britain, and Sweden, since World War II U.S. corporations have achieved greater control over a product market, as measured by the percentage of total sales, assets, or output of the four largest industries. Particularly during recent years, mergers, conglomerate formations, and divestitures have increased the market power of concentrated industries.

Oligopolies wield extensive power over economic decision-making by U.S. government agencies. In both Democratic and Republican administrations most Cabinet members are either industrial executives or corporate lawyers. Large industrialists and company directors who serve on two or more different corporation boards take the major positions in federal administrative agencies. Lobbyists for large manufacturing industries also play the most effective role in Congress, as measured by their success in pressuring Congress to pass bills they favor. These powerful corporations include the national defense industry, highly concentrated firms, industries with large annual sales, and firms with plants in several different states. Smaller industries gain less access to either the federal executive or the Congress; as a result, they score less striking policy successes.[28]

Despite the dominant role played by business organizations, we should not exaggerate the organizational cohesion or class awareness of the U.S. business sector. Various cleavages split the U.S. capitalist class. Large industries compete with each other and with smaller firms. Domestic enterprises pursue divergent interests from exporters. Manufacturing industries, financial enterprises (banks, insurance companies), and trading establishments voice diverse policy preferences and organize different pressure groups. Whereas large-scale banks prefer flexible interest rates and deregulation of financial institutions, smaller banks oppose deregulation and support fixed interest rates. Regional and political party cleavages also fragment the capitalist class. Nearly all corporate executives share some policy objectives—e.g., private enterprise autonomy from government control and lower taxes on business; virtually none seeks a top limit on incomes, more generous welfare payments, or expanded worker participation in a firm's management. Nevertheless, on other policy positions—federal creation of jobs for the unemployed, taxes on polluting industries, increased political power for the poor, local control over social service programs, deregulation of industries, wage-price controls—business leaders take more divided stands.[29] In sum, the diversity of the large U.S. market, the role played by U.S. multinationals in the world capitalist system, and the fragmentation of U.S. political institutions all contribute to the cleavages in the capitalist class. Even if the business sector wields greater power over the policy process than do other social groups, it lacks the cohesion to dictate every specific enacted policy.

Canadian business executives exert a less decisive impact on public policies than do U.S. corporate heads. The Canadian economy is subordinate to U.S. enterprises. During the late 1970s most large-scale manufacturing industries—machinery, petroleum, chemicals, electrical products, transport equipment, rubber products—came under foreign, especially U.S., ownership. Most Canadian exports of oil, food, and manufactured products go to the United States. Canadian manufacturers must ally with provincial and federal officials to prevent extended U.S. economic control. The fragmentation of the Canadian capitalist class also weakens its political power. Independent farmers in western Canada, small entrepreneurs, technocratic managers, Ontario manufacturers, and Albertan oil executives compete for influence. Contending interests also separate Anglo-Canadian from French-Canadian executives, Liberal from Conservative businesspeople, and national capitalists from those linked to U.S. corporations. Financial institutions have established greater cohesion than the manufacturing sector. The five largest Canadian banks—the Royal Bank of Canada, the Canadian Imperial Bank of Commerce, the Bank of Montreal, the Bank of Nova Scotia, and the Toronto-Dominion Bank—hold over 90 percent of all bank assets. Bank directors serve on the boards of large industrial corporations. This financial control gives them the leverage to shape economic policies, particularly decisions about the money supply, interest rates, and capital investment.[30] On the whole, however, Canadian business executives play a more passive policy role than do their U.S. counterparts. Canadian private groups seem more willing to depend on the federal and provincial governments to help realize their goals.

In both Canada and the United States labor unions take a subordinate part in the policy process. When framing economic policies dealing with taxation, investment, wage freezes, and price controls, the Canadian federal and provincial government leaders usually seek the participation of business heads rather than union activists. Neither major political party—Liberal or Progressive-Conservative—maintains close ties with labor unions; instead the major Canadian unions show greater support for the New Democratic party. Because union heads lack close ties with the partisan leadership that holds federal government office, their involvement in the policy process remains limited. Similarly in the United States most unions maintain weak lines with the two major parties. Although the dominant labor federation—the AFL-CIO—has allied with the Democrats since the New Deal era, it represents only one of several factions within the Democratic party. The largest union, the Teamsters, encourages its members to vote Republican in most presidential elections. With limited access to the party holding government office, most U.S. union activists play a comparatively passive role; government leaders consult far more frequently with business executives about crucial economic policies. Particularly since the early 1970s unions have failed to secure legislation that would strengthen union power in a firm. Only when unions have allied with sympathetic agencies like civil rights organizations, consumer groups, churches, and the Democratic party have they attained their policy goals, such as expanded pensions, higher minimum wages, increased unemployment compensation, progressive income taxes, federal aid to education, racial integration, Medicare, Medicaid, and the establishment of OSHA and the Mine Safety and Health Administration.

Neither U.S. nor Canadian unions possess the resources and organizational cohesion needed to shape public policies. U.S. unions, but not those in Canada, have experienced declining membership since World War II (see Table 5.2). Whereas during the early 1960s about 25 percent of the U.S. labor force belonged to a union, by the late 1970s that proportion had declined to under 20 percent. Powerful business opposition weakened union efforts to organize U.S. workers, especially private-sector employees. Although Canadian

Table 5.2

CIVILIAN LABOR FORCE IN LABOR UNIONS, 1960-80

(Percent)

Country	1960-66	1967-73	1974-80
Canada	22.2%[a]	26.0%	29.4%
France	19.7	21.8	23.6
West Germany	25.5	30.5	34.5
Italy	31.6	33.8	37.0
Sweden	55.1	65.4	76.9
United Kingdom	40.5	43.4	48.9
United States	23.4	23.1	20.6

Sources: *Canada Year Book 1980-81* (Ottawa: Statistics Canada, 1981), 285; *Canada Year Book 1976-77* (Ottawa: Statistics Canada, 1977), 407; *Europa Year Book* (London: Europa Publications, 1960-81); George Ross, *Workers and Communists in France: From Popular Front to Eurocommunism* (Berkeley: University of California Press, 1982), 277; J. R. Hough, "France," in *Trade Unions in the Developed Economies*, ed. E. Owen Smith (New York: St. Martin's Press, 1981), 51-54; *Statistisches Jahrbuch für die Bundesrepublik Deutschland* (Herausgeber: Statistisches Bundesamt, 1963-82); *Statistical Abstract of Sweden; 1961-1981* (Stockholm: National Central Bureau of Statistics, 1961-81); *Social Trends*, No. 13, 1983 ed. (London: HMSO, 1982), 152; *British Labour Statistics Year Book 1976* (London: HMSO, 1978), 305; United States Department of Labor, Bureau of Labor Statistics, *Handbook of Labor Statistics* (Washington, D.C.: Government Printing Office, 1980), 412; OECD: *Labour Force Statistics 1969-1980* (Paris, 1982), 24-25; *Labour Force Statistics 1964-1975* (Paris, 1977), 28-29; *Labour Force Statistics 1956-1966* (Paris, 1968), 18.

[a]Figures are average annual percentages for each seven-year period.

managers lack the legal authority to conduct campaigns against unionization, U.S. labor legislation gives managers greater leeway to delay collective bargaining elections, decertify unions, and recruit legal consultants that help defeat unionization drives. The illegal dismissal of pro-union workers brings only weak penalties. Today in both the United States and Canada unions wield the greatest strength in the public sector, especially the postal service, schools, hospitals, and police and fire departments. Yet even in these government agencies no single union unites all U.S. employees; instead several competing unions fragment workers' solidarity. For example, the National Education Association (NEA) competes against the American Federation of Teachers (AFT) to organize elementary and secondary teachers. The Service Employees International Union, the American Nurses Association, the National Union of Hospital and Health Care Workers, and the American Federation of State, County, and Municipal Employees struggle to represent the interests of hospital personnel; they have scored the greatest victories in the New England, Middle Atlantic, and Pacific states.

Canadian unions are also fragmented but more along territorial than occupational lines. The dominant Canadian Labour Congress (CLC) represents English-speaking employees; nearly 60 percent of its members ally with the AFL-CIO, while the other 40 percent maintain ties with the national union headquarters. French-speaking workers in Quebec join the Confederation of National Trade Unions (CNTU). Around one-quarter of union members participate in local unions that retain independence from both the CLC and CNTU. The decentralized government system means that most unions carry out their basic activities within each province. For instance, teachers' unions organize at the provincial rather than the national level. The Alberta Teachers' Association, the British Columbia Teachers' Federation, the Ontario School Teachers' Federation, and the Centrale de l'Enseignement du Québec (CEQ) maintain few close ties with each other; all except the CEQ have refrained from allying with a larger labor movement.

Public-sector unions wield greater impact in Canada than in the United States. Between 40 and 50 percent of U.S. public employees belong to a union; in Canada, however, that figure is over 75 percent. Whereas Canadian public-sector unions have greater authority to strike, most U.S. unions of government employees lack that right. Thus Canadian unions have a crucial veto power over the wage policies formulated by government officials.

Most Canadian and U.S. unions concentrate on securing greater economic benefits for their members; higher wages, expanded fringe benefits, and improved working conditions represent the crucial demands. Although agreed on these goals, union leaders and members show less attitudinal solidarity on issues that extend beyond the factory or office. For example, although most AFT and NEA leaders prefer the liberal Democratic stands on issues before Congress and allied with Jimmy Carter during the 1980 election, members of these two teachers' unions take less liberal policy positions; only 40 percent of NEA members voted for President Carter; 43 percent supported Ronald Reagan, and the remaining 17 percent backed independent candidate John Anderson. The Canadian Labour Congress officials align their union with the socialist New Democratic party; they seek expanded social welfare programs, government regulation of foreign and domestic private investment, the nationalization of private banks, and the creation of more state-owned firms. All these policy stands propose more sweeping changes than preferred by most Canadian union members, who concentrate on immediate, particularistic economic demands.[31]

Compared with both North American societies, Britain has a more activist labor movement, socialist party, and central government; yet national government officials wield less extensive power than do their continental European counterparts. British civil servants must remain politically neutral; unlike French bureaucrats, they cannot serve in Parliament and rarely become directors of private enterprises. Local governments, especially those in Scotland, maintain some autonomy from the London central government to make education and health policies. Like local governments, labor, business, and other social groups operate independently of strong state control. Nonetheless, as in her two former colonies, the United States and Canada, policymaking in Britain features a comparatively weak central government, a fragmented business class, and an incohesive union movement—all structural characteristics associated with a market model.[32]

Although during the nineteenth century British firms dominated the world capitalist economy, today they exert less political power than business organizations in North America. Since the end of World War II British manufacturing firms have faced growing difficulties selling their exports overseas. More and more enterprises have gone bankrupt. By the end of the 1970s British manufacturers earned a lower return on their capital investment than did other industries in West Europe, the United States, and Canada. Yet during the postwar period the banking establishment became more centralized and profitable. Today the four largest banks— Barclays, National Westminster, Midland, and Lloyds—control the financial sector. Dominated by these four clearing banks, London functions as the leading financial center in Europe.

Despite the high banking concentration, British businesses as a whole lack organizational cohesion, attitudinal solidarity, and even ready access to government. Several cleavages split the business sector, including divisions between large-scale industries and small enterprises, banks and manufacturing industries, and domestic firms and multinational corporations. The major employer organization— the Confederation of British Industries (CBI)—operates as a weak pressure group that plays only a limited role in framing incomes policies or reaching collective bargaining agreements. Dominated by the large manufacturing industries but still fragmented, the CBI lacks the resources to impose its general policy preferences on government ministers. Instead it concentrates on making recommendations about the legislative details of industrial policies. Generally the CBI has favored some government involvement in the economy, especially higher government expenditures for public works and the economic infrastructure. By contrast, the Institute of Directors, the Aims of Industry, the Association of Independent Businesses, and the Association of British Chambers of Commerce, which represent smaller business interests, have thrown more support behind the laissez-faire preferences of the Thatcher government. Prodded by such research organizations as the Adam Smith Institute and the Centre for Policy Studies, these businesses led the drive to reduce government control over the private market.

The structural fragmentation of the private business sector leads to attitudinal disunity. Small businesses seek lower interest rates. Exporters want a devalued British pound, which will facilitate the selling of their goods at an inexpensive price overseas. The powerful financial community, however, prefers high interest rates that will profit the banks. Since the multinational British banks favor investing their funds overseas rather than at home, they raise no objections to an overvalued pound. Business organizations also disagree on the best strategy for dealing with the influential but decentralized trade unions. When the Labour party controlled the government during the 1970s, most business executives tried to accommodate their interests with union leaders. Yet demoralized by high inflation, strike actions, falling profit ratios, and wage increases that exceeded labor productivity, corporate leaders welcomed the Conservative party victory in 1979. Although resenting Tory policies that led to high interest rates, an overvalued pound, low economic growth, and business bankruptcies, most businessmen favored restraints on workers' wages, government restrictions on union power, lower social service benefits, tax reductions on corporate income, a stable monetary policy, and the Tories' ideological stress on free enterprise, competition, productivity, and profits.

Compared with U.S. or Canadian businessmen, British business representatives secure fewer ministerial posts in the Cabinet. Hence British executives have recently relied on the Conservative party to represent general business interests. Today the Tory party and government have assumed the dominant responsibility for leading the British economy toward a more competitive, profitable position in the world market.[33]

Although Britain has a reputation for union dominance over government decision-making, trade unions actually play a weaker role than usually assumed. The few resources and low organizational cohesion limit the power of unions to impose their policy preferences on government officials. Union membership is fairly high; in 1980 nearly one-half the civilian labor force belonged to a union. Yet the economic recession that struck Britain during the mid-1970s and the decline of the manufacturing sector caused falling memberships at the start of the 1980s. Today, as in Canada, unions wield greater strength in the public than in the private sector. Fewer than 20 percent of private service employees have joined a union. Moreover, British members contribute a lower share of their weekly earnings to their unions than do West German or Swedish unionists.

Decentralization and organizational fragmentation also restrict trade union power. National Trades Union Congress leaders exert limited influence over plant and shop stewards, who make the key decisions about strikes, wage demands, and collective bargaining arrangements. Even within the same occupation, rival unions compete for dominance. For example, the Transport and General Workers' Union struggles with the Amalgamated Union of Engineering Workers to organize the automobile industry. The National Union of Public Employees represents semi-skilled and unskilled workers in hospitals. The Confederation of Health Service Employees organizes mainly nurses and their assistants. Other unions involved in public health care include the Transport and General Workers' Union, the General and Municipal Workers' Union, the National and Local Government Officers' Association, and the Association of Scientific, Technical, and Managerial Staffs. Within the teaching profession the National Union of Teachers, National Association of Schoolmasters/ Union of Women Teachers, Assistant Masters and Mistresses Association, National Association of Head Teachers, Secondary Heads Association, National Association of Teachers in Further and Higher Education, and Professional Association of Teachers all negotiate collective bargaining agreements with representatives from the local education authorities and the Department of Education and Science. Status differentials split these rival teachers' unions and hinder agreement on salary demands. By staging strikes and protests about working conditions, all these unions exercise some veto power over public policymaking and limit central government control. Yet they lack the organizational solidarity to initiate new policies.

Even under a Labour party administration British unions seldom actively participate in either formulating a policy or carrying it out. They usually try to veto policies decided by the Cabinet. As in English-speaking Canada and the United States, the common law tradition encourages both labor and business to maintain an adversary stance toward the state. Opposed to the accommodationist orientation of the corporate state, unions assert their independence from government control, especially over their right to strike. Most union members seek neither representation on governing boards nor joint participation in decision-making with management. For them workers' freedom means the right to oppose managers when they act contrary to working class interests. Preferring that unions and the Labour party give highest priority to reducing unemployment, increasing workers' real disposable income, and securing higher living standards, union members reject any incomes policy that

173

limits wage hikes to increases below consumer price rises. Although from 1975 to 1977 unions did accept the Labour government's "social contract" program to restrain wage increases, after 1977 union officials opposed the Labour leaders' attempts to impose a 5 percent limit on wage gains. Led by the powerful public employee unions, workers went on strike demanding action against a fall in their real income. Disenchanted with the strikes that hit Britain during the 1978-79 winter, voters in May 1979 elected the Conservative party to office. Embittered by the Labour party's pay restraint policy, many union members even voted for the Tories. Compared with Labour party leaders, Conservative government officials express less enthusiasm about union participation in framing an incomes policy. They want to rely on the "free market" to set wages. By opposing the closed shop, strikes in the public sector, and the alignment of most unions with the Labour party, the Conservative government has tried to weaken union power.

In sum, Britain has shown less movement toward the corporatist model than has West Germany or especially Sweden. Today the administration of public policies reflects a stronger commitment to the market model. Government, business, and labor prefer to maintain their specialized functions rather than become more interdependent in the policy process.[34]

Democractic Corporatism. Unlike the market model, which assumes a clear distinction between state and society, the democratic corporatist model merges government, business, and labor into a social partnership. Government officials, especially the civil servants, play a dominant role in the policy process. They manage, plan, supervise, and regulate economic activities. Seeking to gain cooperation from centralized interest groups, government agencies authorize particular private organizations to represent group interests. These organizations, especially centralized business corporations and labor unions, gain the right to participate in the formulation and implementation of government decisions. Under the corporatist model the system of territorial representation, whereby each voter makes policy demands on an elected legislator, no longer seems so operative. Instead, to exert influence over the policy process, people must become members of organized groups that maintain access to government officials. State and nongovernment professional bureaucrats—

technocrats, specialists, managers—coordinate government decision-making. Legislators play a less important role. When framing economic policies, the corporate technocrats stress the need for government and social groups to cooperate for the public good, not resort to the divisive conflict associated with a market economy. Business firms come under pressure to maintain labor peace by granting sufficient wages and fringe benefits. Labor union officials are discouraged from staging costly strikes.

In the democratic nations of contemporary Western Europe government leaders pursue an inclusionary corporate strategy toward social groups. Several political parties compete for power. Allied with a social democratic party, trade unions can freely press their claims before government agencies. Private enterprises own a large share of the industrial sector; thus government needs their support for realizing its economic objectives. By coopting both business and labor into decision-making agencies like advisory committees, consultation boards, associational chambers, and commissions, government officials hope to maximize collective goal attainment. Because these group leaders operate highly organized, disciplined, and cohesive organizations, they retain the political power required for shaping the policy process.[35]

During the post-World War II period leaders in Sweden and West Germany have most enthusiastically followed the democratic corporatist strategy. Swedish policymakers have sought to reconcile conflicts that split business from labor. The need for Swedish corporations to produce competitively priced goods for sale overseas encourages cooperative relations between business and union leaders. Highly organized unions participate in economic decisions. Through the works councils union officials consult with company managers about a wide range of issues: working hours, wages, plant safety, recruitment of new workers, employee layoffs, manpower training, and investment plans. Even when the Social Democratic party controls the government, business organizations like the Swedish Employers' Federation (SAF) secure tradeoffs with the unions. The Social Democrats implement public policies that produce high wage increases, extensive social services, and low unemployment. In exchange, business obtains investment funds, low corporate income taxes, and subsidies to promote exports. The accommodationist policies have deterred labor strikes.

Swedish civil servants wield extensive influence. Committed to a pragmatic, consensual, problem-solving style of making decisions, they consult with all groups and try to secure accommodations among the different interests. From their perspective the parliament (Riksdag) represents diverse interests, the Cabinet formulates the general policies, and the central administration implements the general policies by adapting them to specific situations.[36]

Swedish policymakers have established a vast array of institutions for representing group interests; particularly under Social Democratic administrations labor unions have secured a powerful role unmatched in most other Western democratic societies. At all stages of the policy process social group representatives help shape government decisions about public issues. For instance, most government departments have planning councils that communicate advice to public officials. More politically influential than the planning councils, royal commissions investigate an issue and then make recommendations to the Riksdag. Composed of civil servants, Riksdag members, and interest group leaders, these commissions give both labor and business the opportunity to advocate their policy preferences. After a royal commission issues a report, groups often circulate written commentaries that propose changes in the commission's recommendations for proposed legislation. At the policy implementation stage groups also can exert some formal influence. Group leaders sit on boards of administrative agencies, including the Labor Market Board. This board makes decisions about vocational guidance, job training, employment for handicapped workers, and wage subsidies to firms that hire new employees. It also formulates guidelines for wages and prices. The Labor Market Board supervises laws dealing with unemployment compensation; however, trade union funding agencies, subject to Board approval, issue benefits to jobless workers. Because labor unions choose nearly half the membership on the Labor Market Board, they have concentrated on using this agency to attain their policy preferences. By contrast, business leaders rely more on direct consultation with administrative agencies; through this mechanism they supply the technical advice and information needed by government technocrats who administer policies. Other institutions providing a participatory role for labor and business groups include labor courts, which handle labor disputes, and citizen boards that oversee the performance of national government agencies, county governments, and public enterprises. Through all these institutional mechanisms unions and business firms can bargain with government officials about the best way to implement specific programs.[37]

In Sweden business and labor have attained a greater balance of power than in most other Western industrial societies. Although most Swedish firms are privately owned, labor unions have the power to shape the distribution of economic resources. Particularly since the 1930s labor and business have negotiated a tradeoff that has brought advantages to each group. Under Social Democratic administrations export firms secured investment funds, low corporate income taxes, and government subsidies designed to make a firm more technologically efficient and to promote the sale of manufactured goods on the world market. Government policies also encouraged the movement of workers from unproductive to more productive, profitable enterprises. In exchange for moderating wage demands, refraining from costly strikes, and accepting private ownership of industry, unionized workers received concrete policy benefits: generous social services (pensions, family allowances, health care), wage subsidies, job retraining opportunities, and labor-intensive public service employment. High expenditures for social service programs, high social security taxes paid by employers, and moderate wage hikes secured by the unions also meant that Swedish manufacturing industries, compared with their counterparts in the United States, Canada, and West Germany, secured a lower profit rate from 1955 through 1976.

Despite their need to share power with unions, Swedish entrepreneurs still possess the power to shape economic policies. Swedish industries are more concentrated than U.S., British, French, German, Italian, or Canadian firms. The Wallenberg family controls the largest enterprises and the largest private bank. Organizational cohesion in the capitalist class remains strong. Interest conflicts divide small, less productive enterprises from the larger, export-oriented corporations, mainly because the smaller firms gain fewer policy benefits from the government and face greater dangers of bankruptcy. Nevertheless, most business executives belong to the highly centralized SAF that oversees collective bargaining with the trade unions. Business organizations, like the unions, secure ready access to government decision-makers. During the 1970s civil servants and members of parliament most frequently contacted private industrialists, followed by leaders of the Swedish Federation of Trade Unions (LO), which represents manual workers, and white-collar union activists in the Central Organization of Salaried Employees (TCO) and the Swedish Federation of Professional Associations (SACO). Civil servants and parliamentarians least often consulted representatives from banks and insurance companies.

Until the late 1970s, when strikes, currency devaluations, government deficits, and oil price hikes struck Sweden, business executives maintained high ideological cohesion; since that time, however, important attitudinal divisions have arisen. Most managers, board members, and company directors seek government expenditures for reducing industrial pollution and assisting economically depressed regions. They seem willing to delegate slightly more power to employees but not to union representatives. The major attitudinal cleavages revolve around the extent of cooperation with the LO and Social Democrats. One segment of the SAF wants a close alliance with the Conservative party, which obtains its greatest support from managers, business owners, independent professionals, and senior civil servants. It supports tax cuts, reduced social service spending, wage restraints, and reduced union power. Another faction within the SAF favors a more accommodationist strategy. It seeks ties not just with the Conservatives but with all nonsocialist parties, including the Liberals and Centrists, which represent small business-people, white-collar employees, and farmers. This faction wants to maintain cooperation with the industrial unions, particularly over the wage-earners' fund issue.[38] In sum, a growing division within Sweden's capitalist class has hindered the prospects for negotiating accommodations between business and labor.

Swedish labor unions command extensive resources and exert centralized control over collective bargaining. The three major unions—the LO, TCO, and SACO—enroll around 80 percent of the civilian labor force, the highest proportion in any Western country. Unlike the British labor movement, Swedish unions possess the finances and staff to press their policy demands on government officials. The LO central headquarters appoints shop stewards and concludes collective bargaining agreements. Although the central leadership consults local union members about these agreements, they do not ratify the final settlement.

The Swedish unions maintain higher organizational cohesion and attitudinal solidarity than do unions in most other Western societies. The largest union, the LO, organizes blue-collar workers along industrial rather than craft lines—a structural feature promoting working class solidarity. The TCO represents white-collar employees who work for private firms, the central government, and municipalities. SACO unites professionals like senior civil servants, university professors, doctors, lawyers, engineers, and armed forces officers. Although LO, TCO, and SACO operate separate organizations and voice different interests, the LO works closely with the TCO. These two unions share similar policy preferences. They want the government to secure full employment, provide comprehensive social services, regulate multinational investment in Sweden, control industrial pollution, provide economic assistance to depressed regions, and expand workers' participation in the management of factories, offices, and government agencies. Their major disagreements arise over the issue of wage equality. Whereas LO members prefer policies that extend wage equality, TCO members, who hold higher-status jobs, seek to retain salary differentials and even struck for higher pay in 1985.

The LO maintains closer ties with the Social Democratic party than does the TCO, the second largest union. The TCO remains neutral from all political parties, yet its members usually vote for the Social Democrats, the Centrists, or the Liberals. Since its founding in 1898, the LO has allied with the Social Democrats; this alliance has strengthened its power over the policy process.

Under Social Democratic administrations the government implemented several policies that enhanced the power of employees and union activists to shape decisions in government agencies, privately owned firms, state enterprises, schools, and hospitals. According to the Industrial Safety Act of 1974, a safety steward appointed by the union has the authority to stop work in a factory if he suspects that employees face an immediate, serious health hazard. Factory operations do not resume until an inspector from the National Swedish Workers Safety Board visits the work site to examine safety practices. The 1974 Employment Security Act placed restraints on managerial power over layoffs. Under this law managers must state "reasonable grounds" for firing an employee, who must receive at least a month's notice prior to dismissal. Before firing workers over the age of forty-four, managers must inform them six months in advance. The 1976 Act on Workers Codetermination further expanded union rights at the expense of traditional managerial prerogatives. Unions can elect representatives to corporate boards of directors, gain information about enterprise activities (financial transactions, personnel policies, production plans), and participate in decisions about personnel recruitment, work assignments, work schedules, and employee dismissals. This law gives unions authority to negotiate all issues with management, including investment, production, and labor force activities. The Codetermination Act also widened Union decision-making powers within hospitals and schools. The hospital workers' union bargains with the Swedish Medical Association, the County Council Federation, and government agencies about salaries, working conditions, and employee rights. Teachers' unions negotiate with municipal government officials about work schedules, salaries, use of resources, and general educational conditions.[39] In short, Swedish public policies have enhanced the power of unions to shape the basic decisions made in economic, educational, and health institutions.

The West German federal government after World War II also pursued a democratic corporatist strategy for expanding group participation in decision-making. During the early 1950s the Christian Democratic administration instituted a social partnership among government, business corporations, and labor unions that decreased consumer goods production and concentrated major efforts on expanding heavy industry and armaments. Since that time both Christian Democratic and Social Democratic administrations have involved business and labor in the administration of social service programs. Independent agencies, composed of elected employer and employee members, implement work-injury benefits and disability pensions. Government officials, union leaders, and business executives participate on the boards administering unemployment compensation. As in Sweden, tripartite labor courts comprising professional judges, employer representatives, and workers arbitrate disputes at the local, Länder, and federal levels.

The West German "codetermination" policies give workers in large enterprises some say in formulating economic decisions. The two major laws on codetermination passed in 1951 and 1976 instituted employee participation on the governing boards of large enterprises, both private and public. Generally employees and stockholders now have equal representation on most supervisory boards. Despite the drive toward parity representation, managers still retain dominant authority. German labor unions wield less influence than do their Swedish counterparts. Until the 1980s, when unemployment grew severe, union participants on supervisory boards rarely challenged managerial decisions about capital investment, use of plant equipment, or even plant closures and layoffs. However, particularly in the large factories, unions have negotiated wages and organized the works councils, which settle grievances, recruit personnel, and bargain with management over piece work rates, working hours, and length of vacations.

Since the end of World War II German business executives have helped shape the economic policies made by both the Christian Democratic and Social Democratic administrations. Most postwar federal governments have comprised a two-party coalition. The pro-business Free Democratic party usually holds a few seats in Cabinet, often heading the economics ministry. Under these power-sharing conditions, business preferences receive a sympathetic hearing, even when the Social Democrats dominate the coalition. The two major business organizations – the Federation of German Industries (BDI) and the Confederation of German Employers' Associations (BDA) – represent most enterprises. Maintaining close ties with officials heading the finance and economics ministries, BDA leaders voice the policy preferences favored by corporate executives and bankers. Because the banks own or control several large industries, bankers' sentiments usually prevail. As a result of this business access to government leaders, economic policies have brought the large industrial-financial sector numerous concrete benefits: subsidies, investment loans, low corporate income taxes, and moderate but stable increases in the money supply. Government opposition to nationalizing private industries and to establishing wage-price controls also reflects the policy preferences of business organizations. Yet German business executives lack the independent power to force their economic choices on a resistant government. Instead their influence over the policy process depends on their associations with sympathetic party politicians, Cabinet ministers, and technocrats from the Christian Democratic and Free Democratic parties.

West German unions show greater decentralization, less organizational cohesion, and lower membership ratios than does the

Swedish labor movement; hence their power over the policy process seems weaker. In the social partnership that has governed West Germany since the late 1940s, unions serve as junior partners to business executives and government officials. During the late 1970s union members comprised only 35 percent of the civilian labor force—less than half the Swedish ratio. Although the unions hold extensive financial resources that derive from their ownership of banks and life insurance companies, several different unions fragment the labor movement. The dominant German Trade Union Federation (DGB) represents blue-collar workers, particularly metal workers and public service employees. The German Salaried Employees' Union (DAG) organizes white-collar workers, primarily in private industry. Civil servants, military officers, police, teachers, and university professors belong to the Confederation of German Civil Service Officials (DBB). The Confederation of Christian Trade Unions of Germany enrolls manual workers, private white-collar employees, and public employees who lean toward the CDU. Compared with Swedish unions, these four organizations maintain looser ties with each other and with political parties. The DGB formally allies with no party. Even though its members usually vote for the Social Democrats, their support falls below the backing LO members give to the Swedish Social Democratic party. The more limited access of German unions to party leaders and government officials means that union activists have faced greater difficulty than their Swedish colleagues in wielding decisive influence over public policy-making. Because the conservative party exerts greater strength in Germany than in Sweden, union power remains more limited.[40]

Compared with Sweden or even West Germany, contemporary Italy less fully typifies the democratic corporatist model. During the 1930s Mussolini attempted to establish a Fascist corporate state. Although he excluded unions from political or economic power, private industrialists retained extensive independence from state control. After the Fascist defeat during World War II, corporatism held ill repute among Christian Democrats, Socialists, and Communists—the three largest political parties. The Italian government has little power to regulate interest groups. Conflicting party and ideological attachments divide the labor movements. Even the industrialists wield less political influence today than during the 1930s.

The Italian business sector is highly fragmented. As a late-developing industrial society, Italy has a sizable proportion of the civilian work force employed as independent proprietors. Large-scale retail organizations – department stores, consumer cooperatives, mail order houses, and multiple shop firms – control a lower share of the total retail trade than in Britain, France, or West Germany. Given the strength of the small business sector, the major employer interest group, the General Confederation of Italian Industry (Confindustria), remains too divided to wield decisive power over government economic policies. The contemporary Italian political system is pluralistic. Several different groups – the Christian Democratic party, the Communist party, the Socialist party, the Roman Catholic Church, and labor unions – share power along with business organizations, which can translate their policy preferences into government decisions only if they gain support from party politicians, Cabinet ministers, civil servants, and heads of the state-holding companies.

Although the Italian labor movement is weaker than in Sweden, since the late 1960s unions have grown more powerful in pressing their claims on business executives and central government officials. Trade union membership as a proportion of the civilian labor force grew from 30 percent in 1960 to nearly 40 percent twenty years later (see Table 5.2). Three major unions compete for influence. The largest – the Confederazione Generale Italiana del Lavoro – allies with the Communist party but also includes some Socialist party sympathizers. The Confederazione Italiana Sindicati Lavoratori represents workers who support the Christian Democratic party. Republican, Social Democratic, and Socialist voters belong to the smallest union, the Unione Italiana del Lavoro. These three unions struggle to gain members from the same occupation. Yet since the early 1970s union ties with the political parties have loosened; the three labor organizations have established more cooperative relationships with each other in their efforts to secure higher wages, improved working conditions, and more favorable fringe benefits. The governing Christian Democrats need labor cooperation as they seek to lower unemployment, curb inflation, and expand exports. Thus at the policy formulation stage labor unions have gained the right to consult with party leaders, Cabinet ministers, and senior civil servants. Union officials help implement government policies that allocate pensions, work-injury benefits, and unemployment insurance. Boards of directors that operate the railways and postal service comprise both public managers and union officials. Workers' councils give employees participatory rights at the local plant level. All these developments signify a trend toward a more democratic corporatist style of policymaking.[41]

State Planning. Of the seven Western industrialized nations France best fulfills the assumptions of the state planning model. Since the seventeenth century French policymakers have pursued a *dirigiste* strategy toward economic development. Under the regime of Louis XIV and his finance minister Jean Baptiste Colbert, the state nationalized the tobacco industry, regulated commerce, built transportation facilities (roads, canals), promoted the merchant fleet, subsidized exports, and established a trading company that went into East India. Neither the French Revolution of 1789 nor the frequent changes of political system that occurred since then diminished the state's planning role. Particularly after World War II, the central government increased its power over the economy. General Charles de Gaulle, provisional president of France after the Nazi defeat, authorized extensive nationalizations, imposed price controls, and instituted national economic planning. Later postwar governments, whether Gaullist, neo-liberal, or Socialist, continued this state planning tradition.

According to the French orientation toward planning, the state—actually the senior civil servants and technocrats—decides the general interest for society. Social groups voice specific interests and exchange information with state officials. Both trade unionists and business executives depend on state policies for support. Until after World War II, French businessmen excluded factory workers from collective bargaining. Political parties representing the working class rarely gained government office. Attracted initially toward anarcho-syndicalism and later toward Marxism, workers sought government policies that rectified their economic grievances; yet they resisted strong state control. Like the trade unionists, business leaders wanted to preserve their autonomy from state manipulation; however, they depended on the state for investment subsidies, tax credits, licenses, technical training, and other benefits needed in an industrialized economy. Under every administration since World War II, the central government has granted special benefits to business firms and directed them toward a more modernized, rationalized economy. Unlike the democratic corporatist model, the state planning model thus assumes a conflict, not a consensus, between state officials' views and group leaders' interests. Just as interest groups seek independence from state domination, so state bureaucrats want to preserve their autonomy from group leaders.

Whatever their party affiliation or ideological orientation, all French presidents during the Fifth Republic have followed a state planning strategy. De Gaulle, president from 1958 through 1969, preferred indicative planning. For him the five-year plans should specify national goals, indicate the state's priorities, and reduce economic uncertainties. However, he left the detailed execution of the plans to private enterprises. Planning occurred in a mixed market economy; both state officials and private business leaders participated in the planning process. A major goal was to expand free trade—that is, make French exports more competitive on the world market. When Valéry Giscard d'Estaing became president in 1974, he adopted a more neo-liberal perspective that showed slightly less enthusiasm for a directive role by the government. According to him and his prime minister Raymond Barre, the government should concentrate on setting monetary targets, limiting the expansion of credit, promoting a stronger franc, and strengthening France's competitive position in world trade.

The election of Socialist president François Mitterrand in 1981 reactivated the state planning process. Mitterrand wants to combine centralized formulation of plans with decentralized implementation. For him state planning agencies fulfill comprehensive tasks. They should organize communication among national technocrats, regional officials, local government leaders, trade unionists, and director-managers in both public and private enterprises. The planners also finance public investments, formulate rules for spending state funds, and mediate disputes about ways to allocate scarce resources. Through nationalizations, government subsidies, state-financed capital investment, and business reorganizations, Mitterrand hopes to promote such advanced technological industries as computers, electronics, semiconductors, and microchips.

Under the Socialist administration the expansion of the public sector has inolved three major features. First, the eighth five-year plan (1981-85) promotes decentralized implementation by elected regional officials, state civil servants, and heads of interest groups. Managers and union representatives help administer the unemployment insurance program. Interest groups, including unions, participate with elected political leaders and government technocrats to formulate national economic plans. Representatives from government, business, and labor frame policies intended to train young workers and retrain the unemployed for jobs in technologically advanced industries. Second, although Socialist officials have abandoned their previous commitment to autogestion (workers' self-management), they have encouraged greater participation by employees and trade union activists in economic decision-making. Employers in large industries must grant workers released time to discuss job conditions. Managers must supply information about a plant's activities to the works councils, the *comités d'entreprise,* which handle welfare and recreation, negotiate profit-sharing agreements with managers, and promote safer working conditions. Safety commissions have greater authority to secure a healthier workplace. Third, the Mitterrand government has extended the publicly owned sector by nationalizing most private banks, financial institutions, and basic industries.

Despite the extensive state ownership, planning in socialist France diverges from the state socialism followed in Eastern Europe. There the central government maintains direct, detailed control over policy implementation. Few private enterprises exist; instead state-owned firms dominate the economy. Labor unions retain little independence from the central government and the communist party. By contrast, Mitterrand, like his predecessors, remains dedicated to a decentralized implementation of plans, a mixed market economy, and trade union autonomy. State planning occurs in a political context of civil liberties, competitive elections, and voluntary group participation. Private industries can choose whether or not to sign planning contracts under the national economic plan.

In France the disunity of business organizations hinders their effectiveness in achieving policy goals. Family entrepreneurs, small retail traders, and self-employed businesspeople still retain extensive influence over the market. They voice different policy preferences from those held by managers of the large-scale domestic corporations and French multinationals, which give greater support to free trade. The dominant employers' organization—the National Council of French Employers—represents mainly large-scale industries. Other organizations like the General Confederation of Small and Medium Enterprises as well as the Chambers of Commerce pressure the government for tax credits and business subsidies that favor self-employed entrepreneurs and family firms. Committed to state planning, French government officials, particularly the civil servants, want the state to preserve its independence from all interest groups, including business organizations. Moreover, business executives distrust the state. Nevertheless, government officials and business leaders have regularly consulted with each other about economic policies, such as price controls, capital investment, and export promotion. During the late 1970s interest group leaders perceived that business and especially farmers' representatives had secured greater success in shaping government policies than had trade union activists.

The fragmentation of labor unions limits their influence over public policies. Union members comprise between 20 and 25 percent of the civilian labor force—the lowest ratio in any nation except the United States. Divergent ideological tendencies—communist vs. socialist vs. Catholic—hinder working class solidarity. Around one-half the unionists belong to the Confédération Générale du Travail (CGT), which the French Communist party (PCF) dominates. It organizes mainly blue-collar workers in large private industrial corporations and state enterprises. Although allied with the PCF, the CGT members want less political polarization among the unions and a greater concentration on economic goals, such as higher wages, improved working conditions, and narrowed income differences. One Socialist union, the Force Ouvrière, represents the interests of public employees. Another pro-Socialist union, the Confédération Française Démocratique du Travail, originally articulated a pro-Catholic orientation. Today it most enthusiastically supports auto-gestion; it has a following among white-collar employees. Most teachers belong to the Fédération de l'Éducation Nationale (FEN). It maintains the tightest alliance with the Socialist party, which gains major backing from teachers, managers, and professionals. Like other French unions, FEN pursues primarily economic demands: higher salaries, fewer students in courses, greater job security, and more paid leaves of absence for educational activities. Except for the CGT cadre, French unionists lean toward the Socialist party, although they maintain only loose ties with it. Middle class professionals, particularly teachers and civil servants, comprise the Socialist party base. Represented by the CGT, industrial workers lack direct influence over government policy. Thus even under a Socialist presidency, the state planners, not the factory workers, dominate the French policy process.[42]

In conclusion, the state planning, democratic corporatist, and market models assume diverse relationships among the government, business groups, and labor unions. In the state planning model the central government defines the general interest for the society, organizes the market, and retains its independence from both labor and business. Similarly each interest group remains autonomous from the state. Conflict, not consensus, guides interactions with other groups and government officials. By contrast, the democratic corporatist model in Sweden and West Germany expects greater harmony among interest groups and the state. Powerful government agencies incorporate centralized trade unions and concentrated business groups in the policy process. Rather than remaining autonomous, all participants — senior civil servants, trade union officials, business leaders — become dependent on each other for realizing policy objectives. The central government performs the least active role under the market model. Civil servants lack the power to dominate the policy process. Like the state planning model, the market model assumes interest groups will engage in conflict and maintain autonomy from tight state control. However, compared with France, in market-oriented societies like Britain, Canada, and especially the United States, business groups exert a more decisive impact on government decisions. Particularly in the two North American nations labor unions wield less political influence than in continental European societies where political leaders remain committed to democratic corporatist principles.

EVALUATION OF POLICY PERFORMANCE

Evaluation is a basic purpose of policy analysis, but it poses problems for the investigator. As we saw in Chapter 4, the evaluation process arouses controversy because of the vague criteria used to assess policy performance and the difficulties in finding objective indicators that will measure these criteria. The subjective nature of policy evaluation also means that different analysts will rarely agree on the standards for making the assessments. This section will use the following evaluative criteria to assess economic, education, and health policy performance: institutional goal attainment, equality, efficiency, and public satisfaction.

The four criteria illustrate the problems of making insightful evaluations. Institutional goal attainment can refer to various dimensions, including the policy success in reducing unemployment and inflation rates, increasing economic growth, promoting cognitive performance, lowering infant mortality, and raising life expectancy. Although people expect their economic, education, and health care institutions to fulfill some of these objectives, not everyone agrees on the goals that should take priority. Young unskilled workers probably evaluate economic policy performance according to the success in lowering unemployment. Creditors show greater concern for inflation. Professionals and administrators expect educational systems to produce students who show high cognitive performance on standardized tests. Young parents seek health care policies that reduce infant mortality. Older citizens will more likely give favorable ratings to health programs that lengthen life expectancy. Obviously institutions attain goals other than the foregoing. People want schools to teach youths the dominant social values. Physicians and hospital staffs are expected to provide high quality health care, not just increase life expectancy. Equality, efficiency, and public satisfaction are also vague standards. How do we verbally define them and devise empirical operational indicators that measure the degree to which several nations' policies actually reached these standards? Despite these analytic difficulties, the four criteria we have chosen are useful for assessing policy performance. Whatever the subjective problems, empirical indicators of these criteria are available so that we can make tentative cross-national judgments.

INSTITUTIONAL GOAL ATTAINMENT

Measures of economic goal attainment indicate that all nations do not achieve the same success in lowering unemployment, reducing inflation, and expanding the growth rate; policy performance on these three evaluative criteria show extensive cross-national differences.

As Tables 2.10, 2.11, and 2.12 revealed, from 1960 through 1980 Sweden and West Germany reached the lowest unemployment rates. Canada, the United States, and especially West Germany attained relatively low inflation. Italy, Canada, and France had a high growth rate. On these three indicators the United Kingdom performed the worst. Its real growth rate was the lowest. Along with Italy, Britain faced the highest consumer price rises. Particularly after 1980 British workers had to contend with a higher jobless rate than did other Western citizens. (Before the early 1980s the two North American countries experienced the largest unemployment rates.) Thus all good economic things did not necessarily go together. Although Swedish public policies helped produce low unemployment, they may have stimulated moderate inflation and lower growth rates, mainly during the 1970s. The United States and Canada attained relatively low inflation rates yet at the expense of higher unemployment. Italy compensated for its high inflation by securing a rapid growth rate.

Cross-national standardized tests give some clues about cognitive proficiency among primary and secondary school students. According to IEA examination results that compared the top 4 or 5 percent of students in the last year of secondary school in each nation, Swedish youths performed the best on mathematics tests. English and French students did moderately well on the math examination, but U.S. and West German students scored the lowest. On the science examination Swedish secondary seniors, along with the English, made the best scores; U.S., West German, and French students showed moderately high performance. Italians received the lowest science scores. At the sixth-grade level, Swedish students obtained higher scores on science, mathematics, and geography examinations than did students in England, Canada, the United States, and France.[43]

Swedish policymakers have compiled a favorable record for health care performance. In 1980 Sweden had the lowest infant mortality and the highest life expectancy (see Tables 4.1 and 4.2). On these two measures France and Canada ranked behind Sweden but ahead of England and West Germany. The United States and West Germany experienced the highest infant mortality rates. U.S. women lived longer than did English or West German females; however, the typical U.S. man died before the average male in all other countries except West Germany.

190

In sum, the various nations show mixed results on the institutional goal attainment scale. Generally Swedish policymakers have scored the greatest success in lowering unemployment, reducing infant mortality, raising life expectancy, and expanding students' knowledge, yet the Swedish inflation and economic growth rates are less impressive. Britain's policy record appears the worst among the seven nations. During the last twenty years it has faced high inflation, low economic growth, high infant mortality, and low life expectancy; however, sixth-grade students and secondary school seniors did quite well on mathematics, geography, and science examinations. According to these indicators of economic, education, and health care policy performance, the French usually achieved an intermediate ranking ahead of the Italians but behind the Swedes.

EQUALITY

As a standard for evaluating policy performance, equality arouses controversy among partisan contenders. Whereas right-wing parties generally oppose government efforts to promote greater equality, leftists place a higher priority on the extension of egalitarian benefits. This ideological controversy partly stems from the ambiguous nature of equality. Three dimensions seem especially crucial: access, use, and outcome. First, egalitarian access means that all individuals have a similar opportunity to secure economic, education, and health care benefits. The second dimension focuses on the extent to which people make the same use of public services. Third, equality of outcome designates people's life conditions — that is, the degree of similarity in their income, educational competence, and health.[44]

Policy analysts cannot easily make cross-national evaluations of a government's commitment to these three dimensions of equality, mainly because in every country the social stratification system conditions access to policy benefits, the use of these benefits, and policy outcomes. Individuals at the bottom of the social hierarchy — those with the least political power, wealth, and status — usually gain limited access to a university education and to high-quality public health care. They make less extensive use of many public services. As implied by their lower socioeconomic background,

191

they possess less income, complete fewer years of education, and experience more sickness. These conditions hold true even in relatively equalitarian societies like Sweden. Although we can measure the inequalities faced by different individuals and groups, comparisons of inequalities across nations become difficult to validate. Hence cross-national judgments about egalitarian policy performance must remain tentative, subject to future clarification.

Compared with the other six nations, the United States ensures the least access to public policy benefits, especially income maintenance and health care services. Means-tested programs prevail. Even though all elderly persons receive a social security pension and Medicare benefits, only those classified as "truly needy" or economically impoverished gain access to family allowances and health treatments under Medicaid. Other people must rely on private benefits, which reinforce the social inequalities. Highly paid, unionized senior workers in large oligopolistic corporations like General Motors receive generous fringe benefits while employees in smaller, more competitive, non-unionized firms secure less generous and extensive health care, unemployment compensation, paid vacations, and pensions. By contrast, in Canada and Western Europe all individuals secure family allowances and public health care. Public benefits as a proportion of a worker's income are more generous and comprehensive. Because private benefits assume less importance, greater equality results. Unlike public health care and income maintenance services, access to higher public education seems more widespread in the United States. Until recently nearly all students had the opportunity to attend an inexpensive community college. However, in Western Europe, especially England, West Germany, and France, the higher education system is more elitist; low-income youths cannot easily secure a post-secondary college or university education.[45]

In all Western nations a person's position in the social stratification system influences the use of public policy programs. While the introduction of national public health systems equalized the use of physician and hospital services by all people, major inequalities now derive from the tendency of wealthier individuals to receive higher-quality treatments from a trained specialist. Youths from upper-status families still comprise the major group attending upper secondary schools and universities. Poorer children show lower enrollments in post-compulsory schools; hence they gain fewer benefits from government expenditures for higher education. In the United States a large share of poor people fail to receive certain income maintenance benefits, despite their legal eligibility. During the mid-1970s only about 60 percent of the nonaged poor under a specified poverty line obtained any monetary payments from public assistance, AFDC, Supplemental Security Income, and food stamps. Only 30 percent of all Medicare and Medicaid transfers went to low-income citizens. Medicare financed the health expenses of the wealthy as well as the poor. The main beneficiaries of Medicaid have been the elderly, white, urban poor who live in the northern states; young, nonwhite, rural poor in the southern states fare less well. In short, even the means-tested U.S. transfer programs have shown unequal use. The elderly have gained the most benefits, mainly from such programs as Medicare and Social Security. Impoverished youths and adults who work part-time at low-paying jobs received the lowest cash transfers as a share of their income.[46] Except for old-age pensions, U.S. public policies have exerted a limited impact on income equality.

On measures of income equality Sweden ranks higher than the other six countries. According to studies of post-tax incomes during the 1970s, Sweden was the most equal, followed by the United Kingdom, West Germany, Italy, Canada, the United States, and France (see Table 5.3). If we assume that personal income taxes constitute the most progressive (pro-poor) tax measure and that social service expenditures for income-maintenance and health care benefit poorer citizens, then nations most committed to these two fiscal policies should attain the greatest income equality. According to Table 5.4, this assumption holds true. The Swedish government levies the highest personal income taxes as a share of the GDP. Social service expenditures take a larger percentage of the GDP in Sweden than in any other country among the seven. Both fiscal policies have exerted an egalitarian impact. Dedicated to income equality, the Social Democratic party has long controlled the central government and has implemented egalitarian programs. Labor unions, particularly the LO, strive for greater wage solidarity. By contrast, the other nations have weaker socialist parties, less powerful unions, and a more muted commitment to income equality. France remains the most economically elitist society among these seven.

Table 5.3

POST-TAX INCOME EQUALITY, 1970s

Country	Year	Ginis[a]	Share of Post-Tax Income[b] Possessed by	
			Poorest 20%	Wealthiest 20%
Sweden	1979	.30	7.2%	37.2%
United Kingdom	1979	.32	7.3	39.3
West Germany	1978	.36	6.3	42.8
Italy	1977	.36	6.2	43.9
Canada	1977	.38	3.8	42.0
United States	1971	.39	5.0	44.6
France	1975	.39	5.3	45.8

Sources: *World Development Report 1983* (New York: Oxford University Press, 1983), 201; ILO, *World Labour Report,* vol. 1 (Geneva, 1984), 206-7; Wouter van Ginneken and Jong-goo Park, eds., *Generating Internationally Comparable Income Distribution Estimates* (Geneva: ILO, 1984), 5, 67, 176.

[a]Low *ginis* indicate low inequality.

[b]Post-tax income includes wages and salaries, entrepreneurial income, property incomes, investment income, and social security and private insurance transfers. Personal income taxes, property taxes and social security contributions are excluded.

The tax system is regressive; wealthy groups like technocrats, public notaries, bank employees, independent businesspeople, and civil servants evade paying income taxes, which comprise a relatively low proportion of the GDP. High expenditures for pensions and family allowances wield some equalizing effects; yet non-unionized manual workers employed in small firms receive the fewest economic benefits. In the United States as well, neither expenditure nor tax policies have significantly raised income equality since World War II. Here democratic socialist parties exert no influence. Labor unions have lost strength and now represent under 20 percent of the labor force. Public employment as a share of total civilian employment has recently decreased. Compared with private enterprises, government agencies hire a larger proportion of women and ethnic minorities, employ more professionals, and pay more equal salaries. Hence

Table 5.4

EGALITARIAN IMPACT OF FISCAL POLICIES, 1970s

Country	Year	Personal Income Taxes (Percent of GDP)	Social Service Expenditures (Percent of GDP)	Egalitarian Fiscal Impact[a] (Percent of GDP)	Ginis
Sweden	1979	21.2%	29.9%	6.3%	.30
United Kingdom	1979	10.5	17.1	1.8	.32
West Germany	1978	11.3	22.6	2.6	.36
Italy	1977	6.2	20.5	1.3	.36
Canada	1977	10.4	14.2	1.5	.38
United States	1971	9.7	9.8	1.0	.39
France	1975	5.0	20.9	1.0	.39

Sources: *Revenue Statistics of OECD Member Countries, 1965-1982* (Paris: OECD, 1983), 72; ILO: *The Cost of Social Security,* 9th and 10th eds. (Geneva, 1979, 1981), table 2, and *World Labour Report,* vol. 1 (Geneva, 1984), 207, 213; *World Development Report 1983* (New York: Oxford University Press, 1983), 201; Wouter van Ginneken and Jong-goo Park, eds., *Generating Internationally Comparable Income Distribution Estimates* (Geneva: ILO, 1984), 5, 67, 176.

[a]Egalitarian fiscal impact has been calculated by multiplying personal income taxes (percent of GDP) times social service expenditures (percent of GDP).

Note: The Pearson correlation coefficient between the egalitarian fiscal impact and income inequality *(gini)* is -.82, which indicates that nations with higher personal income taxes and social service expenditures as proportions of the GDP have lower income inequality.

during the 1980s declining opportunities for public employment, combined with tax cuts for the wealthy, tax increases for the poor, and reduced social service expenditures for low-income people, exacerbated the U.S. trend toward greater income inequality. The growing interest payments on the federal government debt, which go mainly to the wealthy holders of government bonds, also reduced income equality.[47]

ECONOMIC EFFICIENCY

Like equality, efficiency conveys diverse, ambiguous meanings; most generally it refers to input/output ratios. The most efficient enterprise produces the greatest output (goods, services) with the fewest inputs (money, labor time, resources). Although analysts can easily measure the relative efficiencies of different manufacturing enterprises, judgments about the efficiency of an entire national economy become difficult. One commonly used indicator measures manufacturing productivity—the annual percentage changes in output per hour (see Table 2.7). In this case manufactured goods are the output; the inputs include workers' labor time, managerial skills, energy sources, and capital.[48]

Despite some U.S. officials' contention that income equality leads to economic inefficiencies, the cross-national data for the seven nations show no clear relationship between productivity and equality. For example, from 1960 through 1980 Sweden's manufacturing output per hour increased by 5 percent each year—a comparatively high productivity gain. Yet Sweden also attained the greatest income equality. The United States demonstrated the lowest manufacturing productivity but also fairly high income inequality. British productivity was lower than the West German; however, Britons lived in a more egalitarian society. Among the seven countries only France, Italy, and West Germany revealed the expected linkage between high efficiency and low income equality.

Input/output ratios also provide useful indicators for making cross-national evaluations about education and health care policy performance. The human capital approach to educational investment equates efficiency with the rate of income returns from formal education. According to this approach, individual earnings constitute the output; years of schooling comprise the main input. Other relevant inputs, which serve as control variables, include labor market experience, occupation, and age. Presumably the education gained in secondary schools and universities represents an investment that teaches individuals certain economic skills as well as certain norms: hard work, discipline, punctuality, and responsibility for task attainment. All these skills and norms—human capital—should increase productivity. Cross-national analyses carried out between 1960 and 1972 suggest that Canadian, U.S., Italian, and French citizens make the greatest income gains by completing each additional year of secondary and higher education. People from the more egalitarian nations such as Sweden and the United Kingdom secure a lower rate of economic return from the time spent in educational institutions.[49]

Measurements of a government's health care policy performance show a complex relationship between income equality and efficiency, as measured by cost-benefit ratios. Canada, the United States, and West Germany rank fairly high on measures of income inequality. U.S. and West German health policy officials have operated a less efficient system than have the Canadian health administrators. Of all seven nations Canada secures the greatest health care efficiencies; the quality of health services is high, but government officials have managed to limit the costs. Although the English NHS provides low-cost care, inner-city hospital staff and physicians administer lower quality treatments than in Canada. Sweden operates a technically competent but expensive system; yet its costs are lower than in France, a more economically elitist society.

PUBLIC SATISFACTION WITH POLICY PERFORMANCE

Public satisfaction with economic, education, and health care policy performance depends on the degree to which government leaders help realize the other three evaluative standards. If they reduce inflation, decrease unemployment, raise the economic growth rate, promote efficiency, secure high student proficiency, lower infant mortality, raise life expectancy, and make policy benefits available to all citizens, then most citizens will favorably evaluate a nation's policy record. Sample surveys conducted in different countries enable us to make comparative evaluations of popular attitudes toward policy performance.

Citizens in all Western countries favorably evaluate social service programs that provide pensions, job training, education, and health care; most people seem willing to maintain or increase these expenditures even if higher taxes result. Policies to nationalize more private industries, however, arouse less popular support.

The greatest backlash against welfare state programs has occurred in the United States, Britain, and some Canadian provinces. More than other Western publics, many U.S. and British citizens want to reduce taxes, expenditures for social service programs, and the size of the government bureaucracy. In these two countries the private business sector wields more political influence than do the decentralized craft unions. Rightist political parties possess the cohesion needed to shape economic policies and citizens' policy preferences. Conservative party leaders, along with private business executives, articulate beliefs about individualism and self-reliance that attract widespread acceptance among the people, who rank personal freedom over social equality. Social service programs provide the least generous benefits. In the four continental European nations popular satisfaction with the welfare state remains higher. Sweden, West Germany, and France all have influential socialist parties. Although excluded from the central government, the Italian Communist party plays an important policy role in several regional and city governments, especially throughout the northern industrial areas. Except in France, labor unions show sufficient organizational cohesion to influence their members' attitudes toward the welfare state. When framing public policies, business executives share power with trade union leaders. Individualistic political beliefs based on "free enterprise" ideology arouse less enthusiasm than in the United States, Britain, and parts of Canada. Compared with North Americans and the British, continental Europeans place a higher value on social equality. Because social service programs provide comprehensive, generous benefits to all citizens, not just the economically needy, these policies generally evoke positive evaluations.[50]

Over the last decade a growing disillusionment with public schools has emerged. For example, in 1974 nearly half the U.S. public gave the local public schools an A or B grade; in 1983, however, only 31 percent offered such a favorable rating. During this period confidence in educational leadership waned. Before 1965 around three-fourths of U.S. voters approved local public school bonds; during the 1970s school bonds rarely won approval from more than half the electorate. The major reasons for the growing disenchantment revolved around the perceived lack of school discipline, the use of drugs on campuses, the low educational standards, and the failure to provide the schools sufficient financial assistance. Similarly in Canada popular satisfaction with public education has recently declined. Whereas in 1971 63 percent of a national sample believed that children were receiving a better education than had the survey respondents, by 1983 that figure had fallen to only 41 percent. Despite this decreasing support, Canadians evaluated the public schools more favorably than did respondents in the United States. Although Canadians perceived that teachers showed less interest in their students today than before, people in Canada believed that the curriculum and opportunities for public school involvement in school board meetings had changed for the better over the past generation. In Britain as well, public confidence in education has waned. From 1973 through 1979 fewer Britons assumed that primary, secondary, or university education offered a "good value" for the expenditures. By 1983 over 40 percent expressed little confidence in the education system; only 12 percent had "a great deal" of confidence.

Except in the United States and Italy, satisfaction with the public health system has remained higher than with the public schools. As we saw in Chapter 4, citizens favorably assess public health care performance. In the United States, however, respondents express greater discontent with the government's medical care performance than do either the British or the West Germans. Especially for low-income U.S. citizens, the mounting health care costs and the unavailability of physician care in rural and inner-city areas bring acute suffering.

Whatever the satisfaction with education and health policies, most people in the industrialized nations want to increase expenditures for education and health care. For example, in 1980 the Swedes preferred to cut their spending on private consumption for television sets, cars, restaurants, and vacations, rather than reduce expenditures for health care or education. Of all public programs, education and the NHS drew the greatest British support for increased spending in 1982. Even during the Reagan administration most people in the United States have favored higher federal government assistance to finance health care, elementary schooling, and secondary education, despite the higher taxes that might result.[51] In short, in all Western nations support for public education and health care policies remains high, as indicated by voters' willingness to increase both expenditures and taxes for these programs.

CONCLUSION

This analysis of policy performance in Western industrial societies has stressed three general themes. First, although all these societies operate private enterprise market economies, the public policies in the "capitalist camp" show great variety. Structural administration, government expenditures, finances, and benefits vary from one country to another. The contrasts between Sweden and the United States seem especially striking. Whereas U.S. policymakers rely on private institutions to help resolve human problems, Swedish officials express a stronger commitment to governmental routes to goal attainment. The weight of variables used to explain policy contents also diverges across nations. For example, although private business organizations wield greater policy influence in the United States, labor unions and the government civil service play a more powerful role in Sweden. Comparative evaluations reveal that all good things do not necessarily go together. No nation secures a highly favorable ranking on all the evaluative criteria.

Second, a reciprocal interaction occurs between social stratification and policy performance. Social stratification both shapes public policies and is affected by them. Groups at the top of the social hierarchy—managers, administrators, professionals—have greater resources to influence public policies than do individuals with less political power, wealth, and status. In all societies, no matter how egalitarian, the most active participants in the policy process comprise those with the most education, income, and organizational ties. In turn, public policies shape the social stratification system. Since World War II government policies have expanded access to social services, widened educational opportunities, and made health care more available to all citizens. Lower-income groups have benefited from these programs. Nevertheless, throughout most countries economic, education, and health programs have failed to produce substantially greater income equality. Except in Sweden, public policies have reinforced or slightly modified income distribution patterns rather than brought about a significant rise in the proportion of income possessed by the poor.

Third, public policymakers face limits in realizing the objectives of full employment, low inflation, rapid economic growth, high student performance, and a healthy population. The public policies chosen for implementation reflect the interaction between leaders' subjective will and objective conditions less subject to policy manipulation. The objective conditions include a nation's historical context, its position in the international politico-economic system, the power of labor unions and private businesses in the market economy, and cultural values transmitted from past generations. In democratic societies government cannot easily control family and peer group environments, which profoundly affect an individual's economic status, educational performance, and health. All these conditions limit government leaders' efforts to transform their policy preferences into binding public decisions. Even after the implementation of a policy, its outcomes may diverge from the original intentions of its formulators. Effective goal attainment depends on clear policy preferences, agreed-upon policy priorities, a strong will to realize objectives, and the organizational means to reach policy goals. Swedish policymakers have probably achieved the greatest success in goal attainment, mainly because the Swedish political system embodies these prerequisites. A powerful Social Democratic party has controlled a fairly centralized government for a lengthy period. Strong labor unions (especially the LO), cooperatives, workers' education associations, newspapers, and student unions helped the Socialists educate the populace, implement policies, and attain egalitarian objectives. By contrast, other nations have stronger conservative parties, more influential business organizations, weaker unions, and more fragmented governments that give groups the opportunity to veto policies preferred by the national leadership. Hence decision-makers' objectives never become fully realized in the national policy performance of most Western industrial societies.

NOTES

Chapter 1

1. Seymour Martin Lipset, "The Limits of Social Science," *Public Opinion* 4 (October/November 1981): 2-9; W. G. Runciman, *A Treatise on Social Theory*, vol. 1: *The Methodology of Social Theory* (New York: Cambridge University Press, 1983), 145-341.

2. George C. Homans, "The Present State of Sociological Theory," *Sociological Quarterly* 23 (Summer 1982): 285-89.

3. James G. March, "Theories of Choice and Making Decisions," *Society* 20 (November/December 1982): 29-39; Lennart J. Lundqvist, *The Hare and the Tortoise: Clean Air Policies in the United States and Sweden* (Ann Arbor: University of Michigan Press, 1980), 22-36.

4. See Duncan MacRae, Jr. and James A. Wilde, *Policy Analysis for Public Decisions* (North Scituate, Mass.: Duxbury Press, 1979), 63; Garry D. Brewer and Peter deLeon, *The Foundations of Policy Analysis* (Homewood, Ill.: Dorsey Press, 1983), 335-36.

Chapter 2

1. See Marie Jahoda, *Employment and Unemployment: A Social-Psychological Analysis* (Cambridge: Cambridge University Press, 1982), 33-61 and 83-101; *OECD Economic Outlook*, no. 32 (December 1982): 163, 165; Helen Chappell, "The Family Life of the Unemployed," *New Society* 62 (14 October 1982): 76-79; Catherine Hakim, "The Social Consequences of High Unemployment," *Journal of Social Policy* 11 (October 1982): 433-67; R. E. Pahl, review of *Coping with Unemployment: The Effects on the Unemployed Themselves*, by Economist Intelligence Unit, *New Society* 63 (6 January 1983): 27; Jane Millar, "Family Life on the Dole," *New Society* 64 (7 April 1983): 16-17.

2. Czeslaw Milosz, "The Nobel Lecture, 1980," *New York Review of Books* 28 (5 March 1981): 11.

3. Henrietta J. Duvall, Karen W. Goudreau, and Robert E. Marsh, "Aid to Families with Dependent Children: Characteristics of Recipients in 1979," *Social Security Bulletin* 45 (April 1982): 3-9, 19; *Social Security Bulletin* 45 (December 1982): 40.

4. Ruth Leger Sivard, *World Military and Social Expenditures, 1981* (Leesburg, Va.: World Priorities, 1981), 28-33; OECD, *The 1981 Tax/Benefit Position of a Typical Worker in OECD Member Countries* (Paris, 1982), 33-51;

Jonathan Aldrich, "The Earnings Replacement Rate of Old-Age Benefits in 12 Countries, 1969-80," *Social Security Bulletin* 45 (November 1982): 3-11; Michael D. Packard, "Retirement Options under the Swedish National Pension System," *Social Security Bulletin* 45 (November 1982): 12-22.

5. See OECD, *Employment in the Public Sector* (Paris, 1982), 9-15, 77-79; "Big Government—How Big Is It?" *OECD Observer*, no. 121 (March 1983): 9-10; Leila Pathirane and Derek W. Blades, "Defining and Measuring the Public Sector: Some International Comparisons," *Review of Income and Wealth* 28 (September 1982): 261-89; Göran Therborn, "The Prospects of Labour and the Transformation of Advanced Capitalism," *New Left Review*, no. 145 (May-June 1984): 33-34; John T. Tucker, "Government Employment: An Era of Slow Growth," *Monthly Labor Review* 104 (October 1981): 19-25; Dan Butler and Bruce D. Macnaughton, "Public Sector Growth in Canada: Issues, Explanations and Implications," in *Canadian Politics in the 1980s*, ed. Michael S. Whittington and Glen Williams (Toronto: Methuen, 1981), 93-97.

6. Friedrich A. Hayek, *The Constitution of Liberty* (Chicago: University of Chicago Press, 1960), 305. See also Friedrich A. Hayek, *The Road to Serfdom* (Chicago: University of Chicago Press, 1976), esp. iii-xxi, 119-33, and Dan Usher, *The Economic Prerequisite to Democracy* (New York: Columbia University Press, 1981), 105-41. Milton Friedman even sees the welfare state as inimical to national security: "The real threat to our national security is not the Soviet Union. It is the growth of the welfare state, which has increasingly absorbed the taxable capacity of the nation and is inexorably driving the United States into the state of impotence in international affairs that [C. Northcote] Parkinson ascribed to Britain" ("High Taxes, Low Security," *Newsweek*, 18 April 1983, 64).

7. See Patricia Capdevielle, Donato Alvarez, and Brian Cooper, "International Trends in Productivity and Labor Costs," *Monthly Labor Review* 105 (December 1982): 3-14; "The Productivity Slowdown," *Dollars and Sense*, no. 69 (September 1981): 12-14; Ira C. Magaziner and Robert E. Reich, *Minding America's Business* (New York: Vintage Books, 1983), 1-8, 29-59, 143-54.

8. Ivo K. Feierabend, Betty Nesvold, and Rosalind L. Feierabend, "Political Coerciveness and Turmoil: A Cross-National Inquiry," *Law and Society Review* 5 (August 1970): 93-118; Raymond D. Gastil, *Freedom in the World: Political Rights and Civil Liberties 1979* (New York: Freedom House, 1979), 15-24. For data on government social service expenditures in 1977, see ILO, *The Cost of Social Security: Tenth International Inquiry, 1975-1977* (Geneva: International Labour Office, 1981), 58-61. In both the Feierabend, Nesvold, and Feierabend and Gastil investigations, Italy, France, and West Germany rank lower on the civil liberties scale than do Sweden, the United States, Canada, and the United Kingdom.

9. See Robert D. Putnam, "The Political Attitudes of Senior Civil Servants in Western Europe: A Preliminary Report," *British Journal of Political Science*

3 (July 1973): 257-90; Joel D. Aberbach, Robert D. Putnam, and Bert A. Rockman, *Bureaucrats and Politicians in Western Democracies* (Cambridge, Mass.: Harvard University Press, 1981), 84-114, 170-237; Thomas J. Anton, *Administered Politics: Elite Political Culture in Sweden* (The Hague: Martinus Nijhoff, 1980); Royston Greenwood, "Relations between Central and Local Government in Sweden: The Control of Local Government Expenditure," *Public Administration* 57 (Winter 1979): 457-70; Douglas Johnson, "Waiting for the Balance-Sheet: France and the Socialists," *Encounter* 60 (March 1983): 66-75; Theodore Zeldin, *The French* (New York: Pantheon Books, 1982), 161-84; Alfred Diamant, "Bureaucracy and Public Policy in Neocorporatist Settings," *Comparative Politics* 14 (October 1981): 101-24.

10. See James O'Connor: *The Fiscal Crisis of the State* (New York: St. Martin's Press, 1973); "The Meaning of Crisis," *International Journal of Urban and Regional Research* 5 (September 1981): 301-29; and "The Fiscal Crisis of the State Revisited: A Look at Economic Crisis and Reagan's Budget Policy," *Kapitalistate*, no. 9 (1981): 41-61; Ian Gough, *The Political Economy of the Welfare State* (London: Macmillan, 1979), esp. 11-15, 122-53; Ian Gough and Anne Steinberg, "The Welfare State, Capitalism and Crisis," in *Political Power and Social Theory*, vol. 2, ed. Maurice Zeitlin (Greenwich, Conn.: JAI Press, 1981), 141-71; Mark Kesselman, "Prospects for Democratic Socialism in Advanced Capitalism: Class Struggle and Compromise in Sweden and France," *Politics and Society* 11, no. 4 (1982): 397-438; Ulf Himmelstrand, Göran Ahrne, Leif Lundberg, and Lars Lundberg, *Beyond Welfare Capitalism* (London: Heinemann, 1981), 17-21. For the Marxist interpretation of "contradiction," see Robert L. Heilbroner, *Marxism: For and Against* (New York: W. W. Norton, 1980), 39-40, 77-78.

11. For data on profit shares in industrial societies, see T. P. Hill, *Profits and Rates of Return* (Paris: OECD, 1979), 113-23; *OECD Economic Outlook*, no. 33 (July 1983): 57.

12. For analyses of the backlash against the welfare state, see the following: Harold L. Wilensky: *The Welfare State and Equality: Structural and Ideological Roots of Public Expenditures* (Berkeley: University of California Press, 1975), 28-69, 107-19; *The "New Corporatism," Centralization, and the Welfare State*, vol. 2; Sage Professional Papers in Contemporary Political Sociology, series no. 06-020 (Beverly Hills, Calif.: Sage Publications, 1976); and "Democratic Corporatism, Consensus, and Social Policy: Reflections on Changing Values and the 'Crisis' of the Welfare State," in *The Welfare State in Crisis* (Paris: OECD, 1981), 185-95; Richard M. Coughlin, *Ideology, Public Opinion and Welfare Policy: Attitudes toward Taxes and Spending in Industrialized Societies* (Berkeley: Institute of International Studies, 1980); Sara A. Rosenberry, "Social Insurance, Distributive Criteria and the Welfare Backlash: A Comparative Analysis," *British Journal of Political Science* 12 (October 1982): 421-47; Douglas A. Hibbs, Jr. and Henrik Jess Madsen, Public Reactions to the Growth of Taxation and Government Expenditure," *World Politics* 33 (April 1981): 413-35; Hélène Riffault and Jacques-René

Rabier, *The Perception of Poverty in Europe* (Brussels: Commission of the European Communities, 1977); "Public Opinion in the European Community at the End of 1981," *Eurobarometer*, no. 16 (December 1981): A43-44; *World Opinion Update* 6 (November/December 1982): 149-50; Gosta Esping-Andersen, "Comparative Social Policy and Political Conflict in Advanced Welfare States: Denmark and Sweden," *International Journal of Health Services* 9, no. 2 (1979): 269-93; Stanley Feldman: "Economic Self-Interest and Political Behavior," *American Journal of Political Science* 26 (August 1982): 446-66, and "Economic Individualism and American Public Opinion," *American Politics Quarterly* 11 (January 1983): 3-29; Garth Stevenson, "Quasi-Democracy in Alberta," *Canadian Forum* 62 (February 1983): 14-15, 24.

13. Information about popular attitudes toward government social service expenditures appears in the following: Elizabeth Hann Hastings and Philip K. Hastings, eds., various issues of *Index to International Public Opinion* (Westport, Conn.: Greenwood Press, 1980-84)—vol. 1 (1978-79), 41, 174, 293-94; vol. 2 (1979-80), 71-74, 277, 295, 297; vol. 3 (1980-81), 29, 63, 114-15, 117-19, 122, 142-47, 364-66; vol. 4 (1981-82), 37, 85, 150, 166-68; and vol. 5 (1982-83), 37, 183; Coughlin, *Ideology, Public Opinion and Welfare Policy*, 17-126; *World Opinion Update* 5 (July/August 1981): 99, and 6 (September/October 1982): 126-28; Barbara G. Farah, Samuel H. Barnes, and Felix Heunks, "Political Dissatisfaction," in *Political Action: Mass Participation in Five Western Democracies*, ed. Samuel H. Barnes and Max Kaase (Beverly Hills, Ca.: Sage Publications, 1979), 412-14; Olof Petersson and Henry Valen, "Political Cleavages in Sweden and Norway," *Scandinavian Political Studies* 2, no. 4 (1979): 316; Paul Whiteley, "Public Opinion and the Demand for Social Welfare in Britain," *Journal of Social Policy* 10 (October 1981): 453-76; Stewart Lansley and Stuart Weir, "Towards a Popular View of Poverty," *New Society* 65 (25 August 1983): 283-84; Peter Taylor-Gooby: "Two Cheers for the Welfare State: Public Opinion and Private Welfare," *Journal of Public Policy* 2 (October 1982): 319-46, and "Public Belt and Private Braces," *New Society* 64 (14 April 1983): 51-53; Paul Beedle and Peter Taylor-Gooby, "Ambivalence and Altruism: Public Opinion about Taxation and Welfare," *Policy and Politics* 11 (January 1983): 15-39; Kathleen Maurer Smith and William Spinrad, "The Popular Political Mood," *Social Policy* 11 (March/April 1981): 37-45; David M. Alpern, "Polarizing the Nation?" *Newsweek* 99 (8 February 1982): 33-34; Warren E. Miller and J. Merrill Shanks, "Policy Directions and Presidential Leadership: Alternative Interpretations of the 1980 Presidential Election," *British Journal of Political Science* 12 (July 1982): 312, 320, 323; Vicente Navarro, "Where Is the Popular Mandate? A Reply to Conventional Wisdom," *International Journal of Health Sciences* 13, no. 1 (1983): 169-74; David O. Sears and Jack Citrin, *Tax Revolt: Something for Nothing in California* (Berkeley: University of California Press, 1982), 233.

14. For analyses of the relationships between economic conditions and voting behavior, see the following: Martin Paldam, "A Preliminary Survey of the

Theories and Findings on Vote and Popularity Functions," *European Journal of Political Research* 9 (June 1981): 181-99; Seymour Martin Lipset, "No Room for the Ins: Elections around the World," *Public Opinion* 5 (October/November 1982): 41-43; Kendall Baker, Russell J. Dalton, and Kai Hildebrandt, *Germany Transformed: Political Culture and the New Politics* (Cambridge, Mass.: Harvard University Press, 1981), 73-104; Werner Pommerehne, Friedrich Schneider, and Jean-Dominique Lafay, "Les Interactions entre économie et politique: Synthèse des analyses théoriques et empiriques," *Revue Économique* 32 (January 1981): 110-62; Bruno S. Frey and Friedrich Schneider: "Politico-Economic Models in Competition with Alternative Models: Which Predict Better?" *European Journal of Political Research* 10 (September 1982): 241-54, and "Recent Research on Empirical Politico-Economic Models," in *Contemporary Political Economy*, ed. Douglas A. Hibbs, Jr., Heino Fassbender, and R. Douglas Rivers (New York: North-Holland, 1981), 11-26; Richard R. Lau and David O. Sears, "Cognitive Links between Economic Grievances and Political Responses," *Political Behavior* 3, no. 4 (1981): 279-302; M. Stephen Weatherford: "How Economic Events Affect Electoral Outcomes: A Model of Political Translation," *Micropolitics* 1, no. 3 (1981): 269-93, and "Economic Voting and the 'Symbolic Politics' Argument: A Reinterpretation and Synthesis," *American Political Science Review* 77 (March 1983): 158-74; Volkmar Lauber, "From Growth Consensus to Fragmentation in Western Europe: Political Polarization over Redistribution and Ecology," *Comparative Politics* 15 (April 1983): 329-49; Paul Whiteley, "Inflation, Unemployment and Government Popularity—Dynamic Models for the United States, Britain and West Germany," *Electoral Studies* 3 (April 1984): 3-24.

15. Hastings and Hastings, eds., *Index to International Public Opinion, 1978-1979*, 172; *1980-1981*, 115-19; and *1982-1983*, 373; Frances Williams, Chris Pond, Ruth Lister, Jane Morton, and Helen Chappell, "An Anatomy of Thatcherism," *New Society* 57 (24 September 1981): 519-20; Frances Williams, "Sir Geoffrey Takes the Low Road," *New Society* 58 (10 December 1981): 452-54; David Walker, "Public Spending: Sleight of Hand," *New Society* 62 (18 November 1982): 299-300; W. B. Reddaway, "The Government's Economic Policy—An Appraisal," *Three Banks Review*, no. 136 (December 1982): 3-18; Ken Livingstone, "Monetarism in London," *New Left Review*, no. 137 (January-February 1983): 68-76; James Bishop, "Programme for the 1980s: Interview with Prime Minister Margaret Thatcher," *Illustrated London News* 271 (May 1983): 22-24; Tom Forester, "The Tale of the Working Class Tory," *New Society* 58 (15 October 1981): 97-99; David Thomas, "Will the Man Who Put Mrs. Thatcher In Do So Again?" *New Society* 64 (26 May 1983): 291-93; "The Policies of the Parties," *New Society* 64 (26 May 1983): 298-300; *The Economist*, 4 June 1983, pp. 39-40, and 18 June 1983, pp. 13-14, 33-41; *World Opinion Update* 7 (January 1983): 6; Peter Kellner, "Anatomy of a Landslide," *New Statesman* 105 (17 June 1983): 7-8; Alan Ryan, "The Slow Death of Labour England?" *New Society* 64 (18 June 1983): 419-21; Ivor Crewe: "Why Labour Lost

the British Elections," *Public Opinion* 6 (June/July 1983): 7-9, 56-60, and "The Electorate: Partisan Dealignment Ten Years On," *West European Politics* 6 (October 1983): 183-215; Richard Rose, "Two and One-Half Cheers for the Market in Britain," *Public Opinion* 6 (June/July 1983): 10-15; Hugh Berrington, "Notes on Recent Elections: The British General Election of 1983," *Electoral Studies* 2 (December 1983): 263-69. Data on unemployment and inflation rates appear in *OECD Economic Outlook*, no. 34 (December 1983): 161, 163. For information about recent electoral returns, see *European Journal of Political Research*, September issues.

16. Rainer Eisfeld, "The West German Elections: Economic Fears and the Deployment Debate," *Government and Opposition* 18 (Summer 1983): 291-303; Baker, Dalton, and Hildebrandt, *Germany Transformed*, 88-103; Paul Peretz, "The Effect of Economic Change on Political Parties in West Germany," in D. Hibbs, Fassbender, and Rivers, eds., *Contemporary Political Economy*, 101-20; Hans Rattinger, "Unemployment and the 1976 Election in Germany: Some Findings at the Aggregate and the Individual Level of Analysis," in *ibid.*, 121-35; Geoffrey Pridham, "Party Politics and Coalitions in Bonn," *World Today* 39 (January 1983): 21-29; Caroline Bray, "The West German Election," *World Today* 39 (April 1983): 123-25; Lauber, "From Growth Consensus to Fragmentation in Western Europe," 343-45; Mark Danser Hibbs, "Changing the Guard in Germany," *Challenge* 26 (May/June 1983): 50-57; Max Kaase, "The West German General Election of 6 March 1983," *Electoral Studies* 2 (August 1983): 158-66; Hastings and Hastings, eds., *Index to International Public Opinion, 1982-1983*, 399-400; Andrei S. Markovits, "West Germany's Political Future: The 1983 Bundestag Elections," *Socialist Review* 13 (July-August 1983): 67-98.

17. Patricia Capdevielle and Donato Alvarez, "International Comparisons of Trends in Productivity and Labor Costs," *Monthly Labor Review* 104 (December 1981): 17; Charles F. Andrain, *Foundations of Comparative Politics: A Policy Perspective* (Monterey, Calif.: Brooks/Cole, 1983), 240-42; Larry and Roberta Garner, "Problems of the Hegemonic Party: The PCI and the Structural Limits of Reform," *Science and Society* 45 (Fall 1981): 257-73; Sidney Tarrow, "Transforming Enemies into Allies: Non-Ruling Communist Parties in Multiparty Coalitions," *Journal of Politics* 44 (November 1982): 924-54; Marzio Barbagli and Piergiorgio Corbetta, "After the Historic Compromise: A Turning Point for the PCI," *European Journal of Political Research* 10 (September 1982): 213-39; John S. Eisenhammer: "The PCI Congress—What Alternative?" *World Today* 39 (April 1983): 126-28, and "The Italian General Election of 1983," *Electoral Studies* 2 (December 1983): 280-85; *The Economist*, 2 July 1983, p. 41; *New York Times*, 29 June 1983, p. 3; Lawrence Garner, "A Change in Italy's Choirmaster?" *Current History* 83 (April 1984): 160-63, 181-83; Michael S. Lewis-Beck and Paolo Bellucci, "Economic Influences on Legislative Elections in Multiparty Systems: France and Italy," *Political Behavior* 4, no. 1 (1982): 93-107.

18. Miller and Shanks, "Policy Directions and Presidential Leadership," 299-356;
    Gregory B. Markus, "Political Attitudes during an Election Year: A Report
    on the 1980 NES Panel Study," *American Political Science Review* 76 (Sep-
    tember 1982): 538-60; Paul R. Abramson, John H. Aldrich, and David W.
    Rohde, *Change and Continuity in the 1980 Elections* (Washington, D.C.:
    Congressional Quarterly Press, 1982), 95-185; *New York Times*, 9 November
    1980, p. 18; John S. Jackson III, Barbara Leavitt Brown, and David Bositis,
    "Herbert McClosky and Friends Revisited: 1980 Democratic and Republican
    Party Elites Compared to the Mass Public," *American Politics Quarterly* 10
    (April 1982): 158-80; Joan D. Borum, "Wage Increases in 1980 Outpaced
    by Inflation," *Monthly Labor Review* 104 (May 1981): 55-56; Douglas A.
    Hibbs, Jr., "President Reagan's Mandate from the 1980 Elections: A Shift
    to the Right?" *American Politics Quarterly* 10 (October 1982): 387-420;
    D. Roderick Kiewiet, *Macroeconomics and Micropolitics: The Electoral
    Effects of Economic Issues* (Chicago: University of Chicago Press, 1983).

19. William P. Irvine: "The Canadian Voter" and "Epilogue: The 1980 Elec-
    tion," both in *Canada at the Polls, 1979 and 1980: A Study of the General
    Elections*, ed. Howard R. Penniman (Washington, D.C.: American Enterprise
    Institute, 1981), 55-85 and 337-98; Harold D. Clarke, Jane Jenson, Lawrence
    LeDuc, and Jon Pammett, "Voting Behaviour and the Outcome of the 1979
    Federal Election: The Impact of Leaders and Issues," *Canadian Journal of
    Political Science* 15 (September 1982): 517-52.

20. Hastings and Hastings, eds., *Index to International Public Opinion, 1980-
    1981*, 276; Johnson, "Waiting for the Balance-Sheet: France and the Social-
    ists," 66-75; Jean-Dominique Lafay, "The Impact of Economic Variables on
    Political Behavior in France," in D. Hibbs, Fassbender, and Rivers, eds., *Con-
    temporary Political Economy*, 137-49; Douglas A. Hibbs, Jr. and Nicholas
    Vasilatos, "Economics and Politics in France: Economic Performance and
    Mass Political Support for Presidents Pompidou and Giscard d'Estaing,"
    European Journal of Political Research 9 (June 1981): 133-45; Michael S.
    Lewis-Beck, "Economics and the French Voter: A Microanalysis," *Public
    Opinion Quarterly* 47 (Fall 1983): 347-60.

21. Peter Walters, "Sweden's Public Sector Crisis, Before and After the 1982
    Elections," *Government and Opposition* 18 (Winter 1983): 23-39; Lars
    Jonung and Eskil Wadensjö, "The Effect of Unemployment, Inflation and
    Real Income Growth on Government Popularity in Sweden," *Scandinavian
    Journal of Economics* 81, no. 2 (1979): 343-53; Douglas A. Hibbs, Jr. and
    Henrik Jess Madsen, "The Impact of Economic Performance on Electoral
    Support in Sweden, 1967-1978," *Scandinavian Political Studies* 4, no. 1
    (1981): 33-50; Olof Ruin, "The 1982 Swedish Election: The Re-Emergence
    of an Old Pattern in a New Situation," *Electoral Studies* 2 (August 1983):
    166-71; Svante Ersson and Jan-Erik Lane, "Polarisation and Political Econ-
    omy Crisis: The 1982 Swedish Election," *West European Politics* 6 (July
    1983): 287-96.

22. OECD, *The Challenge of Unemployment: A Report to Labour Ministers* (Paris, 1982); Joyanna Moy, "Unemployment and Labor Force Trends in 10 Industrial Nations: An Update," *Monthly Labor Review* 105 (November 1982): 17-21; "Employment Dislocations," *OECD Observer*, no. 119 (November 1982): 19; Constance Sorrentino, "Youth Unemployment: An International Perspective," *Monthly Labor Review* 104 (July 1981): 3-15; Jim Tomlinson, "Unemployment and Policy in the 1930s and 1980s," *Three Banks Review*, no. 135 (September 1982): 17-33; Marillyn A. Hewson and Michael A. Urquhart, "The Nation's Employment Situation Worsens in the First Half of 1982," *Monthly Labor Review* 105 (August 1982): 8; Michael A. Urquhart and Marillyn A. Hewson, "Unemployment Continued to Rise in 1982 as Recession Deepened," *Monthly Labor Review* 106 (February 1983): 8; Sunder Magun, "Unemployment Experience in Canada: A 5-Year Longitudinal Analysis," *Monthly Labor Review* 106 (April 1983): 36-38; Helen Ginsburg, *Full Employment and Public Policy: The United States and Sweden* (Lexington, Mass.: D. C. Heath, 1983), 21-54, 113-21, 162, 179, 185; Paul G. Schervish, *The Structural Determinants of Unemployment: Vulnerability and Power in Market Relations* (New York: Academic Press, 1983), 78-114, 190-93.

23. Angus Maddison, *Phases of Capitalist Development* (New York: Oxford University Press, 1982), 44.

24. See Maddison, *Phases of Capitalist Development*; Paul M. Sweezy and Harry Magdoff, "The Deepening Crisis of U.S. Capitalism," *Monthly Review* 33 (October 1981): 1-16; Paul Sweezy, "Why Stagnation?" *Monthly Review* 34 (June 1982): 1-10; A. P. Thirlwall, "Deindustrialisation in the United Kingdom," *Lloyds Bank Review*, no. 144 (April 1982): 22-37; W. W. Rostow, "Technology and Unemployment in the Western World," *Challenge* 26 (March/April 1983): 6-17; Donald Tomaskovic-Devey and S. M. Miller, "Can High-Tech Provide the Jobs?" *Challenge* 26 (May-June 1983): 57-63; Jeffrey J. Schott, "Can World Trade Be Governed?" *Challenge* 25 (March/April 1982): 43-49; David R. Cameron, "On the Limits of the Public Economy," *Annals of the American Academy of Political and Social Science* 459 (January 1982): 46-62.

25. See Charles F. Andrain, *Politics and Economic Policy in Western Democracies* (North Scituate, Mass.: Duxbury Press, 1980), 64-84, 140-72; Guy Standing: "The Notion of Structural Unemployment," *International Labour Review* 122 (March-April 1983): 137-53, and "The Notion of Technological Unemployment," *International Labour Review* 123 (March-April 1984): 127-47; "Structural Unemployment: Policies for Job Creation," *OECD Observer*, no. 127 (March 1984): 28-32; A. P. Thirlwall, "Keynesian Employment Theory Is Not Defunct," *Three Banks Review*, no. 131 (September 1981): 14-29; James E. Meade, "Stagflation in the United Kingdom," *Atlantic Economic Journal* 7 (December 1979): 1-10.

26. Robert Malcolm Campbell, "Post-Keynesian Politics and the Post-Schumpeterian World," *Canadian Journal of Political and Social Theory* 8 (Winter/Spring 1984): 72-75.

27. "Social Expenditure: Erosion or Evolution?" *OECD Observer*, no. 126 (January 1984): 5; Lillian Liu, "Social Security Problems in West European Countries," *Social Security Bulletin* 47 (February 1984): 20; *OECD Observer*, no. 121 (March 1983): 21; "28½ Million Unemployed," *OECD Observer*, no. 115 (March 1982): 8-16; Douglas Webber, "Combatting and Acquiescing in Unemployment? Crisis Management in Sweden and West Germany," *West European Politics* 6 (January 1983): 23-43; Helen Ginsburg: "How Sweden Combats Unemployment among Young and Older Workers," *Monthly Labor Review* 105 (October 1982): 22-27, and *Full Employment and Public Policy*, 127-55.

28. Andrain, *Politics and Economic Policy*, 85-172; Wallace C. Peterson: *Our Overloaded Economy: Inflation, Unemployment and the Crisis in American Capitalism* (Armonk, N.Y.: M. E. Sharpe, 1982), 91-120; "Power and Economic Performance," *Journal of Economic Issues* 14 (December 1980): 827-69; and "Economic Stabilization and Inflation," *Journal of Economic Issues* 18 (March 1984): 69-100; William L. Hemphill, "Inflationary Momentum and Stabilization Policy: A US Perspective," *Journal of Public Policy* 2 (August 1982): 193-215; Joan Robinson, *What Are the Questions? and Other Essays* (Armonk, N.Y.: M. E. Sharpe, 1981), 15-26, 38, 199.

29. Basil J. Moore, "Monetary Factors," in *A Guide to Post-Keynesian Economics*, ed. Alfred S. Eichner (White Plains, N.Y.: M. E. Sharpe, 1979), 131, 133.

30. European Economic Community (EEC), *Basic Statistics of the Community*, 19th ed. (Luxembourg: Office for Official Publications of the EEC, 1981), 17; Sidney Weintraub, *Capitalism's Inflation and Unemployment Crisis* (Reading, Mass.: Addison-Wesley, 1978), 43-64; Joan Robinson, *Aspects of Development and Underdevelopment* (London: Cambridge University Press, 1979), 78-79.

31. Capdevielle, Alvarez, and Cooper, "International Trends in Productivity and Labor Costs," 4, 7; H. Sonmez Atesoglu, "Inflation and Its Acceleration: Evidence from the Postwar United States," *Journal of Post Keynesian Economics* 3 (Fall 1980): 105-15; Antonio Fazio, "Inflation and Wage Indexation in Italy," *Banca Nazionale del Lavoro*, no. 137 (June 1981): 147-70; Tran Van Hoa, "Causality and Wage Price Inflation in West Germany, 1964-1979," *Weltwirtschaftliches Archiv*, no. 117 (no. 1, 1981): 110-24.

32. M. A. Akhtar, "Recent Experience with Monetary Growth and Inflation in Germany, Japan, and the United States," *Journal of Post Keynesian Economics* 2 (Summer 1980): 585-92; George S. Tavlas, Danny M. Leipziger, Dae Choi, and Victor Filatov, "Interest Rate Policies and Inflation in Interdependent Economies: Recent Policy Dilemmas," *Journal of Policy Modeling* 3 (February 1981): 1-18.

33. Mark J. Johnson, "U.S. Foreign Trade Policies in 1982: Import Index Falls, Export Indexes Mixed," *Monthly Labor Review* 106 (May 1983): 23; OECD, *Quarterly Oil Statistics*, 2d quarter 1982, no. 3, and 2d quarter 1981, no. 3 (Paris, 1981-82); *OECD Observer*, no. 121 (March 1983): 17; U.S. Central Intelligence Agency, Directorate of Intelligence, *International Energy Statistical Review* (25 January 1983): 3-19.

34. Robinson, *Aspects of Development and Underdevelopment*, 81-101; Nicholas Kaldor and James Trevithick, "A Keynesian Perspective on Money," *Lloyds Bank Review*, no. 139 (January 1981): 1-19; James S. Earley, "What Caused Worldwide Inflation: Excess Liquidity, Excessive Credit, or Both?" *Weltwirtschaftliches Archiv*, no. 117 (no. 2, 1981): 213-43; J. Barkley Rosser, Jr., "The Emergence of the Megacorpstate and the Acceleration of Global Inflation," *Journal of Post Keynesian Economics* 3 (Spring 1981): 429-39; "Borrowing from Abroad," *Dollars and Sense*, no. 97 (May/June 1984): 3-5.

35. Andrain, *Foundations of Comparative Politics*, 33-39, 171-76; Plato, *The Republic*, trans. Francis MacDonald Cornford (New York: Oxford University Press, 1945), 195-96.

36. Lester C. Thurow, *Dangerous Currents: The State of Economics* (New York: Random House, 1983), 24.

Chapter 3

1. Charles Dickens, *Hard Times* (New York: New American Library, 1961), 31.

2. *Ibid.*, 11.

3. The following section on the school curriculum draws on material in Charles F. Andrain, *Children and Civic Awareness: A Study in Political Education* (Columbus, Ohio: Charles E. Merrill, 1971), esp. 20-22, 73-74, 119-20.

4. See Samuel H. Barnes and Max Kaase, eds., *Political Action: Mass Participation in Five Western Democracies* (Beverly Hills, Calif.: Sage Publications, 1979), 27-96.

5. Judith V. Torney, A. N. Oppenheim, and Russell F. Farnen, *Civic Education in Ten Countries* (New York: John Wiley and Sons, 1975), 237, 248, 272, 278; H. Dean Nielsen, *Tolerating Political Dissent: The Impact of High School Social Climates in the United States and West Germany* (Stockholm: Almqvist and Wiksell, 1977).

6. Otto Klineberg, Marisa Zavalloni, Christiane Louis-Guérin, and Jeanne BenBrika, *Students, Values, and Politics: A Crosscultural Comparison* (New York: Free Press, 1979), 44, 73-79, 94-98; W. B. Devall, "Support for Civil Liberties among English-Speaking Canadian University Students," *Canadian Journal of Political Science* 3 (September 1970): 447; Robert D. Putnam, "Elite Transformation in Advanced Industrial Societies: An Empirical Assessment of the Theory of Technocracy," *Comparative Political Studies* 10 (October 1977): 399; Harvey E. Rich, "Tolerance for Civil Liberties among

College Students: A Multivariate Analysis," *Youth and Society* 12 (September 1980): 17-32; Ruth S. Jones, "Democratic Values and Preadult Virtues: Tolerance, Knowledge, and Participation," *Youth and Society* 12 (December 1980): 189-220.

7. Michael S. Lewis-Beck, "Explaining Peasant Conservatism: The West European Case," *British Journal of Political Science* 7 (October 1977): 458-61; Edward N. Muller, Pertti Pesonen, and Thomas O. Jukam, "Support for the Freedom of Assembly in Western Democracies," *European Journal of Political Research* 8 (September 1980): 265-88; Alan Marsh and Max Kaase, "Background of Political Action," in Barnes and Kaase, eds., *Political Action*, 100, 112-17; Stephen F. Szabo: "Contemporary French Orientations toward Economic and Political Dimensions of Human Rights," *Universal Human Rights* 1 (July-September 1979): 61-76, and "Social Perspectives and Support for Human Rights in West Germany," *Universal Human Rights* 1 (January-March 1979): 81-98; Ursula Feist and Klaus Liepelt, "New Elites in Old Parties: Observations on a Side Effect of German Educational Reform," *International Political Science Review* 4, no. 1 (1983): 71-83; Michael D. Ornstein, H. Michael Stevenson, and A. Paul Williams, "Region, Class and Political Culture in Canada," *Canadian Journal of Political Science* 13 (June 1980): 257-58; E. M. Schreiber, "Cultural Cleavages between Occupational Categories: The Case of Canada," *Social Forces* 55 (September 1976): 16-29; Edward G. Grabb, "Working-Class Authoritarianism and Tolerance of Outgroups: A Reassessment," *Public Opinion Quarterly* 43 (Spring 1979): 36-47; David Knoke, "Stratification and the Dimensions of American Political Orientations," *American Journal of Political Science* 23 (November 1979): 772-79; James A. Davis, "Communism, Conformity, Cohorts, and Categories: American Tolerance in 1954 and 1972-73," *American Journal of Sociology* 81 (November 1975): 491-513; Clyde Z. Nunn, Harry J. Crockett, Jr., and J. Allen Williams, Jr., *Tolerance for Nonconformity* (San Francisco: Jossey-Bass, 1978), 60-82; Herbert H. Hyman and Charles R. Wright, *Education's Lasting Influence on Values* (Chicago: University of Chicago Press, 1979), 32-37, 87-106; Marvin E. Olsen and Mary Anna Baden, "Legitimacy of Social Protest Actions in the United States and Sweden," *Journal of Political and Military Scoiology* 2 (Fall 1974): 187-88; Seymour Martin Lipset, *Political Man: The Social Bases of Politics*, expanded and updated ed. (Baltimore, Md.: Johns Hopkins University Press, 1981), 87-126, 476-88; Herbert McClosky and Alida Brill, *Dimensions of Tolerance: What Americans Believe about Civil Liberties* (New York: Russell Sage Foundation, 1983), 255, 370-403, 415-38. For a dissenting interpretation of the direct positive effects of advanced education on support for civil liberties in the United States, see John L. Sullivan, James Piereson, and George E. Marcus, *Political Tolerance and American Democracy* (Chicago: University of Chicago Press, 1982).

8. Robert Jackman, "Political Elites, Mass Publics, and Support for Democratic Principles," *Journal of Politics* 34 (August 1972): 772. For a rebuttal, see Hyman and Wright, *Education's Lasting Influence on Values*, 12-17.

9. M. Kent Jennings and Richard G. Niemi, *Generations and Politics: A Panel Study of Young Adults and Their Parents* (Princeton: Princeton University Press, 1981), 210, 257-70; Arnold Vedlitz, "The Impact of College Education on Political Attitudes and Behaviors: A Reappraisal and Test of the Self-Selection Hypothesis," *Social Science Quarterly* 65 (March 1983): 145-53; Paul R. Abramson, *Political Attitudes in America: Formation and Change* (San Francisco: W. H. Freeman, 1983), 241-59.

10. Russell F. Farnen and Dan B. German, "Youth, Politics, and Education: England, Italy, Sweden, the United States, and West Germany," in *Political Youth, Traditional Schools: National and International Perspectives*, ed. Byron G. Massialas (Englewood Cliffs, N. J.: Prentice-Hall, 1972), 170-74; Torney, Oppenheim, and Farnen, *Civic Education in Ten Countries*, 81; Marshall W. Conley and Kenneth Osborne, "Political Education in Canadian Schools: An Assessment of Social Studies and Political Science Courses and Pedagogy," *International Journal of Political Education* 6 (April 1983): 65-85; Ed Sullivan and Clive Beck, "Moral Education," in *Must Schools Fail? The Growing Debate in Canadian Education*, ed. Niall Byrne and Jack Quarter (Toronto: McClelland and Stewart, 1972), 126-41; Lawrence Kohlberg, "Moral Education: A Response to Thomas Sobol," *Educational Leadership* 28 (October 1980): 19-32.

11. Torney, Oppenheim, and Farnen, *Civic Education in Ten Countries*, 73-74; Henry W. Ehrmann, *Politics in France*, 4th ed. (Boston: Little, Brown, 1983), 82-85; Richard F. Tomasson, *Sweden: Prototype of Modern Society* (New York: Random House, 1970), 116; Frances FitzGerald, *America Revised: History Schoolbooks in the Twentieth Century* (New York: Vintage, 1980); John I. Goodlad, "A Study of Schooling: Some Findings and Hypotheses," *Phi Delta Kappan* 64 (March 1983): 465-70; Gail L. Zellman, "Antidemocratic Beliefs: A Survey and Some Explanations," *Journal of Social Issues* 31 (Spring 1975): 37-38, 45-47; W. Lance Bennett, *The Political Mind and the Political Environment* (Lexington, Mass.: Lexington Books, 1975), 125; David G. Lawrence, "Procedural Norms and Tolerance: A Reassessment," *American Political Science Review* 70 (March 1976): 80-100; Lee H. Ehman, "The American School in the Political Socialization Process," *Review of Educational Research* 50 (Spring 1980): 99-119; Michael Corbett, "Education and Contextual Tolerance: Group-Relatedness and Consistency Reconsidered," *American Politics Quarterly* 8 (July 1980): 345-59; Sullivan, Piereson, and Marcus, *Political Tolerance and American Democracy*, 114-26, 209-58.

12. Charles F. Andrain, *Foundations of Comparative Politics: A Policy Perspective* (Monterey, Calif.: Brooks/Cole, 1983), 338-39; *World Opinion Update* 2 (July 1978): 85-86; Frederick D. Weil, "Tolerance of Free Speech in the United States and West Germany, 1970-79: An Analysis of Public Opinion Survey Data," *Social Forces* 60 (June 1982): 973-92; Volkmar Lauber, "From Growth Consensus to Fragmentation in Western Europe," *Comparative Politics* 15 (April 1983): 344; Maya Pines, "Unlearning Blind Obedience

in German Schools," *Psychology Today* 15 (May 1981): 59-65; Nielsen, *Tolerating Political Dissent*, 66-67, 94-110; Siegfried George, "Society and Social Justice: Problems of Political Education in West Germany," *Teaching Political Science* 8 (April 1981): 281-96; David P. Conradt: "Political Culture, Legitimacy and Participation," *West European Politics* 4 (May 1981): 18-34, and *The German Polity*, 2d ed. (New York: Longman, 1982), 63-82; Ivo K. Feierabend, Betty Nesvold, and Rosalind L. Feierabend, "Political Coerciveness and Turmoil: A Cross-National Inquiry," *Law and Society Review* 5 (August 1970): 93-118; Raymond D. Gastil, *Freedom in the World: Political Rights and Civil Liberties, 1979* (New York: Freedom House, 1979), 15-24.

13. Torsten Husén, "Are Standards in U.S. Schools Really Lagging Behind Those in Other Countries?" *Phi Delta Kappan* 64 (March 1983): 455-61; Alex Inkeles, "National Differences in Scholastic Performance," *Comparative Education Review* 23 (October 1979): 386-407; *San Diego Union*, 12 December 1983, p. A-10; Arnold J. Heidenheimer, Hugh Heclo, and Carolyn Teich Adams, *Comparative Public Policy: The Politics of Social Choice in Europe and America*, 2d ed. (New York: St. Martin's Press, 1983), 34. For a dissenting interpretation of the cross-national effects of the educational curriculum, see Barbara Lerner, "American Education: How Are We Doing?" *Public Interest*, no. 69 (Fall 1982): 59-82.

14. Torney, Oppenheim, and Farnen, *Civic Education in Ten Countries*, 114-19, 141-52, 334-35.

15. Hans D. Klingemann, "The Background of Ideological Conceptualization," in Barnes and Kaase, eds., *Political Action*, 258-62; Gabriel A. Almond and Sidney Verba, *The Civic Culture: Political Attitudes and Democracy in Five Nations* (Princeton: Princeton University Press, 1963), 380-87; Ronald Inglehart, *The Silent Revolution: Changing Values and Political Styles among Western Publics* (Princeton: Princeton University Press, 1977), 72-84, 93, 339-40; Hyman and Wright, *Education's Lasting Influence on Values*, 64; Herbert H. Hyman, Charles R. Wright, and John Shelton Reed, *The Enduring Effects of Education* (Chicago: University of Chicago Press, 1975), 80-92; David G. Winter, Abigail J. Stewart, and David C. McClelland, "Grading the Effects of a Liberal Arts Education," *Psychology Today* 12 (September 1978): 69-72, 106.

16. Torney, Oppenheim, and Farnen, *Civic Education in Ten Countries*, 267, 282-89; Farnen and German, "Youth, Politics and Education," 170-75; Gunnell Gustafsson, "Environmental Influence on Political Learning," in *The Politics of Future Citizens*, ed. Richard G. Niemi (San Francisco: Jossey-Bass, 1974), 149-66; Conley and Osborne, "Political Education in Canadian Schools," 65-85; Goodlad, "A Study of Schooling," 468; George B. Levenson, "The School's Contribution to the Learning of Participatory Responsibility," in Massialas, ed., *Political Youth, Traditional Schools*, 123-36; M. Kent Jennings and Richard G. Niemi, *The Political Character of*

Adolescence: The Infleunce of Families and Schools (Princeton: Princeton University Press, 1974), 191-93; 201-6, 215-16; Byron G. Massialas: "The Inquiring Activist: Citizenship Objectives for the '70s," in Massialas, ed., *Political Youth, Traditional Schools*, 251-52, and "Some Propositions about the Role of the School in the Formation of Political Behavior and Political Attitudes of Students," *Comparative Education Review* 19 (February 1975): 171-72.

17. Marsh and Kaase, "Background of Political Action," 100-35; Almond and Verba, *The Civic Culture*, 379-87; Paul Burstein, "Social Structure and Individual Political Participation in Five Countries," *American Journal of Sociology* 77 (May 1972): 1087-1110; Sidney Verba, Norman H. Nie, and Jae-on Kim, *Participation and Political Equality: A Seven-Nation Comparison* (New York: Cambridge University Press, 1978), 67, 287; Lester W. Milbrath and M. L. Goel, *Political Participation*, 2d ed. (Chicago: Rand McNally, 1977), 98-101; Alan Marsh, *Protest and Political Consciousness* (Beverly Hills, Calif.: Sage Publications, 1977), 70-72, 125; Olsen and Baden, "Legitimacy of Social Protest Actions in the United States and Sweden," 184-88; Edward G. Grabb, "Class, Conformity and Political Powerlessness," *Canadian Review of Sociology and Anthropology* 18 (Augsut 1981): 362-69; Ronald D. Lambert and James E. Curtis, "Education, Economic Dissatisfaction, and Nonconfidence in Canadian Social Institutions," *Canadian Review of Sociology and Anthropology* 16 (February 1979): 47-59; W. Russell Neuman, "Differentiation and Integration: Two Dimensions of Political Thinking," *American Journal of Sociology* 86 (May 1981): 1236-68; Abramson, *Political Attitudes in America*, 177-83, 232-33; Jennings and Niemi, *Generations and Politics*, 239-54; Michele Micheletti, "Democracy and Political Power in Denmark, Norway and Sweden: A Review-Essay," *Western Political Quarterly* 37 (June 1984): 324-42.

18. David Glass, Peverill Squire, and Raymond Wolfinger, "Voter Turnout: An International Comparison," *Public Opinion* 6 (December 1983/January 1984): 49-55; G. Bingham Powell, Jr., *Contemporary Democracies: Participation, Stability, and Violence* (Cambridge, Mass.: Harvard University Press, 1982), 111-22; Ivor Crewe, "Electoral Participation," in *Democracy at the Polls*, ed. David Butler, Howard R. Penniman, and Austin Ranney (Washington, D.C.: American Enterprise Institute, 1981), 216-63; Verba, Nie, and Kim, *Participation and Political Equality*, 172-214, 286-309; Abramson, *Political Attitudes in America*, 5-8.

19. See James Davis, "Up and Down Opportunity's Ladder," *Public Opinion* 5 (June/July 1982): 11-15, 48-51; Russell W. Rumberger, "The Influence of Family Background on Education, Earnings, and Wealth," *Social Forces* 61 (March 1983): 755-73; Michael Hout, "Status, Autonomy, and Training in Occupational Mobility," *American Journal of Sociology* 89 (May 1984): 1379-1409; Christopher Jencks, et al., *Who Gets Ahead: The Determinants of Economic Success in America* (New York: Basic Books, 1979), 175, 223-24; Robert M. Hauser and David L. Featherman, *The Process of Stratifica-*

tion: Trends and Analyses (New York: Academic Press, 1977), 290; Peter M. Blau and Otis Dudley Duncan, *The American Occupational Structure* (New York: Wiley, 1967), 402-30; Monica Boyd, John Goyder, Frank E. Jones, Hugh A. McRoberts, Peter C. Pineo, and John Porter, "Status Attainment in Canada: Findings of the Canadian Mobility Study," *Canadian Review of Sociology and Anthropology* 18 (December 1981): 657-73; Monica Boyd, "Sex Differences in the Canadian Occupational Attainment Process," *Canadian Review of Sociology and Anthropology* 19 (February 1983): 1-28; Donald J. Treiman and Hermit Terrell, "The Process of Status Attainment in the United States and Great Britain," *American Journal of Sociology* 81 (November 1975): 563-83; Donald J. Treiman, "Toward Methods for a Quantitative Sociology: Reply to Burawoy," *American Journal of Sociology* 82 (March 1977): 1042-56, esp. 1045; John Papanicolaou and George Psacharopoulos, "Socioeconomic Background, Schooling and Monetary Rewards in the United Kingdom," *Economica* 46 (November 1979): 435-39; "Social Mobility," *New Society* 54 (2 October 1980): ii-iv; A. H. Halsey, "Towards Meritocracy? The Case of Britain," in *Power and Ideology in Education,* ed. Jerome Karabel and A. H. Halsey (New York: Oxford University Press, 1977), 173-82; Marvin E. Olsen, "Social Classes in Contemporary Sweden," *Sociological Quarterly* 15 (Summer 1974): 327; Seppo Pöntinen and Hannu Uusitalo, "Socioeconomic Background and Income," *Acta Sociologica* 18, no. 4 (1975): 322-29; Richard Scase, "Images of Inequality in Sweden and Britain," *Human Relations* 28 (April 1975); 264-66; Maurice Garnier and Lawrence E. Hazelrigg: "Father-to-Son Occupational Mobility in France: Evidence from the 1960's," *American Journal of Sociology* 80 (September 1974): 478-502, and "La Mobilité professionnelle en France comparée à celle d'autres pays," *Revue française de sociologie* 15 (July-September 1974): 377; Maurice Garnier and Michael Hout, "Inequality of Educational Opportunity in France and the United States," *Social Science Research* 5 (September 1976): 225-46.

20. John Angle, Steven R. Steiber, and David A. Wissmann, "Educational Indicators and Occupational Achievement," *Social Science Research* 9 (March 1980): 64. See also R. P. Dore, "Human Capital Theory, the Diveristy of Societies and the Problem of Quality in Education," *Higher Education* 5 (February 1976): 79-102; Randall Collins, *Conflict Sociology: Toward an Explanatory Science* (New York: Academic Press, 1975), 449-54; Lester C. Thurow, *Dangerous Currents: The State of Economics* (New York: Random House, 1983), 173-81, 196-200; OECD, *Selection and Certification in Education and Employment* (Paris, 1977).

21. France, Ministry of Economy and Finance, *Annuaire statistique de la France 1981,* vol. 86 (Paris: Institut national de la statistique et des études économiques, 1981), 107-10; Ehrmann, *Politics in France,* 80-95; Françoise Oeuvrard, "Démocratisation ou élimination différée?" *Actes de la recherche en sciences sociales,* no. 30 (November 1979): 87-97; Benoit Millot, "Social Differentiation and Higher Education: The French Case," *Comparative*

Education Review 25 (October 1981): 353-68; Jean-Jacques Paul, "Education and Employment: A Survey of French Research," *European Journal of Education* 16 (March 1981): 95-119; Emmanuelle Pautler, "The Links between Secondary and Higher Education in France," *European Journal of Education* 16 (June 1981): 185-95; Roger Duclaud-Williams, "Centralization and Incremental Change in France: The Case of the Haby Educational Reform," *British Journal of Political Science* 13 (January 1983): 71-91; Michael Hout and Maurice A. Garnier, "Curriculum Placement and Educational Stratification in France," *Sociology of Education* 52 (July 1979): 146-56; Michelle Patterson, "Governmental Policy and Equality in Higher Education: The Junior Collegization of the French University," *Social Problems* 24 (December 1976): 173-83; William R. Schonfeld, *Obedience and Revolt: French Behavior toward Authority* (Beverly Hills, Calif.: Sage Publications, 1976), 205-14; Michele Tournier, "Towards a Transformation of the French Educational System in the 1980s?" *Comparative Education* 16 (October 1980): 281-90; Guy Neave, "The Changing Balance of Power: Recent Developments in Provision for the 16-19 Years Age Range in Europe," *Comparative Education* 16 (June 1980): 96-98; Corrado de Francesco and Jean-Pierre Jarousse, "Under-utilisation and Market Value of University Degrees: Findings of a Survey in France and Italy," *European Journal of Education* 18 (March 1983): 65-79; Hilary Steedman, "The Reorganisation of Upper Secondary Education in Italy: The Political and Educational Context," *Compare* 9 (April 1979): 71-84; Corrado de Francesco, "Myths and Realities of Mass Secondary Schooling in Italy," *European Journal of Education* 15 (June 1980): 139-51; Richard L. Merritt and Robert L. Leonardi, "The Politics of Upper Secondary School Reform in Italy: Immobilism or Accommodation?" *Comparative Education Review* 25 (October 1981): 369-83.

22. Jürgen Baumert and Dietrich Goldschmidt, "Centralization and Decentralization as Determinants of Educational Policy in the Federal Republic of Germany (FRG)," *Social Science Information* 19 (December 1980): 1029-98; Diana Geddes, "Germany Dips a Toe in Comprehensives," *New Society* 51 (14 February 1980): 336-38; Lewis J. Edinger, *Politics in West Germany*, 2d ed. (Boston: Little, Brown, 1977), 52-54; W. Williamson, "Patterns of Educational Inequality in West Germany," *Comparative Education* 13 (March 1977), 29-44.

23. Colin Brock, "Problems of Articulation between Secondary and Higher Education in England and Wales," *European Journal of Education* 16 (June 1981): 153-73; Peter Godsen, "The Educational System of England and Wales since 1952," *British Journal of Educational Studies* 30 (February 1982): 108-21; Rick Rogers and Anna Coote, "Who Knows Where the Tech Is?" *New Statesman* 103 (30 April 1982): 10-12; Paul E. Peterson, "The Politics of Education in England and the United States," *Comparative Education Review* 17 (June 1973): 170-71; Diana Geddes, "What Will Happen to Grammar Schools?" *New Society* 49 (5 July 1979): 12-14; Michael Useem, *The Inner Circle* (New York: Oxford University Press, 1984), 67.

24. Samuel Bowles and Herbert Gintis, *Schooling in Capitalist America* (New York: Basic Books, 1976), 203-20; Caroline Hodges Persell, *Education and Inequality* (New York: Free Press, 1977); Canada, Minister of Supply and Services: *Canada Year Book 1980-81* (Ottawa: Statistics Canada, 1981), 209-28, and *Education in Canada: A Statistical Review for 1980-81* (Ottawa: Statistics Canada, 1982), 14-19; Lillemor Kim, "Widened Admission to Higher Education in Sweden (the 25/5 Scheme)," *European Journal of Education* 14 (June 1979): 181-92; Dietrich Goldschmidt, "Power and Decision Making in Higher Education," *Comparative Education Review* 22 (June 1978): 217; Rune Premfors, "Analysis in Politics: The Regionalization of Swedish Higher Education," *Comparative Education Review* 28 (February 1984): 85-104.

25. George Z. F. Bereday, "Social Stratification and Education in Industrial Countries," *Comparative Education Review* 21 (June/October 1977): 195-210; Torsten Husén, *Social Influences on Educational Attainment* (Paris: OECD, 1975), 73-157.

26. Anthony Heath, *Social Mobility* (Glasgow: Fontana Paperbacks, 1981), 208; Seymour Martin Lipset, "Social Mobility in Industrial Societies," *Public Opinion* 5 (June/July 1982): 41-44; Robert Erikson, John Goldthorpe, and Lucienne Portocarero, "Intergenerational Class Mobility in Three Western European Societies: England, France, and Sweden," *British Journal of Sociology* 30 (December 1979): 415-44.

27. Raymond Boudon and Janina Lagneau, "Inequality of Educational Opportunity in Western Europe," *Prospects* 10, no. 2 (1980): 181-88; Heidenheimer, Heclo, and Adams, *Comparative Public Policy*, 44-51; OECD, *Employment in the Public Sector* (Paris, 1982), 12, 23; "Big Government—How Big Is It?" *OECD Observer*, no. 121 (March 1983): 10.

28. Dean Jaros and Bradley C. Canon, "Transmitting Basic Political Values: The Role of the Educational System," *School Review* 77 (June 1969): 94-107; Petter Cuttance, "Do Schools Consistently Influence the Performance of Their Students?" *Educational Review* 32, no. 3 (1980): 267-80; Richard J. Murnane, "Interpreting the Evidence on School Effectiveness," *Teachers College Record* 83 (Fall 1981): 19-35.

29. Seymour Martin Lipset and William Schneider, *The Confidence Gap: Business, Labor, and Government in the Public Mind* (New York: Free Press, 1983), 403-6; Steven H. Chaffee, Marilyn Jackson-Beeck, Jean Durall, and Donna Wilson, "Mass Communication in Political Socialization," in *Handbook of Political Socialization*, ed. Stanley Allen Renshon (New York: Free Press, 1977), 223-58.

30. David A. Walker, *The IEA Six Subject Survey: An Empirical Study of Education in Twenty-One Countries* (New York: John Wiley, 1976), 200-26; Torney, Oppenheim, and Farnen, *Civic Education in Ten Countries*, 332-33; Jennings and Niemi, *Generations and Politics*, 242; James Murphy, "Class Inequality in Education: Two Justifications, One Evaluation, but No Hard

Evidence," *British Journal of Sociology* 32 (June 1981): 185; Henry M. Levin, "Educational Opportunity and Social Inequality in Western Europe," *Social Problems* 24 (December 1976): 148-72; Husén, *Social Influences on Educational Attainment*, 78-157.

31. "Education and Work: The Views of the Young," *OECD Observer*, no. 118 (September 1982): 12; Sara L. Silbiger, "Peers and Political Socialization," in Renshon, ed., *Handbook of Political Socialization*, 172-89.

32. Torney, Oppenheim, and Farnen, *Civic Education in Ten Countries*, 158.

Chapter 4

1. U.S. Congress, Senate, Subcommittee on Health and Scientific Research of the Committee on Human Resources, *National Health Insurance, 1978*, 95th Cong., 2d sess., 9 October 1978, 42. See also 24-26, 31-33, 37-40, 43-44.

2. See Rudolf Klein, "Performance, Evaluation and the NHS: A Case Study in Conceptual Perplexity and Organizational Complexity," *Public Administration* 60 (Winter 1982): 385-407.

3. Alwyn Smith, "Are We Any Healthier?" *New Society* 41 (8 September 1977): 485; *Perspective Canada II: A Compendium of Social Statistics 1977* (Ottawa: Statistics Canada, 1977), 88; World Bank, *World Development Report 1982* (New York: Oxford University Press, 1982), 111.

4. Quoted in Irving Leveson, "Some Policy Implications of the Relationship between Health Services and Health," *Inquiry* 16 (Spring 1979): 9; James Thurber, *Fables for Our Time and Famous Poems Illustrated* (New York: Harper, 1940), 22.

5. For analyses of the individual and environmental causes of illnesses, see the following: Ronald Labonté, "Good Health: Individual or Social," *Canadian Forum* 63 (April 1983): 10-13; James F. Blumstein and Michael Zubcoff, "Perspectives on Government Policy in the Health Sector," *Milbank Memorial Fund Quarterly/Health and Society* 51 (Summer 1973): 395-431, esp. 400; Vicente Navarro, "Social Class, Political Power and the State, and Their Implications in Medicine," *Social Science and Medicine* 10 (September-October 1976): 446-47; Aaron Wildavsky, "Richer Is Safer," *Public Interest*, no. 60 (Summer 1980): 23-39; Mick Carpenter, "Left Orthodoxy and the Politics of Health," *Capital and Class*, no. 11 (Summer 1980): 92-96; "What's in a Name? Workers Seek Truth about Workplace Chemicals," *Dollars and Sense*, no. 86 (April 1983): 6-7, 18; "Carcinogens at Large," *Dollars and Sense*, no. 80 (October 1982): 13-15.

6. Aaron Wildavsky, "Doing Better and Feeling Worse: The Political Pathology of Health Policy," *Daedalus* 106 (Winter 1977): 122-23.

7. K. Robert Keiser, "The New Regulation of Health and Safety," *Political Science Quarterly* 95 (Fall 1980): 490; Donald Gould, "The Springs of

Suffering," *New Statesman* 94 (28 October 1977): 574-77; Ruth Levitt, "Can the Health Service Be Cured? *New Statesman* 98 (19 October 1979): 582-85; Marvin M. Kristein, Charles B. Arnold, and Ernst L. Wynder, "Health Economics and Preventive Care," *Science* 195 (4 February 1977): 457-62.

8. Richard F. Tomasson, "The Mortality of Swedish and U.S. White Males: A Comparison of Experience, 1969-1971," *American Journal of Public Health* 66 (October 1976): 968-74; Helen M. Wallace and Hyman Goldstein, "The Status of Infant Mortality in Sweden and the United States," *Journal of Pediatrics* 87 (December 1975): 995-1000; P. Harker, "Child Health Services in Sweden," *Public Health* 94 (May 1980): 144-48; Alex Gerber, "Headaches Ahead for Healthy Swedes?" *American Medical News Impact*, 27 March 1978, 9-10; Victor W. Sidel and Ruth Sidel, *A Healthy State* (New York: Pantheon Books, 1977), 122; Don Hinrichsen, "Smoking Ourselves to Death," *Sweden Now* 15, no. 1 (1981): 32-35; Harold L. Wilensky, *The Welfare State and Equality* (Berkeley: University of California Press, 1975), 98-104.

9. *Canada Year Book 1980-81* (Ottawa: Statistics Canada, 1981), 123-24, 147-51, 165-86.

10. Anne Corbett, "France's Mark Two Welfare State," *New Society* 51 (3 January 1980): 13-15; *Social Security and National Health Insurance in France*, no. 80/69, *Health Insurance*, no. 80/70, *Family Allowance Benefits* (New York: French Embassy Press and Information Division, 1980).

11. Kurt Winter, "Health Services in the German Democratic Republic Compared to the Federal Republic of Germany," *Inquiry* 12 (June 1975 Supplement): 63-68; Tomasson, "The Mortality of Swedish and U.S. White Males," 970-71; *World Development Report 1982*, 111.

12. Milton I. Roemer, *Comparative National Policies on Health Care* (New York: Marcel Dekker, 1977), 153-56; Lu Ann Aday, Ronald Andersen, and Gretchen V. Fleming, *Health Care in the U.S.: Equitable for Whom?* (Beverly Hills, Calif.: Sage Publications, 1980), 118; *The Indian Health Program of the U.S. Public Health Service* (Washington, D.C.: U.S. Department of Health, Education, and Welfare, Public Health Service, Health Services and Mental Health Administration, 1969), 21; Steven L. Gortmaker: *Poverty, Race, and Infant Mortality in the United States* (Madison: University of Wisconsin Institute for Research on Poverty, Discussion Paper No. 404, 1977), and "Poverty and Infant Mortality in the United States," *American Sociological Review* 44 (April 1979): 280-97, esp. 295; *U/S: A Statistical Portrait of the American People*, ed. Andrew Hacker and Lorrie Millman (New York: Penguin Books, 1983), 68; National Center for Health Statistics, *Monthly Vital Statistics Report, Advance Report of Final Mortality Statistics, 1980* 32 (11 August 1983): 7-8; Mary Grace Kovar, "Mortality of Black Infants in the United States," *Phylon* 38 (December 1977): 374-75; C. Arden Miller and Elizabeth J. Coulter, "The World Economic Crisis and the Children: A United States Case Study," *World Development* 12 (March 1984): 353;

Harker, "Child Health Services in Sweden," 147; Barbara Preston, "Further Statistics of Inequality," *Sociological Review* 27 (May 1979): 343-50; Margaret Wynn and Arthur Wynn, "Some Developments in Child Health Care in Europe," *Royal Society of Health Journal* 99 (December 1979): 259-64; John R. Ashton, "Poverty and Health in Britain Today," *Public Health* 93 (March 1979): 89-94; Margaret Stacey, "Health and Class: People Who Are Affected by the Inverse Law of Care," *Health and Social Service Journal* 87 (3 June 1977): 898-902; "Infant Mortality and Class," *New Society* 63 (31 March 1983): 511.

13. Aaron Antonovsky and Judith Bernstein, "Social Class and Infant Mortality," *Social Science and Medicine* 11 (May 1977): 453-70; A. Leclerc, P. Aiach, A. Phillippe, M. Vennin, and D. Cebe, "Morbidité, mortalité et classe sociale: Revue bibliographique portant sur divers aspects de la pathologie, et discussion," *Revue d'épidémiologie et de santé publique* 27, no. 4 (1979): 331-58; France, Ministère de la Solidarité Nationale, Ministère de la Santé, *Santé sécurité sociale: statistiques et commentaires*, no. 3 (May-June 1982): 29; Alastair McIntosh Gray, "Inequalities in Health, The Black Report: A Summary and Comment," *International Journal of Health Services* 12, no. 3 (1982): 349-80; Joel W. Gregory and Victor Riche, "Inequality and Mortality: Demographic Hypotheses Regarding Advanced and Peripheral Capitalism," *International Journal of Health Services* 13, no. 1 (1983): 89-106; J. Rogers Hollingsworth, "Inequality in Levels of Health in England and Wales, 1891-1971," *Journal of Health and Social Behavior* 22 (September 1981): 268-83; Jon Stern, "Does Unemployment Really Kill?" *New Society* (10 June 1982): 421-22; Paul Starr, "The Politics of Therapeutic Nihilism," *Working Papers for a New Society* 4 (Summer 1976): 52-53; Julian Le Grand, "The Distribution of Public Expenditures: The Case of Health Care," *Economica* 45 (May 1978): 126-29; Ashton, "Poverty and Health in Britain Today," 92; Preston, "Further Statistics of Inequality," 343-50; Emanuel de Kadt, "Wrong Priorities in Health," *New Society* 36 (3 June 1976): 525; Jill Turner, "Black Mark for the Nation's Health," *New Society* 53 (4 September 1980): 454-55; Peter Townsend, *Poverty in the United Kingdom: A Survey of Household Resources and Standards of Living* (Berkeley: University of California Press, 1979), 710-11, 736-38; Pranlal Manga and Geoffery R. Weller, "The Failure of the Equity Objective in Health: A Comparative Analysis of Canada, Britain, and the United States," in *Comparative Social Research*, vol. 3, ed. Richard F. Tomasson (Greenwich, Conn.: JAI Press, 1980), 243; *Perspective Canada II*, 284; Gortmaker: *Poverty, Race, and Infant Mortality in the United States*, 47-54, and "Poverty and Infant Mortality in the United States," 280-95; *Monthly Vital Statistics Report*, 17 September 1980, p. 11; Kovar, "Mortality of Black Infants in the United States," 374-75; Joseph Eyer, "Does Unemployment Cause the Death Cycle Peak in Each Business Cycle: A Multifactor Model of Death Rate Change," *International Journal of Health Services* 7, no. 4 (1977): 630; *The Indian Health Program of the U.S. Public Health Service*, 21; Jerry L. Weaver, *National Health Policy and the Underserved: Ethnic Minorities,*

Women, and the Elderly (Saint Louis, Mo.: C. V. Mosby, 1976), 74-78; Aday, Andersen, and Fleming, *Health Care in the U.S.*, 118; Sidel and Sidel, *A Healthy State*, 17, 65-66; U.S. Congress, House of Representatives, Subcommittee on Health of the Committee on Ways and Means, *National Health Insurance Resource Book*, rev. ed., 30 August 1976, 76-81, 251-52, 257, 261-63; Anders Steen Lunde, "Health in the United States," *Annals of the American Academy of Political and Social Science* 453 (January 1981): 44-47.

14. J. Paul Leigh, "Direct and Indirect Effects of Education on Health," *Social Science and Medicine* 17, no. 4 (1983): 227-34; Antonovsky and Bernstein, "Social Class and Infant Mortality," 458-59; Ann Cartwright and Maureen O'Brien, "Social Class Variations in Health Care and in the Nature of General Practitioner Consultations," in *Sociological Review Monograph* 22, ed. Margaret Stacey (Keele, England: University of Keele, 1976), 77-98; Leveson, "Some Policy Implications of the Relationship between Health Services and Health," 17; Victor R. Fuchs, "The Economics of Health in a Post-Industrial Society," *Public Interest*, no. 56 (Summer 1979): 3-20.

15. Antonovsky and Bernstein, "Social Class and Infant Mortality," 458-59; Wildavsky, "Richer Is Safer," 23-39; Peter Draper, Gordon Best, and John Dennis, "Health and Wealth," *Royal Society of Health Journal* 97 (June 1977): 123; "The Unequal Ranks of Workers: Health Hazards," *New Society* 49 (9 August 1979): 302; Torkel Alfthan, "Level of Living Surveys in Sweden: Some Issues and Findings," *International Labour Review* 117 (September-October 1978): 602-4; Matt Witt and Steve Early, "The Worker as Safety Inspector," *Working Papers for a New Society* 7 (September-October 1980): 21-29; "Deregulating Workers' Health," *Dollars and Sense*, no. 70 (October 1981): 3-5; Richard P. Appelbaum, "Housing Supply and Regulation: A Study of the Rental Housing Market," *Journal of Applied Behavioral Science* 19 (February 1983): 1-18, esp. 15; Susan S. Fainstein and Norman I. Fainstein, "National Policy and Urban Development," *Social Problems* 26 (December 1978): 125-46; Steven Kelman, *Regulating America, Regulating Sweden: A Comparative Study of Occupational Safety and Health Policy* (Cambridge, Mass.: Massachusetts Institute of Technology Press, 1981), esp. 179, 221-37, 253; Vicente Navarro, "The Determinants of Health Policy, A Case Study: Regulating Safety and Health at the Workplace in Sweden," *Journal of Health Politics, Policy and Law* 9 (Spring 1984): 137-56; Arnold J. Heidenheimer, Hugh Heclo, and Carolyn Teich Adams, *Comparative Public Policy: The Politics of Social Choice in Europe and America*, 2d ed. (New York: St. Martin's Press, 1983), 88-121; Manga and Weller, "The Failure of the Equity Objective in Health," 229-67, esp. 251-60; Aday, Andersen, and Fleming, *Health Care in the U.S.*, 107-12; *National Health Insurance Resource Book*, 277; Turner, "Black Mark for Nation's Health," 454-55; Barbara Preston: "Statistics of Inequality," *Sociological Review* 22 (February 1974): 103-18, and "Further Statistics of Inequality," 343-50.

16. Lawrence D. Brown, "The Scope and Limits of Equality as a Normative Guide to Federal Health Quality," *Public Policy* 26 (Fall 1978): 491-96; Aday, Andersen, and Fleming, *Health Care in the U.S.*, 25-41.

17. John Fry, "Primary Care Problems in London," *Journal of Public Health Policy* 3 (March 1982): 101-3; Brian Abel-Smith, "Towards a Healthier Population," *New Society* 58 (15 October 1981): 95-97; Alan Maynard and Anne Ludbrook, "Inequality, the National Health Service and Health Policy," *Journal of Public Policy* 2 (May 1982): 97-116; Hollingsworth, "Inequality in Levels of Health in England and Wales," 268-74; Michael W. Spicer, "The Economics of Bureaucracy and the British National Health Service," *Milbank Memorial Fund Quarterly/Health and Society* 60 (Fall 1982): 665-66; Julian Le Grand, *The Strategy of Equality: Redistribution and the Social Services* (London: George Allen and Unwin, 1982), 23-53; Cartwright and O'Brien, "Social Class Variations in Health Care," 77-98; Ashton, "Poverty and Health in Britain Today," 89-94; Stacey, "Health and Class," 898-902; Levitt, "Can the Health Service Be Cured?" 582-85.

18. Timothy Smeeding and Marilyn Moon, "Valuing Government Expenditures: The Case of Medical Care Transfers and Poverty," *Review of Income and Wealth* 26 (September 1980): 305-24; Mary A. Fruen and James R. Cantwell, "Geographic Distribution of Physicians: Past Trends and Future Influences," *Inquiry* 19 (Spring 1982): 44-50; E. Richard Brown, "Public Hospitals on the Brink: Their Problems and Their Options," *Journal of Health Politics, Policy and Law* 7 (Winter 1983): 927-44; Aday, Andersen, and Fleming, *Health Care in the U.S.*, 47-92, 231-48; Lu Ann Aday, "The Impact of Health Policy on Access to Medical Care," *Milbank Memorial Fund Quarterly/Health and Society* 54 (Spring 1976): 215-33; Peter Singer, "Blood, Markets, and Medical Care," *Working Papers for a New Society* 4 (Summer 1976): 56-64; Starr, "The Politics of Therapeutic Nihilism," 52-55; Theodore R. Marmor, "The Politics of National Health Insurance: Analysis and Prescription," *Policy Analysis* 3 (Winter 1977): 30; Andrew B. Dunham and Theodore R. Marmor, "Federal Policy and Health: Recent Trends and Differing Perspectives," in *Nationalizing Government: Public Policies in America*, ed. Theodore J. Lowi and Alan Stone (Beverly Hills, Calif.: Sage Publications, 1978), 269-71; *National Health Insurance Resource Book*, 271, 276; Louise M. Okada and Thomas T. H. Wan, "Impact of Community Health Centers and Medicaid on the Use of Health Services," *Public Health Reports* 95 (November-December 1980): 520-34; Saad Z. Nagi and Judith Marsh, "Disability, Health Status, and Utilization of Health Services," *International Journal of Health Services* 10, no. 4 (1980): 657-76; Dorothy P. Rice and Douglas Wilson, "The American Medical Economy: Problems and Perspectives," *Journal of Health Politics, Policy and Law* 1 (Summer 1976): 160; Karen Davis and Diane Rowland, "Uninsured and Underserved: Inequities in Health Care in the United States," *Milbank Memorial Fund Quarterly/Health and Society* 61 (Spring 1983): 156-57.

19. Alan Maynard, "The Inefficiency and Inequalities of the Health Care Systems of Western Europe," *Social Policy and Administration* 15 (Summer 1981): 145-63; Winter, "Health Services in the German Democratic Republic," 63-68; Gordon K. MacLeod, "National Health Insurance in the Federal Republic of Germany and Its Implications for U.S. Consumers," *Public Health Reports* 91 (July-August 1976): 345; T. E. Chester, "Health Care in West Germany and France: A Comparative Analysis," *Three Banks Review*, no. 112 (December 1976): 77; *Santé sécurité sociale*, May-June 1982, 38; Jean de Kervasdoué, "Les Politiques de santé sont-elles adaptées à la pratique de la médecine?" *Sociologie du travail* 21 (July-September 1979): 268; Victor G. Rodwin: "On the Separation of Health Planning and Provider Reimbursement: The U.S. and France," *Inquiry* 18 (Summer 1981): 144-48, and "The Marriage of National Health Insurance and *La Médecine Libérale* in France: A Costly Union," *Milbank Memorial Fund Quarterly/Health and Society* 59 (Winter 1981): 16-43; Hjordis M. Foy, "Medical Practice in Sweden: Recent Developments," *Journal of the American Medical Women's Association* 32 (May 1977): 184; Nils Elvander, "Barriers and Opportunities for Primary Care Delivery Systems: A Case Study from the County Council of Uppsala, Sweden," *Scandinavian Political Studies* 4, no. 4 (1981): 302, 311; Finn Diderichsen, "Ideologies in the Swedish Health Sector Today: The Crisis of the Social Democracy," *International Journal of Health Services* 12, no. 2 (1982): 191-200; Geoffrey R. Weller, "The Determinants of Canadian Health Policy," *Journal of Health Politics, Policy and Law* 5 (Fall 1980): 414; Thomas T. H. Wan and Joel H. Broida, "Factors Affecting Variations in Health Services Utilization in Quebec, Canada," *Socio-Economic Planning Sciences* 15, no. 5 (1981): 231-42; Jack Siemiatycki and Lesley Richardson, "Statut socioéconomique et utilisation des services de santé à Montréal," *L'Actualité économique* 56 (April-June 1980): 194-210; Jack Siemiatycki, Lesley Richardson, and Ivan Barry Pless, "Equality in Medical Care under National Health Insurance in Montreal," *New England Journal of Medicine* 303 (3 July 1980): 10-15; Ed Finn, *Medicare on the Critical List* (Ottawa: Canadian Centre for Policy Alternatives, 1983); Milton I. Roemer and Ruth Roemer, *Health Manpower Policies under Five National Health Care Systems*, Department of Health, Education, and Welfare Publication No. (HRA) 78-43 (Washington, D.C.: U.S. Department of Health, Education, and Welfare, Public Health Service, Health Resources Administration, Division of Medicine, 1978), 7.

20. Alan Maynard and Anne Ludbrook, "What's Wrong with the National Health Service?" *Lloyds Bank Review*, no. 138 (October 1980): 28-33; K. C. Gaspari, "The Use and Misuse of Cost-Effectiveness Analysis," *Social Science and Medicine* 17, no. 15 (1983): 1043-46.

21. *Public Expenditure on Health: OECD Studies in Resource Allocation*, no. 4 (Paris, 1977); Joseph G. Simanis and John R. Coleman, "Health Care Expenditures in Nine Industrialized Countries, 1960-76," *Social Security Bulletin* 43 (January 1980): 5; "Public Health Expenditures: Towards a Better

Utilisation of Resources," *OECD Observer*, no. 86 (May 1977): 10-11, 14; Ewe E. Reinhardt, "Can the United States Learn from Foreign Medical Insurance Systems?" *Hospital Progress* 59 (November 1978); 65; Leveson, "Some Policy Implications of the Relationship between Health Services and Health," 12; Brian Abel-Smith, "The Cost of Health Services," *New Society* 49 (12 July 1979): 74-76.

22. Lee Soderstrom, "The Canadian Experience," in *Regulating Health Care: The Struggle for Control*, vol. 33 of *Proceedings of the Academy of Political Science*, ed. Arthur Levin (New York: Academy of Political Science, 1980), 224-38; R. J. Van Loon, "From Shared Cost to Block Funding and Beyond: The Politics of Health Insurance in Canada," *Journal of Health Politics, Policy and Law* 2 (Winter 1978): 473; Eugene Vayda, Robert G. Evans, and William R. Mindell, "Universal Health Insurance in Canada: History, Problems, Trends," *Journal of Community Health* 4 (Spring 1979): 224; Stuart M. MacLeod and Donald Coxe, "Canadian Medicare: Prescription for U.S.A.?" *National Review* 31 (13 April 1979): 469-71; C. S. Redden, "The Impact of Medicare—How It Affects Physicians and Consumers," *Medical Group Management* 24 (November/December 1977): 18-20; Charlotte Gray, "Canada/Medicare Crisis," *New Society* 48 (3 May 1979): 269; Milan Korcok, "Why They're Touting Canada's System in the U.S.," *American Medical News Impact*, 23 January 1978, 2; M. I. Roemer and R. Roemer, *Health Manpower Policies under Five National Health Care Systems*, 48-49, 52; C. Barber Mueller, "Some Effects of Health Insurance in Canada—From Private Enterprise toward Public Accountability," *New England Journal of Medicine* 298 (9 March 1978): 537; Peter J. Banks, "C. M. A. President on Medical Economics," *Ontario Medical Review* 41 (June 1974): 339-46; Eugene Vayda, "Aspects of Medical Manpower under National Health Insurance in Canada," *Journal of Public Health Policy* 4 (December 1983): 504-13; Janet Ableson, Peter Paddon, and Claude Strohmenger, *Perspectives on Health* (Ottawa: Statistics Canada, 1983), 110; "1983: The Year in Review," *Canadian Medical Association Journal* 130 (1 January 1984): 62-64; Robert M. Gibson, Daniel R. Waldo, and Katharine R. Levit, "National Health Expenditures, 1982," *Health Care Financing Review* 5 (Fall 1983): 3-4; Theodore R. Marmor, *Political Analysis and American Medical Care: Essays* (New York: Cambridge University Press, 1983), 179.

23. Robert G. Evans, "Health Care in Canada: Patterns of Funding and Regulation," *Journal of Health Politics, Policy and Law* 8 (Spring 1983): 1-43; Sidney S. Lee, "Health Policy, A Social Contract: A Comparison of the United States and Canada," *Journal of Public Health Policy* 3 (September 1982): 293-301; C. D. Naylor, "In Defence of Medicare," *Canadian Forum* 62 (April 1982): 12-16; Errol Black, "Dealing with the Doctors: The Canadian Experience," *Monthly Review* 33 (September 1981): 27-35; "Medicare Suffers Another Setback," *Maclean's* 96 (11 April 1983): 50-51; Uwe E. Reinhardt, "Health Insurance and Cost-Containment Policies: The Experience Abroad," *American Economic Review* 70 (May 1980): 153; Paul Starr

and Gosta Esping-Andersen, "Passive Intervention," *Working Papers for a New Society* 7 (July-August 1979): 21-24; Peter Williamson, "How Much Canadian Doctors Earn, Spend, and Save," *Medical Economics* 56 (20 August 1979), 133; *National Health Insurance Resource Book*, 48-53.

24. Theodore Allison, "Two Separate Programs Are Involved in Canada's Health Insurance Plan," *Federation of American Hospitals Review* 11 (August 1978): 18; Reinhardt, "Health Insurance and Cost-Containment Policies," 154; Vayda, Evans, and Mindell, "Universal Health Insurance in Canada," 220-26; Soderstrom, "The Canadian Experience," 225-38; Judith Feder and Bruce Spitz, "The Politics of Hospital Payment," *Journal of Health Politics, Policy and Law* 4 (Fall 1979): 453-54; "The Upheaval in Health Care," *Business Week*, no. 2800 (25 July 1983): 44-56; Elliott A. Krause, *Power and Illness: The Political Sociology of Health and Medical Care* (New York: Elsevier, 1977), 68-87; James F. Blumstein and Michael Zubkoff, "Public Choice in Health: Problems, Politics and Perspectives on Formulating National Health Policy," *Journal of Health Politics, Policy and Law* 4 (Fall 1979): 396-97; Martin Feldstein, "The High Cost of Hospitals—and What To Do about It," *Public Interest*, no. 48 (Summer 1977): 40-54; Dunham and Marmor, "Federal Policy and Health," 282-84; Starr and Esping-Andersen, "Passive Intervention," 22-24; Rice and Wilson, "The American Medical Economy," 153-55; Milan Korcok, "The Ontario Hospital Experiment: American Managers March In," *Canadian Medical Association Journal* 128 (15 March 1983): 699.

25. Thomas K. Fulda and Paul F. Dickens III, "Controlling the Cost of Drugs: The Canadian Experience," *Health Care Financing Review* 1 (Fall 1979): 55-64; MacLeod and Coxe, "Canadian Medicare," 470; Milton I. Roemer and John E. Roemer, "The Social Consequences of Free Trade in Health Care: A Public Health Response to Orthodox Economics," *International Journal of Health Services* 12, no. 1 (1982): 121; A. Peter Thompson, "Current Cost Profitability of British and American Industry," *Financial Analysts Journal* 39 (March-April 1983): 78; United States Council of Economic Advisers, *Economic Report of the President, 1979*, p. 281; *1980*, p. 302; *1981*, p. 320; *1982*, p. 332; *1983*, p. 262.

26. Evans, "Health Care in Canada," 3-5; K. C. Charron, "Health Insurance: The Canadian Experience," *AFL-CIO American Federationist* 85 (April 1978): 11-16; Reinhardt, "Can the United States Learn from Foreign Medical Insurance Systems?" 65-66; Soderstrom, "The Canadian Experience," 230; Gordon H. Hatcher, "Canadian Approaches to Health Policy Decisions—National Health Insurance," *American Journal of Public Health* 68 (September 1978): 883; Max Horlick, "Administrative Costs for Social Security Programs in Selected Countries," *Social Security Bulletin* 39 (June 1976): 31; OECD, *Public Expenditures on Health*, 23.

27. David Nowlan, "Medical Migration: Now a European Doctor Can Practise under Nine Flags," *Canadian Medical Association Journal* 116 (8 January

1977): 103-4; Joseph P. Newhouse, "Medical-Care Expenditure: A Cross-National Survey," *Journal of Human Resources* 12 (Winter 1977): 121; Pamela M. McCurdy and David K. McCurdy, "The British Experience: Thirty Years of National Health Service," *Oklahoma State Medical Association Journal* 70 (November 1977): 500-502; Joseph G. Simanis, "The British National Health Service in International Perspective," *Current History* 73 (July/August 1977): 27-29; Linda L. Hughey, "So You Like Social Security? You Will Love National Health Insurance!" *Perspectives in Biology and Medicine* 22 (Summer 1979): 590-92; Rudolf Klein: "Ideology, Class and the National Health Service," *Journal of Health Politics, Policy and Law* 4 (Fall 1979): 477-83, and "International Perspectives on the NHS," *British Medical Journal*, no. 6100 (3 December 1977): 1492-93; A. Krosnick, "British National Health Service in 1977—Part III," *Journal of the Medical Society of New Jersey* 74 (November 1977): 992; Steven Jones and David Banta, "The 1974 Reorganization of the British National Health Service: An Analysis," *Journal of Community Health* 1 (Winter 1975): 93; Spicer, "The Economics of Bureaucracy and the British National Health Service," 657-72; Uwe E. Reinhardt, "Health Insurance and Health Policy in the Federal Republic of Germany," *Health Care Financing Review* 3 (December 1981): 1-14; Chester, "Health Care in West Germany and France," 77, 83; Deborah A. Stone: "Health Care Cost Containment in West Germany," *Journal of Health Politics, Policy and Law* 4 (Summer 1979): 182-97, and *The Limits of Professional Power: National Health Care in the Federal Republic of Germany* (Chicago: University of Chicago Press, 1980), 75-181; Christa Altenstetter, "Hospital Planning in France and the Federal Republic of Germany," *Journal of Health Politics, Policy and Law* 5 (Summer 1980): 326; Hans-Ulrich Deppe, "Some Remarks on the Economic and Political Development of Health Care in the Federal Republic of Germany," *International Journal of Health Services* 7, no. 3 (1977): 356; J.-Matthias Graf Schulenburg, "Report from Germany: Current Conditions and Controversies in the Health Care System," *Journal of Health Politics, Policy and Law* 8 (Summer 1983): 320-51; William A. Glaser, "Lessons from Germany: Some Reflections Occasioned by Schulenburg's 'Report,'" *Journal of Health Politics, Policy and Law* 8 (Summer 1983): 360; John J. Carroll, "National Health Systems in Eight Countries," Summary of Information on Pharmaceuticals from *National Health Systems in Eight Countries* by Joseph G. Simanis, *Journal of the American Pharmaceutical Association* 15 (December 1975): 699; Abel-Smith, "The Cost of Health Services," 75; OECD, *Public Expenditure on Health*, 24.

28. Simone Sandier, "Les Soins médicaux en France et aux U.S.A.," *Consommation—revue de socio-économie*, no. 1 (January-March 1981): 3-36; Victor G. Rodwin: *The Health Planning Predicament: France, Quebec, England, and the United States* (Berkeley: University of California Press, 1984), 72-80, 110-12; "On the Separation of Health Planning and Provider Reimbursement," 139-50; and "The Marriage of National Health Insurance and *La Médecine Libérale* in France," 16-43; J. Gourault, "Relations between

the Free Medical Profession and the Social Security System in France," *International Social Security Review* 30, no. 2 (1977): 156-69; Chester, "Health Care in West Germany and France," 74, 79; *Social Security and National Health Insurance in France*: no. 80/67, 1-3, no. 80/68, 3; Richard M. Hessler and Andrew C. Twaddle, "Sweden's Crisis in Medical Care: Political and Legal Changes," *Journal of Health Politics, Policy and Law* 7 (Summer 1982): 440-59; Ingemar Ståhl, "Can Equality and Efficiency Be Combined? The Experience of the Planned Swedish Health Care System," in *A New Approach to the Economics of Health Care*, ed. Mancur Olson (Washington, D.C.: American Enterprise Institute, 1981), 172-95; Ragnar Berfenstam and Ray H. Elling, "Regional Planning in Sweden: A Social and Medical Problem," *Scandinavian Review* 63 (September 1975): 47-49; Gerber, "Headaches Ahead for the Healthy Swedes?" 11; Bo Hjern, "What about Socialized Medicine in Sweden?" *Archives of Surgery* 111 (September 1976): 941-44; Nowlan, "Medical Migration," 104; Christa Altenstetter and James Warner Björkman, "Planning and Implementation: A Comparative Perspective on Health Policy," *International Political Science Review* 2, no. 1 (1981): 35-36; Theodore R. Marmor and Amy Bridges, "American Health Planning and the Lessons of Comparative Policy Analysis," *Journal of Health Politics, Policy and Law* 5 (Fall 1980): 424-26; Reinhardt, "Health Insurance and Cost-Containment Policies," 154; Carroll, "National Health Systems in Eight Countries," 699; U.S. Department of Health, Education, and Welfare, Social Security Administration, Office of Research and Statistics, *National Health Systems in Eight Countries*, by Joseph G. Simanis (Washington, D.C.: Government Printing Office, 1975), 48-55; OECD, *Public Expenditure on Health*, 22-24.

29. J. Rogers Hollingsworth, "Commentary," in Olson, ed., *A New Approach to the Economics of Health Care*, 196-201; Altenstetter and Björkman, "Planning and Implementation," 23; Stone, *The Limits of Professional Power*, 149-51, 179; Paivi Tripp, "A Comparative Analysis of Health Care Costs in Three Selected Countries: The United States, the United Kingdom, and Australia," *Social Science and Medicine* 15C (March 1981): 19-30.

30. Elizabeth Hann Hastings and Philip K. Hastings, eds.: *Index to International Public Opinion* (Westport, Conn.: Greenwood Press, 1983-84), vol. 4, *1981-1982*, 179, and vol. 5, *1982-1983*, 182, 196; *World Opinion Update* 6 (January/February 1982): 6; Marc Bonnel, "Relationships and Medical Care in France," *Asian Medical Journal* 19 (March 1976): 165; Rudolf Klein, "Public Opinion and the National Health Service," *British Medical Journal*, no. 6173 (12 May 1979): 1296; Timothy B. Norbeck, "Observations on the Canadian Health Care System," *Connecticut Medicine* 43 (March 1979): 162; Korcok, "Why They're Touting Canada's System in the U.S.," 1; Aday, Andersen, and Fleming, *Health Care in the U.S.*, 148; *Public Opinion* 2 (January/February 1979): 24; *Public Opinion* 2 (October/November 1979): 32; Richard M. Coughlin, *Ideology, Public Opinion, and Welfare Policy: Attitudes toward Taxes and Spending in Industrialized Societies* (Berkeley:

Institute of International Studies, University of California, 1980), 74-94; Allan Parachini, "Louis Harris Survey: Doctors Differ on Need for Health Care Change," *Los Angeles Times*, 10 June 1984, part 7, p. 23; Barbara G. Farah, Samuel H. Barnes, and Felix Heunks, "Political Dissatisfaction," in *Political Action: Mass Participation in Five Western Democracies*, ed. Samuel H. Barnes and Max Kaase (Beverly Hills, Calif.: Sage Publications, 1979), 412-19.

31. Hastings and Hastings, eds.: *Index to International Public Opinion*, vol. 2, *1979-1980*, 72, 294; vol. 3, *1980-1981*, 144-47; vol. 4, *1981-1982*, 150, 167, 168; vol. 5, *1982-1983*, 39, 183, 188; *Current Opinion* 5 (February 1977): 19, 22; *Public Opinion* 1 (September/October 1978): 25, 35; *Public Opinion* 3 (December 1979/January 1980): 21; *Public Opinion* 3 (October/November 1980): 22; *World Opinion Update* 3 (January 1979): 20; *World Opinion Update* 4 (May/June 1980): 61; *World Opinion Update* 4 (November/December 1980): 150; *World Opinion Update* 5 (July/August 1981): 109; "Bureaucracy Bad: Welfare Good," *New Society* 54 (4 December 1980): 464-65; Stone, *The Limits of Professional Power*, 89; Norbeck, "Observations on the Canadian Health Care System," 162; *World Opinion Update* 2 (July 1978): 105; Klein, "Public Opinion and the National Health Service," 1296-97; Brian Abel-Smith, "Merrison's Medicine for the Health Service," *New Society* 49 (26 July 1979): 191-92; A. Krosnik, "A View of the British National Health Service in 1977," *Journal of the Medical Society of New Jersey* 74 (September 1977): 787; Aday, Andersen, and Fleming, *Health Care in the U.S.*, 62-63, 71, 91-97; Ronald M. Andersen, Gretchen V. Fleming, and Timothy F. Champney, "Exploring a Paradox: Belief in a Crisis and General Satisfaction with Medical Care," *Milbank Memorial Fund Quarterly/Health and Society* 60 (Spring 1982): 329-54; Vicente Navarro, "Where Is the Popular Mandate? A Reply to Conventional Wisdom," *International Journal of Health Services* 13, no. 1 (1983): 169-74; David M. Alpern, "Polarizing the Nation?" *Newsweek* 99 (8 February 1982): 34; Dorsey Woodson, "Socialized Medicine in Europe: Is the Idyll Over?" *Medical World News* 17 (17 May 1976): 51-71; C. E. B. Frost, "How Permanent Are NHS Waiting Lists?" *Social Science and Medicine* 14C (March 1980): 4.

32. Couglin, *Ideology, Public Opinion, and Welfare Policy*, 130-46; Aday, Andersen, and Fleming, *Health Care in the U.S.*, 150-53; Weaver, *National Health Policy and the Underserved*, 122-26; Warren E. Miller, Arthur M. Miller, and Edward J. Schneider, *American National Election Studies Data Sourcebook, 1952-1978* (Cambridge, Mass.: Harvard University Press, 1980), 171, 185-86; Steven R. Steiber and Leonard A. Ferber, "Support for National Health Insurance: Intercohort Differentials," *Public Opinion Quarterly* 45 (Summer 1981): 179-98.

Chapter 5

1. See Richard M. Hessler and Andrew C. Twaddle, "Sweden's Crisis in Medical Care: Political and Legal Changes," *Journal of Health Politics, Policy and Law* 7 (Summer 1982): 440-59; Nils Elvander, "Barriers and Opportunities for Primary Care Delivery Systems: A Case Study from the County Council of Uppsala, Sweden," *Scandinavian Political Studies* 4, no. 4 (1981): 295-319; Robert J. Maxwell, *Health and Wealth* (Lexington, Mass.: Lexington Books, 1981), 60-61; Sixten Marklund, "Sweden: Setting Up the Comprehensive School," *Prospects* 11, no. 2 (1981): 161-79; *UNESCO Statistical Yearbook 1975* (Paris, 1976), 149; World Bank, *World Development Report 1983* (New York: Oxford University Press, 1983), 197; Harold J. Noah and Joel D. Sherman, *Educational Financing and Policy Goals for Primary Schools: General Report* (Paris: OECD, Centre for Educational Research and Innovation, 1979), 34; Royston Greenwood, "Relations between Central and Local Government in Sweden: The Control of Local Government Expenditure," *Public Administration* 57 (Winter 1979): 457-70; Thomas J. Anton, *Administered Politics: Elite Political Culture in Sweden* (The Hague; Martinus Nijhoff, 1980), 80-100; OECD, *Revenue Statistics of OECD Member Countries, 1965-1982* (Paris, 1983), 164; "Big Government—How Big Is It?" *OECD Observer*, no. 121 (March 1983): 10; OECD, *Employment in the Public Sector* (Paris, 1982), 12, 79; Rune Premfors, "Analysis in Politics: The Regionalization of Swedish Higher Education," *Comparative Education Review* 28 (February 1984): 85-104.

2. David H. McKay, "Fiscal Federalism, Professionalism and the Transformation of American State Government," *Public Administration* 60 (Spring 1982): 10-22; Harrell R. Rodgers, Jr., *The Cost of Human Neglect: America's Welfare Failure* (Armonk, N.Y.: M. E. Sharpe, 1982), 61; Morris Beck, *Government Spending: Trends and Issues* (New York: Praeger, 1981), 88; Charles F. Andrain, *Politics and Economic Policy in Western Democracies* (North Scituate, Mass.: Duxbury Press, 1980), 22-27; John T. Tucker, "Government Employment: An Era of Slow Growth," *Monthly Labor Review* 104 (October 1981): 19-25; OECD: *Employment in the Public Sector*, 79, and "Big Government—How Big Is It?" 6-11; Leila Pathirane and Derek W. Blades, "Defining and Measuring the Public Sector: Some International Comparisons," *Review of Income and Wealth* 28 (September 1982): 261-89; Ann Kallman Bixby, "Social Welfare Expenditures, Fiscal Year 1980," *Social Security Bulletin* 46 (August 1983): 15; Stanley Wohl, *The Medical Industrial Complex* (New York: Harmony Books, 1984): Paul Starr: *The Social Transformation of American Medicine* (New York: Basic Books, 1982), 420-49, and "The Laissez-Faire Elixir," *New Republic* 188 (18 April 1983): 19-23; Division of Health Interview Statistics, "Health Care Coverage under Private Health Insurance, Medicare, Medicaid, and Military or Veterans Administration Health Benefits: United States, 1978," National Center for Health Statistics *Advance Data*, no. 71 (29 June 1981): 1-8; Karen Davis and Diane Rowland, "Uninsured and Underserved: Inequities

in Health Care in the United States," *Milbank Memorial Fund Quarterly/ Health and Society* 61 (Spring 1983): 149-76; "In Poor Health: Crisis in Public Hospitals," *Dollars and Sense*, no. 81 (November 1982): 16-18; Curtis R. Bergstrand, "Big Profit in Private Hospitals," *Social Policy* 13 (Fall 1982): 49-54; E. Richard Brown, "Public Hospitals on the Brink: Their Problems and Their Options," *Journal of Health Politics, Policy and Law* 7 (Winter 1983): 927-44; William Shonick and Ruth Roemer, "Private Management of Public Hospitals: The California Experience," *Journal of Public Health Policy* 3 (June 1982): 182-204; Gretchen Engquist-Seidenberg, "The States' Role in Health Care Cost Containment," *Policy Studies Review* 1 (November 1981): 275-87; Mark S. Freeland and Carol Ellen Schendler: "National Health Expenditure Growth in the 1980's: An Aging Population, New Technologies, and Increasing Competition," *Health Care Financing Review* 4 (March 1983): 15, and "Health Spending in the 1980's: Integration of Clinical Practice Patterns with Management," *Health Care Financing Review* 5 (Spring 1984): 7; Robert Gibson, Daniel R. Waldo, and Katharine R. Levit, "National Health Expenditures, 1982," *Health Care Financing Review* 5 (Fall 1983): 3-5; Maxwell, *Health and Wealth*, 60-61; Russell L. Hanson, "Medicaid and the Politics of Redistribution," *American Journal of Political Science* 28 (May 1984): 313-39; Andrew B. Dunham and Theodore R. Marmor, "Federal Policy and Health: Recent Trends and Differing Perspectives," in *Nationalizing Government: Public Policies in America*, ed. Theodore J. Lowi and Alan Stone (Beverly Hills, Calif.: Sage Publications, 1978), 263-94; Elliott A. Krause, *Power and Illness: The Political Sociology of Health and Medical Care* (New York: Elsevier, 1977), 132-46; Sara S. McLanahan, "Organizational Issues in U. S. Health Policy Implementation: Participation, Discretion, and Accountability," *Journal of Applied Behavioral Science* 16 (July-August-September 1980): 354-69; W. Vance Grant and Leo J. Eiden, eds., *Digest of Education Statistics, 1981* (Washington, D.C.: National Center for Education Statistics, Government Printing Office, 1981), 8, 21; Michael W. Kirst: "United States," in *Educational Financing and Policy Goals for Primary Schools: Country Reports*, vol. 2 (Paris: OECD, Centre for Educational Research and Innovation, 1979), 55-104, and "The States' Role in Education Policy Innovation," *Policy Studies Review* 1 (November 1981): 298-308; Joel D. Sherman, "Changing Patterns of School Finance," *Proceedings of the Academy of Political Science* 33, no. 2 (1978): 69-76; William Lowe Boyd, "The Changing Politics of Curriculum Policy-Making for American Schools," *Review of Educational Research* 48 (Fall 1978): 577-628; Leonard M. Cantor, "The Growing Role of the States in American Education," *Comparative Education* 16 (March 1980): 25-31.

3. Colin Campbell, "Political Leadership in Canada: Pierre Elliott Trudeau and the Ottawa Model," in *Presidents and Prime Ministers*, ed. Richard Rose and Ezra N. Suleiman (Washington, D.C.: American Enterprise Institute, 1980), 50-93; J. Garfield Allen, "The Flaw in Canadian Federalism," *Round Table* 70 (April 1980): 172-76; Aidan R. Vining, "Provincial Ownership of

Government Enterprise in Canada," *Annals of Public and Co-operative Economy* 54 (January-March 1983): 35-55; Dan Butler and Bruce D. Macnaughton, "Public Sector Growth in Canada: Issues, Explanations and Implications," in *Canadian Politics in the 1980s*, ed. Michael S. Whittington and Glen Williams (Toronto: Methuen, 1981), 84-107; John J. Bergen: "The Private School Alternative," *Canadian Administrator* 20 (February 1981): 1-4, and "The Private School Movement in Canada," *Education Canada* 21 (Summer 1981): 5-8; Milton E. March, "Control over Educational Decisions," *Canadian Administrator* 21 (December 1981): 1-5; Stephen B. Lawton, "Political Values in Educational Finance in Canada and the United States," *Journal of Education Finance* 5 (Summer 1979): 1-18; *Advance Statistics of Education, 1980-81* (Ottawa: Statistics Canada, Education, Science and Culture Division, 1980), 12, 18-27; OECD, *Reviews of National Policies for Education: Canada* (Paris, 1976), 23-24, 66-70, 151-55, 203-21; E. Brock Rideout, Lawrence M. Bezeau, and David Wright, "Canada (Province of Ontario)," in *Educational Financing and Policy Goals for Primary Schools: Country Reports*, vol. 1 (Paris: OECD, 1979), 60-84; Margaret Gayfer, *An Overview of Canadian Education* (Toronto: Canadian Education Association, 1974), 11-19; Dennis J. Dibski, "A Federal-Provincial Partnership Is Needed in Canadian Education," *Education Canada* 21 (Spring 1981): 36-41; Robert G. Evans, "Health Care in Canada: Patterns of Funding and Regulation," *Journal of Health Politics, Policy and Law* 8 (Spring 1983): 1-43; Maxwell, *Health and Wealth*, 61; Eugene Vayda, Robert G. Evans, and William R. Mindell, "Universal Health Insurance in Canada: History, Problems, Trends," *Journal of Community Health* 4 (Spring 1979): 217-31; Eugene Vayda and Raisa B. Deber, "The Canadian Health Care System: An Overview," *Social Science and Medicine* 18, no. 3 (1984): 191-96; United States House of Representatives, Subcommittee on Health of the Committee on Ways and Means, *National Health Insurance Resource Book*, rev. ed. (Washington, D.C.: Government Printing Office, 1976), 295-350.

4. David P. Conradt, *The German Polity*, 2d ed. (New York: Longman, 1982), 148-51, 206-25; OECD: "Big Government—How Big Is It?" 6-10, and *Employment in the Public Sector*, 12, 79; Fritz Knauss, "Federal Enterprises as a Boost to the Economy?" *Annals of Public and Co-operative Economy* 48 (July-September 1977): 421-28; Peter Siewert and Helmut Kohler, "Federal Republic of Germany," in *Educational Financing and Policy Goals*, vol. 1, 109-68; Jörg J. R. Becker, "Textbooks and the Political System in the Federal Republic of Germany, 1945-1975," *School Review* 86 (February 1978): 251-70; John J. Bergen, "The Preparation and Selection of Educational Administrators in West Germany," *Canadian and International Education* 5 (June 1976): 47-68; Charles R. Foster, "Civic Education in the United States and the Federal Republic of Germany," *Western European Education* 8 (Fall 1976): 5-29; Uwe E. Reinhardt, "Health Insurance and Health Policy in the Federal Republic of Germany," *Health Care Financing Review* 3 (December 1981): 1-14; Maxwell, *Health*

and Wealth, 61; Deborah A. Stone, *The Limits of Professional Power: National Health Care in the Federal Republic of Germany* (Chicago: University of Chicago Press, 1980); Howard M Leichter, *A Comparative Approach to Policy Analysis: Health Care Policy in Four Nations* (New York: Cambridge University Press, 1979), 110-56; Hans-Ulrich Deppe, "Some Remarks on the Economic and Political Development of Health Care in the Federal Republic of Germany," *International Journal of Health Services* 7, no. 3 (1977): 349-57; J.-Matthias Graf Schulenburg, "Report from Germany: Current Conditions and Controversies in the Health Care System," *Journal of Health Politics, Policy and Law* 8 (Summer 1983): 320-51.

5. See OECD, *National Accounts Statistics, 1963-1980*, vol. 2 (Paris, 1982), tables 9-11; *Revenue Statistics of OECD Member Countries, 1965-1982*, 164; IMF, *Government Finance Statistics Yearbook, 1979* (Washington, D.C., 1979), 141-43, 194-96, 368-70; Maurice Peston, "United Kingdom (England and Wales)," in *Educational Financing and Policy Goals for Primary Schools: Country Reports*, vol. 2, 19-32; Livio Pescia and Yasmine Ergas, "Italy," in *ibid.*, vol. 3, 135-58; Noah and Sherman, *Educational Financing and Policy Goals*, 23-25, 27-29, 57.

6. George Ross and Jane Jenson, "Crisis and France's Third Way," *Studies in Political Economy*, no. 11 (Summer 1983): 71-103; Jonathan Story, "Capital in France: The Changing Pattern of Patrimony?" *West European Politics* 6 (April 1983): 87-127; *Regards sur l'actualité*, no. 79 (March 1982): 41; Michael Keating, "Decentralization in Mitterrand's France," *Public Administration* 61 (Autumn 1983): 237-51; Yves Mény, "Decentralisation in Socialist France: The Politics of Pragmatism," *West European Politics* 7 (January 1984): 65-79; Maxwell, *Health and Wealth*, 61; Victor G. Rodwin, "The Marriage of National Health Insurance and *La Médecine Libérale* in France: A Costly Union," *Milbank Memorial Fund Quarterly/Health and Society* 59 (Winter 1981): 16-43; Simone Sandier, "Les Soins médicaux en France et aux U. S. A.," *Consommation — Revue de Socio-Économie*, no. 1 (January-March 1981): 3-36; *Social Security and National Health Insurance in France*, No. 80/66-73 (New York: French Embassy, Press and Information Division, 1980); Lionel Elvin, ed., *The Educational Systems in the European Community: A Guide* (London: NFER-Nelson Publishing Co., 1981), 111-27, 164-73, 230-47; Anne Corbett, "French Battle on Private Schools," *New Society* 68 (17 May 1984): 286-87; Henry W. Ehrmann, *Politics in France*, 4th ed. (Boston: Little, Brown, 1983), 80-93; J. K. P. Watson, "Curriculum Development: Some Comparative Perspectives," *Compare* 9 (April 1979): 17-31; Pescia and Ergas, "Italy," 135-75; Noah and Sherman, *Educational Financing and Policy Goals*, 23-29; Sabino Cassese, "Is There a Government in Italy? Politics and Administration at the Top," in Rose and Suleiman, eds., *Presidents and Prime Ministers*, 171-202; Hisaaki Izawa, "Comparison between Public Enterprises in Japan and Italy," *Rivista Internazionale di Scienze Economiche e Commerciali* 27 (July-August 1980): 721-34; David Willey, "Italy: The Weakest Government

in Europe," *World Today* 38 (December 1982): 466-70; Robert D. Putnam, Robert Leonardi, Raffaella Y. Nanetti, and Franco Pavoncello, "Explaining Institutional Success: The Case of Italian Regional Government," *American Political Science Review* 77 (March 1983): 55-74; Robert Ballion, "L'Enseignement privé, une 'école sur mesure?'" *Revue française de sociologie* 21 (April-June 1980): 203-31; Charles F. Andrain, *Foundations of Comparative Politics: A Policy Perspective* (Monterey, Calif.: Brooks/Cole, 1983), 191-202; Jerry A. Webman, "Centralization and Implementation: Urban Renewal in Great Britain and France," *Comparative Politics* 13 (January 1981): 127-48; David Thomas, "Stirring up the State Firms," *New Society* 64 (30 June 1983): 505-6; David Heald and David Steel, "The Privatisation of UK Public Enterprises, *Annals of Public and Co-operative Economy* 52 (July-September 1981): 351-67; Mike Goldsmith and Ken Newton, "Central-Local Government Relations: The Irresistible Rise of Centralised Power," *West European Politics* 6 (October 1983): 216-33; OECD, "Big Government—How Big Is It?" 6-11; Peston, "United Kingdom (England and Wales)," 7-53; Richard Rose, *Politics in England,* 3d ed. (Boston: Little, Brown, 1980), 147-55; Colin Brock, "Problems of Articulation between Secondary and Higher Education in England and Wales," *European Journal of Education* 16 (June 1981): 153-73; Central Statistical Office, *Social Trends*, no. 12, 1982 ed. (London: Her Majesty's Stationery Office, 1981), 45-49; Frederick Ruffett, "Secondary Education: Some Primary Matters," *Policy Studies* 2 (April 1982): 217-36; Mark Pattison, "Intergovernmental Relations and the Limitations of Central Control: Reconstructing the Politics of Comprehensive Education," *Oxford Review of Education* 6 (March 1980): 63-89; Vernon Bogdanor, "Power and Participation," *Oxford Review of Education* 5 (June 1979): 157-68; W. F. Dennison, "Expenditure Decision-Making by English Local Education Authorities," *Educational Studies* 5 (October 1979): 241-50; Christopher Phillips and Michael Strain, "The Distribution of Power and Influence in English Education: A Reappraisal," *Public Administration* 59 (Summer 1981): 189-202; James Scotland, "Scottish Education, 1952-1982," *British Journal of Educational Studies* 30 (February 1982): 122-35; *World Development Report 1983*, 197; OECD, *Educational Statistics in OECD Countries* (Paris, 1981), 77; A. Harry Passow, Harold J. Noah, Max A. Eckstein, and John R. Mallea, *The National Case Study: An Empirical Comparative Study of Twenty-One Educational Systems* (Stockholm: Almqvist and Wiksell International, 1976), 48-73; Rudolf Klein, "Control, Participation, and the British National Health Service," *Milbank Memorial Fund Quarterly/Health and Society* 57 (Winter 1979): 70-94; David J. Hunter, "Organising for Health: The National Health Service in the United Kingdom," *Journal of Public Policy* 2 (August 1982): 263-300; Dorothy Wade and Justine Picardie, "Private Gain," *New Statesman* 105 (25 March 1983): 10-11; Jeremy Laurance, "The Collapse of the BUPA Boom," *New Society* 63 (24 February 1983): 295-96; John K. Iglehart, "The British National Health Service under the Conservatives—Part II," *New England Journal of Medicine* 310 (5 January 1984): 63-67; Starr, *The Social Transformation of American Medicine*, 430.

7. See Christa Altenstetter and James Warner Björkman, "Planning and Implementation: A Comparative Perspective on Health Policy," *International Political Science Review* 2, no. 1 (1981): 15; Victor G. Rodwin, *The Health Planning Predicament: France, Québec, England, and the United States* (Berkeley: University of California Press, 1984), 117-47, 191-99; Stone, *The Limits of Professional Power*, 82-85; Gordon K. MacLeod, "National Health Insurance in the Federal Republic of Germany and Its Implications for U. S. Consumers," *Public Health Reports* 91 (July-August 1976): 343-48; *Social Security and National Health Insurance in France*, No. 80/67, 3; Carolyn Sue Beavert, *Citizen Participation and Health Care Politics: A Shift in the Neighborhood Health Center Paradigm;* Ph.D. dissertation, Department of Sociology, University of Missouri at Columbia, 1979; Richard M. Hessler and Carolyn Sue Beavert, "Citizen Participation in Neighborhood Health Centers for the Poor: The Politics of Reform Organizational Change, 1965-77," *Human Organization* 41, no. 3 (1982): 245-55; Barry Checkoway, "Public Participation in Health Planning Agencies; Promise and Practice," *Journal of Health Politics, Policy and Law* 7 (Fall 1982): 723-33; Klein, "Control, Participation, and the British National Health Service," 75; Erica Bates, "Can the Public's Voice Influence Bureaucracy? The Case of Community Health Councils," *Public Administration* 60 (Spring 1982): 92-98; Chris Ham, "Community Health Council Participation in NHS Planning System," *Social Policy and Administration* 14 (Autumn 1980): 221-31; Stuart Haywood and David J. Hunter, "Consultative Processes in Health Policy in the United Kingdom: A View from the Centre," *Public Administration* 60 (Summer 1982): 143-62; Fred S. Coombs and Richard L. Merritt, "The Public's Role in Educational Policy-Making: An International View," *Education and Urban Society* 9 (Feburary 1977): 167-96; Nicholas Beattie, "Formalized Parent Participation in Education: A Comparative Perspective (France, German Federal Republic, England and Wales)," *Comparative Education* 14 (March 1978): 41-48; Pippa Pridham: "Education and the Italian Crisis," *New Society* 45 (21 September 1978): 620-22, and "The Problems of Educational Reform in Italy: The Case of the Decreti Delegati," *Comparative Education* 14 (October 1978): 223-41; Harvey J. Tucker and L. Harmon Zeigler: "The Myth of Lay Control," *Proceedings of the Academy of Political Science* 33, no. 2 (1978): 18-23, and *Professionals versus the Public: Attitudes, Communication, and Response in School Districts* (New York: Longman, 1980); Alfred Diamant, "Industrial Democracy in Western Europe"; paper delivered at the 1982 annual meeting of the American Political Science Association, Denver, Colorado, 4 September 1982.

8. For analyses of the mandate theory of representation, see Hanna Fenichel Pitkin, *The Concept of Representation* (Berkeley: University of California Press, 1972), 144-67; Richard W. Boyd, "Popular Control of Public Policy:

A Normal Vote Analysis of the 1968 Election," *American Political Science Review* 66 (June 1972): 429-49; John L. Sullivan and Robert E. O'Connor, "Electoral Choice and Popular Control of Public Policy: The Case of the 1966 House Elections," *American Political Science Review* 66 (December 1972): 1256-68; Benjamin Ginsberg, *The Consequences of Consent: Elections, Citizen Control, and Popular Acquiescence* (Reading, Mass.: Addison-Wesley, 1982).

9. M. Stephen Weatherford, "Economic Voting and the 'Symbolic Politics' Argument: A Reinterpretation and Synthesis," *American Political Science Review* 77 (March 1983): 171.

10. James E. Alt, Bo Särlvik, and Ivor Crewe, "Partisanship and Policy Choice: Issue Preferences in the British Electorate, February 1974," *British Journal of Political Science* 6 (July 1976): 273-90; David Butler and Donald Stokes, *Political Change in Britain: The Evolution of Electoral Choice,* 2d ed. (New York: St. Martin's Press, 1974), 292-360; Sullivan and O'Connor, "Electoral Choice and Popular Control of Public Policy," 1256-68; Benjamin I. Page and Robert Y. Shapiro, "Effects of Public Opinion on Policy," *American Political Science Review* 77 (March 1983): 175-90; Ginsberg, *The Consequences of Consent,* 62-109; Edith Stokey and Richard Zeckhauser, *A Primer for Policy Analysis* (New York: W. W. Norton, 1978), 287-90; Roisin Pill and Nigel C. H. Stott, "Concepts of Illness Causation and Responsibility: Some Preliminary Data from a Sample of Working Class Mothers," *Social Science and Medicine* 16, no. 1 (1982): 43-52; Andrain, *Foundations of Comparative Politics,* 191-202, 229-69, 281-339; Lawrence LeDuc, "The Dynamic Properties of Party Identification: A Four-Nation Comparison," *European Journal of Political Research* 9 (September 1981): 257-68; David Butler, "Electoral Systems," in *Democracy at the Polls: A Comparative Study of Competitive National Elections,* ed. David Butler, Howard R. Penniman, and Austin Ranney (Washington, D.C.: American Enterprise Institute, 1981), 7-25; Ivor Crewe, "Electoral Participation," in *ibid.,* 225-32; Seymour Martin Lipset, *The First New Nation* (New York: Basic Books, 1962), 286-317; Hugh Berrington, "The British General Election of 1983," *Electoral Studies* 2 (December 1983): 266; Arend Lijphart, *Democracies: Patterns of Majoritarian and Consensus Government in Twenty-One Countries* (New Haven, Conn.: Yale University Press, 1984), 10-11.

11. Andrain, *Foundations of Comparative Politics,* 231-44.

12. John S. Jackson III, Barbara Leavitt Brown, and David Bositis, "Herbert McClosky and Friends Revisited: 1980 Democratic and Republican Party Elites Compared to the Mass Public," *American Politics Quarterly* 10 (April 1982): 158-80; Edward G. Carmines and J. David Gopoian, "Issue Coalitions, Issueless Campaigns: The Paradox of Rationality in American Presidential Elections," *Journal of Politics* 43 (November 1981): 1170-89; Susan Welch and John G. Peters, "Elite Attitudes on Economic-Welfare and Social Issues," *Polity* 14 (Fall 1981): 160-77; George F. Bishop and

Kathleen A. Frankovic, "Ideological Consensus and Constraint among Party Leaders and Followers in the 1978 Election," *Micropolitics* 1, no. 2 (1981): 87-111; David Lowery and Lee Sigelman, "Party Identification and Public Spending Priorities in the American Electorate," *Political Studies* 30 (June 1982): 221-35.

13. "The Policies of the Parties," *New Society* 64 (26 May 1983): 298-304.

14. Ulf Himmelstrand, "Sweden: Toward Economic Democracy," *Dissent* 30 (Summer 1983): 329-36; Peter Walters, "Sweden's Public Sector Crisis, Before and After the 1982 Elections," *Government and Opposition* 18 (Winter 1983): 23-39; Finn Diderichsen, "Ideologies in the Swedish Health Sector Today: The Crisis of the Social Democracy," *International Journal of Health Services* 12, no. 2 (1982): 191-200; Samuel J. Eldersveld, "Motivations for Party Activism: Multi-National Uniformities and Differences," *International Political Science Review* 4, no. 1 (1983): 57-70; Michael Lindén, "Political Dimensions and Relative Party Positions: A Factor Analytical Study of Swedish Attitude Data," *Scandinavian Journal of Psychology* 16, no. 2 (1975): 97-107.

15. Sten G. Borg and Francis G. Castles, "The Influence of the Political Right on Public Income Maintenance Expenditure and Equality," *Political Studies* 29 (December 1981): 604-21; Francis G. Castles, "How Does Politics Matter: Structure or Agency in the Determination of Public Policy Outcomes," *European Journal of Political Research* 9 (June 1981): 119-32; Manfred G. Schmidt, "The Welfare State and the Economy in Periods of Economic Crisis: A Comparative Study of Twenty-Three OECD Nations," *European Journal of Political Research* 11 (March 1983): 1-26; Francis G. Castles, ed., *The Impact of Parties: Politics and Policies in Democratic Capitalist States* (Beverly Hills, Calif.: Sage Publications, 1982).

16. Paul Burstein, "Party Balance, Replacement of Legislators, and Federal Government Expenditures, 1941-1976," *Western Political Quarterly* 32 (June 1979): 203-8; Howard J. Sherman, "Cyclical Behavior of Government Fiscal Policy," *Journal of Economic Issues* 17 (June 1983): 379-88; Bixby, "Social Welfare Expenditures, Fiscal Year 1980," 15; Table A.2 in *The Reagan Record*, ed. John L. Palmer and Isabel V. Sawhill (Cambridge, Mass.: Ballinger, 1984), 350; D. Lee Bawden and John L. Palmer, "Social Policy: Challenging the Welfare State," in *ibid.*, 177-215; Starr, *The Social Transformation of American Medicine*, 394, 411-12.

17. Brian D. Johnson, "Medicare Suffers Another Setback," *Maclean's* 96 (11 April 1983): 50-51; Deborah MacLean, "Bill Bennett's B. C.," *Canadian Forum* 64 (May 1984): 6-7, 40; Jean-Marc Piotte and Bela Egyed, "A Morose Quebec," *Canadian Forum* 62 (March 1983): 12-13; Raymond Murphy, "Teachers and the Evolving Structural Context of Economic and Political Attitudes in Quebec Society," *Canadian Review of Sociology and Anthropology* 18 (May 1981): 170; Frank Gould and Barbara Roweth, "Politics and Public Spending," *Political Quarterly* 49 (April-June 1978):

222-27; Raphaella Bilski, "Secondary Education and the British Parties' Ideologies," *Res Publica* 17, no. 2 (1975): 303-18; Arnold J. Heidenheimer, Hugh Heclo, and Carolyn Teich Adams, *Comparative Public Policy: The Politics of Social Choice in Europe and America*, 2d ed. (New York: St. Martin's Press, 1983), 34-44; Marquis Childs, *Sweden: The Middle Way on Trial* (New Haven, Conn.: Yale University Press, 1980), 78-79, 169; Ulf Himmelstrand, Göran Ahrne, Leif Lundberg, and Lars Lundberg, *Beyond Welfare Capitalism: Issues, Actors and Forces in Societal Change* (London: Heinemann, 1981), 62-63, 119; Elvander, "Barriers and Opportunities for Primary Care Delivery Systems," 307; *The Economist*, 10 December 1983, pp. 74-75; Andrei S. Markovits, "West Germany's Political Future," *Socialist Review* 13 (July-August 1983): 72-77; Douglas Webber, "A Relationship of 'Critical Partnership'? Capital and the Social-Liberal Coalition in West Germany," *West European Politics* 6 (April 1983): 61-86; Lawrence Garner, "A Change in Italy's Choirmaster?" *Current History* 83 (April 1984): 160-63, 181-83.

18. C. F. Pratten, "Mrs. Thatcher's Economic Experiment," *Lloyds Bank Review*, no. 143 (January 1982): 36-51; D. Thomas, "Stirring Up the State Firms," 505-6; Bob Sutcliffe, "Tory Reaganomics," *Dollars and Sense*, no. 82 (December 1982): 12-14; Nick Bosanquet, "Is Social Spending 'Out of Control'?" *New Society* 63 (Feburary 1983): 220-21; Peter Kellner, "Why Mrs. Thatcher Is a Moderate," *New Statesman* 101 (5 June 1981): 5; J. K. P. Watson, "Coping with Educational Change in England and Wales," *Canadian Administrator* 20 (January 1981): 1-4; Eugene Vayda, "Private Practice in the United Kingdom," *Journal of Public Health Policy* 4 (June 1983): 222-34; Geoffrey R. Weller and Pranlal Manga, "The Push for Reprivatization of Health Care Services in Canada, Britain, and the United States," *Journal of Health Politics, Policy and Law* 8 (Fall 1983): 495-518; Rudolf Klein, "The Politics of Ideology vs. the Reality of Politics: The Case of Britain's National Health Service in the 1980s," *Milbank Memorial Fund Quarterly/Health and Society* 62 (Winter 1984): 82-109; Ian Gough, "The Crisis of the British Welfare State," *International Journal of Health Services* 13, no. 3 (1983): 459-77; Julian Le Grand, "The Future of the Welfare State," *New Society* 68 (7 June 1984): 385-86; R. W. Johnson, "One Up to Reagan," *New Society* 66 (6 October 1983): 28; James Tobin, "Supply-Side Economics: What Is It? Will It Work?" *Economic Outlook USA* 8 (Summer 1981): 51-53; John Kenneth Galbraith, "The Market and Mr. Reagan," *New Republic* 185 (23 September 1981): 15-18; Samuel H. Beer, "Ronald Reagan: New Deal Conservative?" *Society* 20 (January-February 1983): 40-44; United States Council of Economic Advisers, *Economic Report of the President, 1985*, pp. 232, 322; C. Arden Miller and Elizabeth J. Coulter, "The World Economic Crisis and the Children: A United States Case Study," *World Development* 12 (March 1984): 339-64; Vicente Navarro: "Selected Myths Guiding the Reagan Administration's Health Policies," *Journal of Public Health Policy* 5 (March 1984): 65-73, and "The Determinants of Social Policy, A Case Study: Regulating

Health and Safety at the Workplace in Sweden," *International Journal of Health Services* 13, no. 4 (1983): 523.

19. Ross and Jenson, "Crisis and France's 'Third Way,'" 71-103; Douglas Johnson, "Waiting for the Balance-Sheet: France and the Socialists," *Encounter* 60 (March 1983): 66-75; Bob Kuttner, "France's Atari Socialism," *New Republic* 188 (7 March 1983): 19-23; Robert Eisner, "Which Way for France?" *Challenge* 26 (July-August 1983): 32-41; Saul Estrin and Peter Holmes, "How Far Is Mitterrand from Barre?" *Challenge* 26 (November-December 1983): 46-50; Michael M. Harrison, "France under the Socialists," *Current History* 83 (April 1984): 153-56, 181; George Ross, "Socialists vs. Workers," *New Republic* 190 (27 February 1984): 14-16.

20. Klaus von Beyme, "Do Parties Matter? The Impact of Parties on the Key Decisions in the Political System," *Government and Opposition* 19 (Winter 1984): 5-29; Anthony King, "What Do Elections Decide?" in Butler, Penniman, and Ranney, eds., *Democracy at the Polls,* 293-324; John Clayton Thomas: "The Changing Nature of Partisan Divisions in the West: Trends in Domestic Policy Orientations in Ten Party Systems," *European Journal of Political Research* 7 (December 1979): 397-413, and "Ideological Trends in Western Political Parties," in *Western European Party Systems: Trends and Prospects,* ed. Peter H. Merkl (New York: Free Press, 1980), 348-66; K. H. F. Dyson, "The Politics of Economic Management in West Germany," *West European Politics* 4 (May 1981): 35-55; Andrain, *Foundations of Comparative Politics,* 262-68; Joel D. Aberbach, Robert D. Putnam, and Bert A. Rockman, *Bureaucrats and Politicians in Western Democracies* (Cambridge, Mass.: Harvard University Press, 1981), 84-169; Heidenheimer, Heclo, and Adams, *Comparative Public Policy,* 21-51; Stockholm International Peace Research Institute, *World Armaments and Disarmament: SIPRI Yearbook 1983* (London: Taylor and Francis, 1983), 171.

21. Charles E. Lindblom: "The Market as Prison," *Journal of Politics* 44 (May 1982): 326-27, and *Politics and Markets* (New York: Basic Books, 1977), 347. See too Michael Useem, *The Inner Circle: Large Corporations and the Rise of Business Political Activity in the U. S. and U.K.* (New York: Oxford University Press, 1984), esp. 76-115.

22. For analyses of the market model, see Andrain, *Foundations of Comparative Politics,* 220-21; Pierre Birnbaum: "State, Centre and Bureaucracy," *Government and Opposition* 16 (Winter 1981): 58-77, and "The State versus Corporatism," *Politics and Society* 11, no. 4 (1982): 477-501; Graham K. Wilson, "Why Is There No Corporatism in the United States?" in *Patterns of Corporatist Policy-Making,* ed. Gerhard Lehmbruch and Philippe C. Schmitter (Beverly Hills, Calif.: Sage Publications, 1982), 219-36.

23. Vivienne Walters, "State, Capital, and Labour: The Introduction of Federal-Provincial Insurance for Physician Care in Canada," *Canadian Review of Sociology and Anthropology* 19 (May 1982): 157-72; David Coburn, George M. Torrance, and Joseph M. Kaufert, "Medical Dominance in Canada in

Historical Perspective: The Rise and Fall of Medicine?" *International Journal of Health Services* 13, no. 3 (1983): 407-32; Robert Presthus, "Aspects of Political Culture and Legislative Behavior: United States and Canada," *International Journal of Comparative Sociology* 18 (March-June 1977): 13; Robert Presthus and William Monopoli, "Bureaucracy in the United States and Canada: Social, Attitudinal, and Behavioral Variables," *International Journal of Comparative Sociology* 18 (March-June 1977): 181.

24. Franz Groemping, *Country Labor Profile: Canada* (Washington, D.C.: U.S. Department of Labor, Bureau of Labor Affairs, 1980), 5; William W. Lammers and Joseph L. Nyomarkay, "The Canadian Cabinet in Comparative Perspective," *Canadian Journal of Political Science* 15 (March 1982): 39-40.

25. See *U.S. News and World Report* 96 (14 May 1984): 50; David Vogel: "Why Businessmen Distrust Their State: The Political Consciousness of American Corporate Executives," *British Journal of Political Science* 8 (January 1978): 45-78, and "The Power of Business in America: A Re-appraisal," *British Journal of Political Science* 13 (January 1983): 19-43; Theda Skocpol, "Political Response to Capitalist Crisis: Neo-Marxist Theories of the State and the Case of the New Deal," *Politics and Society* 10, no. 2 (1980): 155-201.

26. T. P. Hill, *Profits and Rates of Return* (Paris: OECD, 1979), 122-23; *OECD Economic Outlook* 33 (July 1983): 57; Thomas Byrne Edsall, *The New Politics of Inequality* (New York: W.W. Norton, 1984), 107-40; Vogel, "The Power of Business in America," 30-38; Thomas R. Dye, "Oligarchic Tendencies in National Policy-Making: The Role of Private Policy-Planning Organizations," *Journal of Politics* 40 (May 1978): 309-31.

27. Statistical Office of the European Communities, *Basic Statistics of the Community*, 19th ed. (Luxembourg: Office for Official Publications of the European Communities, 1981), 17.

28. Richard E. Caves, "The Structure of Industry," in *The American Economy in Transition*, ed. Martin Feldstein (Chicago: University of Chicago Press, 1980), 501-45; "The Corporate Shuffle," *Dollars and Sense*, no. 72 (December 1981): 3-5; B. Curry and K. D. George, "Industrial Concentration: A Survey," *Journal of Industrial Economics* 31 (March 1983): 227, 247; Michael Useem, "Which Business Leaders Help Govern?" *Insurgent Sociologist* 9 (Fall 1979/Winter 1980): 107-20; Peter J. Freitag, "The Cabinet and Big Business: A Study of Interlocks," *Social Problems* 23 (December 1975): 137-52; Daniel C. Esty and Richard E. Caves, "Market Structure and Political Influence: New Data on Political Expenditures, Activity, and Success," *Economic Inquiry* 21 (January 1983): 24-38.

29. Allen H. Barton: "Consensus and Conflict among American Leaders," *Public Opinion Quarterly* 38 (Winter 1974/1975): 507-30, and "Fault Lines in American Elite Consensus," *Daedalus* 109 (Summer 1980): 1-24; Seymour Martin Lipset and William Schneider, *The Confidence Gap: Business, Labor,*

and Government in the Public Mind (New York: Free Press, 1983), 370-71; Michael Moran, "Politics, Banks and Markets: An Anglo-American Comparison," *Political Studies* 32 (June 1984): 173-89.

30. Allen, "The Flaw in Canadian Federalism," 172-76; Dennis Olsen, *The State Elite* (Toronto: McClelland and Stewart, 1980), 122; Leo V. Panitch, "Elites, Classes and Power in Canada," in Whittington and Williams, eds., *Canadian Politics in the 1980s*, 167-88; Maureen Appel Molot and Glen Williams, "A Political Economy of Continentalism," in *ibid.*, 68-83; William K. Carroll, John Fox, and Michael D. Ornstein, "The Network of Directorate Links among the Largest Canadian Firms," *Canadian Review of Sociology and Anthropology* 19 (February 1982): 44-69; William K. Carroll, "The Canadian Corporate Elite: Financiers or Finance Capitalists?" *Studies in Political Economy*, no. 8 (Summer 1982); 89-114; Jorge Niosi, "The Canadian Bourgeoisie: Towards a Synthetical Approach," *Canadian Journal of Political and Social Theory* 7 (Fall 1983): 128-49.

31. Groemping, *Country Labor Profile: Canada*, 1-7; Minister of Supply and Services, *Canada Year Book 1980-81* (Ottawa: Statistics Canada, 1981), 254-55, 285; David Lewin and Shirley B. Goldenberg, "Public Sector Unionism in the U.S. and Canada," *Industrial Relations* 19 (Fall 1980): 239-56; John Harp and Gordon Betcherman, "Contradictory Class Locations and Class Action: The Case of School Teachers' Organizations in Ontario and Quebec," *Canadian Journal of Sociology* 5 (Spring 1980): 145-62; Rianne Mahon, "Canadian Labour in the Battle of the Eighties," *Studies in Political Economy*, no. 11 (Summer 1983): 149-75; Everett M. Kassalow, "The Closed and Union Shop in Western Europe, An American Perspective," *Journal of Labor Research* 1 (Fall 1980): 323-39; U.S. Department of Labor, Bureau of Labor Statistics, *Handbook of Labor Statistics*, Bulletin 2070 (Washington, D.C.: Government Printing Office, 1980), 412; Richard B. Freeman and James L. Medoff, *What Do Unions Do?* (New York: Basic Books, 1984), 191-206, 221-45; Edsall, *The New Politics of Inequality*, 141-78; Brian E. Becker and Richard U. Miller, "Patterns and Determinants of Union Growth in the Hospital Industry," *Journal of Labor Research* 2 (Fall 1981): 309-28; Stanley M. Elam, "The National Education Association: Political Powerhouse or Paper Tiger?" *Phi Delta Kappan* 63 (November 1981): 169-74; Myron Lieberman, "Teacher Bargaining: An Autopsy," *Phi Delta Kappan* 63 (December 1981): 231-34; "N.E.A. and A.F.T. Put Their Power on the Line for Carter," *American School Board Journal* 167 (November 1980): 30-33; "Union Growth Stopped in the Seventies," *Dollars and Sense*, no. 87 (May/June 1983): 8-9; "Union Busting Today," *Dollars and Sense*, no. 85 (March 1983): 8-9, 18; A. W. J. Thompson, "The United States of America," in *Trade Unions in the Developed Economies*, ed. E. Owen Smith (New York: St. Martin's Press, 1981), 155-77.

32. Birnbaum: "State, Centre and Bureaucracy," 58-77, and "The State versus Corporatism," 477-501.

33. United Kingdom, *A Review of Monopolies and Mergers Policy*, Cmnd. 7198 (London: Her Majesty's Stationery Office, May 1978), 63-64; R. M. Grant, "Recent Developments in the Control of Price Discrimination in Countries outside North America," *Antitrust Bulletin* 26 (Fall 1981): 595; David R. Steel, "Review Article: Government and Industry in Britain," *British Journal of Political Science* 12 (October 1982): 462; Keith Sisson, "The Bosses with No Bark," *New Society* 54 (6 November 1980): 271-72; Lammers and Nyomarkay, "The Canadian Cabinet in Comparative Perspective," 39-40; Anthony Sampson, *The Changing Anatomy of Britain* (New York: Random House, 1982), 272-85, 308-49; David Marsh and Gareth Locksley, "Capital in Britain: Its Structural Power and Influence over Policy," *West European Politics* 6 (April 1983): 36-60; Michael Useem: "Business and Politics in the United States and United Kingdom," *Theory and Society* 12 (May 1983): 281-308, and *The Inner Circle*; Norman Lewis and Paul Wiles, "The Post-Corporatist State?" *Journal of Law and Society* 11 (Spring 1984): 65-90; Wyn Grant: "Business Interests and the British Conservative Party," *Government and Opposition* 15 (Spring 1980): 143-61, and "The Business Lobby: Political Attitudes and Strategies," *West European Politics* 6 (October 1983): 163-82.

34. Central Statistical Office, *Social Trends*, no. 13, 1983 ed. (London: Her Majesty's Stationery Office, 1982), 152-53; Central Statistical Office, *Social Trends*, no. 12, 1982 ed., 195-96; Eileen Barkas Hoffman, *Country Labor Profile: United Kingdom* (Washington, D.C.: U.S. Department of Labor, Bureau of Labor Affairs, 1980), 1-7; Kevin Hawkins, *Trade Unions* (London: Hutchinson, 1981), 78-93, 208-43; E. Owen Smith, "The United Kingdom," in E. O. Smith, ed., *Trade Unions in the Developed Economies*, 123-54; A. W. J. Thompson, "Trade Unions and the Corporate State in Britain," *Industrial and Labor Relations Review* 33 (October 1979): 36-54; Steel, "Review Article: Government and Industry in Britain," 480-84; Andrew Cox and Jack Hayward, "The Inapplicability of the Corporatist Model in Britain and France: The Case of Labor," *International Political Science Review* 4, no. 2 (1983): 217-40; Lewis and Wiles, "The Post-Corporatist State?" 78-84; Rod Hague, "Confrontation, Incorporation and Exclusion: British Trade Unions in Collectivist and Post-Collectivist Politics," *West European Politics* 6 (October 1983): 130-62; Heinz Hartmann and Christoph Lau, "Trade Union Confederations," *International Studies Quarterly* 24 (September 1980): 365-91; Robert J. Thornton, "Teacher Unionism and Collective Bargaining in England and Wales," *Industrial and Labor Relations Review* 35 (April 1982): 377-91; Noel and José Parry, "Professionalism and Unionism: Aspects of Class Conflict in the National Health Service," *Sociological Review* 25 (November 1977): 823-41.

35. Analyses of the corporatist model appear in Harold L. Wilensky: *The "New Corporatism," Centralization, and the Welfare State*; Sage Professional Papers in Contemporary Political Sociology, Series/Number 06-020 (Beverly Hills, Calif.: Sage Publications, 1976), 21-23; "Leftism, Catholicism, and Demo-

cratic Corporatism: The Role of Political Parties in Recent Welfare State Development," in *The Development of Welfare States in Europe and America*, ed. Peter Flora and Arnold J. Heidenheimer (New Brunswick, N.J.: Transaction Books, 1981), 345-82; and "Political Legitimacy and Consensus: Missing Variables in the Assessment of Social Policy," in *Evaluating the Welfare State: Social and Political Perspectives*, ed. S. E. Spirow and E. Yuchtman-Yaar (New York: Academic Press, 1983), 51-74; Andrain, *Foundations of Comparative Politics*, 222-24; Alfred Diamant, "Review Article: Bureaucracy and Public Policy in Neocorporatist Settings—Some European Lessons," *Comparative Politics* 14 (October 1981): 101-24; Gerhard Lehmbruch, "Introduction: Neo-Corporatism in Comparative Perspective," in Lehmbruch and Schmitter, eds., *Patterns of Corporatist Policy-Making*, 1-28.

36. Joachim Israel, "Swedish Socialism and Big Business," *Acta Sociologica* 21, no. 4 (1978): 341-53; Anton, *Administered Politics*, 1-20, 102-57, 182-87.

37. See Marvin E. Olsen, *Participatory Pluralism: Political Participation and Influence in the United States and Sweden* (Chicago: Nelson-Hall, 1982), 181-272; Norman Eiger, "The Expanding Scope of Public Bargaining in Sweden," *Industrial Relations* 20 (Fall 1981): 335-41; Joseph Mire, "Sweden," in *International Labor Profiles* (Detroit: Grand River Books, 1980), 260-65; *Social Security Programs throughout the World, 1981*, Research Report No. 58 (Washington, D.C.: U.S. Department of Health and Human Services, Social Security Administration, Office of Research and Statistics, 1982), 235.

38. See Israel, "Swedish Socialism and Big Business," 341-53; Himmelstrand et al., *Beyond Welfare Capitalism*, 57, 210-44; Hill, *Profits and Rates of Return*, 119-22; Anton, *Administered Politics*, 99; Mire, "Sweden," 261-62; Walters, "Sweden's Public Sector Crisis," 23-39; Richard Scase, "Why Sweden Has Elected a Radical Government," *Political Quarterly* 54 (January-March 1983): 43-53.

39. See Himmelstrand et al., *Beyond Welfare Capitalism*, 196-244; Mire, "Sweden," 264; Sandra L. Albrecht, "Politics, Bureaucracy, and Worker Participation: The Swedish Case," *Journal of Applied Behavioral Science* 16 (July-August-September 1980): 299-315; Harry Trimborn, "Future of Sweden's Ruling Party Could Hinge on Wage-Earner Fund Proposal," *Los Angeles Times*, 26 October 1981, Part IV, 1, 3; Gosta Esping-Andersen, "Sweden's New Designs," *Working Papers for a New Society* 9 (January-February 1982): 15-16; T. L. Johnston, "Sweden," in E. O. Smith, ed., *Trade Unions in the Developed Economies*, 97-122; John D. Stephens: *The Transition from Capitalism to Socialism* (London: Macmillan Press, 1979), and "Class Formation and Class Consciousness: A Theoretical and Empirical Analysis with Reference to Britain and Sweden," *British Journal of Sociology* 30 (December 1979): 389-414; Walter Korpi and Michael Shalev, "Strikes, Industrial Relations and Class Conflict in Capitalist Society," *British Journal of Sociology* 30 (June 1979): 164-87; Norman Eiger, "The Expanding Scope of

Public Bargaining in Sweden," *Industrial Relations* 20 (Fall 1981): 335-41; Elvander, "Barriers and Opportunities for Primary Care Delivery Systems," 303; OECD, *Educational Reforms in Sweden* (Paris, 1981), 67.

40. M. E. Streit, "Government and Business: The Case of West Germany," in *Government, Business and Labour in European Capitalism*, ed. Richard T. Griffiths (London: Europotentials Press, 1977), 120-31; Dyson, "The Politics of Economic Management in West Germany," 35-55; Werner Abelshauser, "West German Economic Recovery, 1945-1951: A Reassessment," *Three Banks Review*, no. 135 (September 1982): 50-51; Franz A. Groemping, *Country Labor Profile: Federal Republic of Germany* (Washington, D.C.: U.S. Department of Labor, Bureau of International Labor Affairs, 1979), 1-7; *Social Security Programs*, 90-91; 124-25; Diamant, "Industrial Democracy in Western Europe," 21-27; Hartmann and Lau, "Trade Union Confederations," 365-91; Andrei S. Markovits and Christopher S. Allen, "Power and Dissent: The Trade Unions in the Federal Republic of Germany Re-Examined," *West European Politics* 3 (January 1980): 68-86; E. Owen Smith, "West Germany," in E. O. Smith, ed., *Trade Unions in the Developed Economies*, 178-207; Wolfgang Streeck, "Organizational Consequences of Neo-Corporatist Cooperation in West German Labour Unions," in Lehmbruch and Schmitter, eds., *Patterns of Corporatist Policy-Making*, 29-78; Klaus von Beyme, "Neo-Corporatism: A New Nut in an Old Shell?" *International Political Science Review* 4, no. 2 (1983): 173-96; Webber, "A Relationship of 'Critical Partnership'?" 61-86; Lewis J. Edinger, *Politics in West Germany*, 2d ed. (Boston, Mass.: Little, Brown, 1977), 222-37, 334-38; Marion Alexis, "Neo-Corporatism and Industrial Relations: The Case of German Trade Unions," *West European Politics* 6 (January 1983): 75-92.

41. Marco Maraffi, "State/Economy Relationships: The Case of Italian Public Enterprise," *British Journal of Sociology* 31 (December 1980): 507-24; Marino Regini, "Changing Relationships between Labour and the State in Italy: Towards a Neo-Corporatist System?" in Lehmbruch and Schmitter, eds., *Patterns of Corporatist Policy-Making*, 109-32; Thomas D. Bowie, *Country Labor Profile: Italy* (Washington, D.C.: U.S. Department of Labor, Bureau of International Labor Affairs, 1979), 1-7; United Kingdom, *A Review of Monopolies and Mergers Policy*, 63-65; R. M. Grant, "Recent Developments in the Control of Price Discrimination," 595; Statistical Office of the European Communities, *Basic Statistics of the Community*, 17; Marino Regini and Gosta Esping-Andersen, "Trade Union Strategies and Social Policy in Italy and Sweden," *West European Politics* 3 (January 1980): 107-23; von Beyme, "Neo-Corporatism," 182-85.

42. See Diana Green, "Individualism versus Collectivism: Economic Choices in France," *West European Politics* 1 (October 1978): 81-96; Birnbaum, "The State versus Corporatism," 477-501; Frank L. Wilson: "French Interest Group Politics: Pluralist or Neocorporatist?" *American Political Science Review* 77 (December 1983): 895-910, and "Alternative Models of Interest Intermediation: The Case of France," *British Journal of Political Science* 12

(April 1982): 173-200; Mark Kesselman, "Prospects for Democratic Social-ism in Advanced Capitalism: Class Struggle and Compromise in Sweden and France," *Politics and Society* 11, no. 4 (1982): 397-438; *Business Week*, 10 January 1983, pp. 47-58; Hubert Prevot, "La Nouvelle Planification Française," *Annals of Public and Co-operative Economy* 53 (June 1982): 161-72; "Forum: Réforme de la Planification Française," *Futuribles*, no. 53 (March 1982): 59-71; James K. Galbraith, "Monetary Policy in France," *Journal of Post Keynesian Economics* 4 (Spring 1982): 388-403; Estrin and Holmes, "How Far Is Mitterrand from Barre?" 46-50; F. Jenny, "From Price Controls to Competition Policy in France," *Annals of Public and Co-operative Economy* 52 (October-December 1981): 477-90; Theodore Zeldin, *The French* (New York: Pantheon Books, 1982), 193, 267-77; Ehrmann, *Politics in France*, 32-51, 181-208; Thomas D. Bowie, *Country Labor Pro-file: France* (Washington, D.C.: U.S. Department of Labor, Bureau of Inter-national Labor Affairs, 1979), 1-7; J. R. Hough, "France," in E. O. Smith, ed., *Trade Unions in the Developed Economies*, 43-70; John Ardagh, *France in the 1980s* (New York: Penguin Books, 1982), 93-115; George Ross, "What Is Progressive about Unions?" *Theory and Society* 10 (September 1981): 609-43; Cox and Hayward, "The Inapplicability of the Corporatist Model in Britain and France," 217-40; Duncan Gallie, "Trade Union Ideology and Workers' Conceptions of Class Inequality in France," in *Trade Unions and Politics in Western Europe*, ed. Jack Hayward (London: Frank Cass, 1980), 10-32; Story, "Capital in France," 87-127; Fred S. Coombs, "The Politics of Educational Change in France," *Comparative Education Review* 22 (October 1978): 480-503.

43. Torsten Husén, "Are Standards in U.S. Schools Really Lagging Behind Those in Other Countries?" *Phi Delta Kappan* 64 (March 1983): 455-61; Ralph W. Tyler, "The U.S. vs. the World: A Comparison of Educational Performance," *Phi Delta Kappan* 62 (January 1981): 307-10; *San Diego Union*, 12 December 1983, p. A-10.

44. See Julian Le Grand, *The Strategy of Equality: Redistribution and the Social Services* (London: George Allen and Unwin, 1982), 14-15.

45. Harold L. Wilensky, *The Welfare State and Equality* (Berkeley: University of California Press, 1975), 50-69; Richard M. Coughlin, *Ideology, Public Opinion and Welfare Policy: Attitudes toward Taxes and Spending in In-dustrialized Societies* (Berkeley: Institute of International Studies, 1980), 120-24; Sara A. Rosenberry, "Social Insurance, Distributive Criteria and the Welfare Backlash: A Comparative Analysis," *British Journal of Political Science* 12 (October 1982): 421-47; Hugh Mosley: "Corporate Social Bene-fits and the Underdevelopment of the American Welfare State," *Contempo-rary Crises* 5 (April 1981): 139-54, and "Social Security in the United States and the Federal Republic of Germany: A Comparison of Public and Private Benefit Systems," *Policy Studies Journal* 11 (March 1983): 492-503.

46. Harrell R. Rodgers, Jr., "Hiding versus Ending Poverty," *Politics and Society* 8, no. 2 (1978): 253-66; Timothy Smeeding and Marilyn Moon, "Valuing

Government Expenditures: The Case of Medical Care Transfers and Poverty," *Review of Income and Wealth* 26 (September 1980): 305-24; Patricia Ruggles and Michael O'Higgins, "The Distribution of Public Expenditure among Households in the United States," *Review of Income and Wealth* 27 (June 1981): 137-64; Michael O'Higgins and Patricia Ruggles, "The Distribution of Public Expenditures and Taxes among Households in the United Kingdom," *Review of Income and Wealth* 27 (September 1981): 298-326; Le Grand, *The Strategy of Equality*, 120-30; *Educational Statistics in OECD Countries*, 77.

47. Richard C. Michel, Frank S. Levy, Marilyn L. Moon, and Isabel V. Sawhill, "Are We Better Off in 1984?" *Challenge* 27 (September/October 1984), 10-17; Andrain: *Politics and Economic Policy in Western Democracies*, 173-202, and *Foundations of Comparative Politics*, 82-89, 160-66; Malcolm Sawyer, "Income Distribution in OECD Countries," *OECD Economic Outlook: Occasional Studies* (Paris, July 1976), 3-36; Christopher Hewitt, "The Effect of Political Democracy and Social Democracy on Equality in Industrial Societies: A Cross-National Comparison," *American Sociological Review* 42 (June 1977): 450-64; Toshiaki Tachibanaki, "A Note on the Impact of Tax on Income Distribution," *Review of Income and Wealth* 27 (September 1981): 327-32; Lester C. Thurow, "The Indirect Incidence of Government Expenditures," *American Economic Review* 70 (May 1980): 82-87; Michael Goldsmith, "French Social System Called Archaic," *Los Angeles Times*, 25 November 1982, part 13, 2; Garey C. Durden and Ann V. Schwarz-Miller, "The Distribution of Individual Income in the U.S. and Public Sector Employment," *Social Science Quarterly* 63 (March 1982): 39-47; Freeman and Medoff, *What Do Unions Do?* 5-25, 61-93; Jeffrey Pfeffer and Jerry Ross, "Unionization and Income Inequality," *Industrial Relations* 20 (Fall 1981): 271-85; Michael Reich, *Racial Inequality: A Political-Economic Analysis* (Princeton: Princeton University Press, 1981); Robert B. Reich, *The Next American Frontier* (New York: Times Books, 1983), 283-84; Robert Lekachman, "Reagan's Joy and Misery Index," *New Society* 68 (3 May 1984): 175-77; "Slimmer Middle, Bigger Bottom: Reagan Rearranges Income Distribution," *Dollars and Sense*, no. 96 (April 1984): 3-5.

48. Donato Alvarez and Brian Cooper, "Productivity Trends in Manufacturing in the U.S. and 11 Other Countries," *Monthly Labor Review* 107 (January 1984): 52-58.

49. George Psacharopoulos, "Returns to Education: An Updated International Comparison," *Comparative Education* 17 (March 1981): 321-41.

50. Wilensky: *The Welfare State and Equality*, 52-69, 107-19, and *The "New Corporatism,"* 8-71; Coughlin, *Ideology, Public Opinion and Welfare Policy*, 118; Rosenberry, "Social Insurance, Distributive Criteria and the Welfare Backlash," 421-47; Douglas A. Hibbs, Jr., and Henrik Jess Madsen, "Public Reactions to the Growth of Taxation and Government Expenditure," *World Politics* 33 (April 1981): 413-35; Gosta Esping-Andersen, "Comparative

Social Policy and Political Conflict in Advanced Welfare States: Denmark and Sweden," *International Journal of Health Services* 9, no. 2 (1979): 269-93; Elizabeth Hann Hastings and Philip K. Hastings, eds., *Index to International Public Opinion* (Westport, Conn.: Greenwood Press, 1981-84), vol. 2, *1979-1980*, 277; vol. 3, *1980-1981*, 29, 111-17, 142-47; vol. 5, *1982-1983*, 546-47, 604; Richard Rose, "Two and One-Half Cheers for the Market in Britain," *Public Opinion* 6 (June/July 1983): 15.

51. Barbara G. Farah, Samuel H. Barnes, and Felix Heunks, "Political Dissatisfaction," in *Political Action: Mass Participation in Five Western Democracies*, ed. Samuel H. Barnes and Max Kaase (Beverly Hills, Calif.: Sage Publications, 1979), 418-21; Giacomo Sani, "The Political Culture of Italy: Continuity and Change," in *The Civic Culture Revisited*, ed. Gabriel A. Almond and Sidney Verba (Boston: Little, Brown, 1980), 310; Richard Rose, "Public Confidence, Popular Consent: A Comparison of Britain and the United States," *Public Opinion* 7 (February/March 1984): 11; Hastings and Hastings, eds., *Index to International Public Opinion, 1979-1980*, 72, 294; *1980-1981*, 114-17, 143-47; *1982-1983*, 182-83; *World Opinion Update* 7 (May 1983): 55; *World Opinion Update* 7 (June 1983): 66; *World Opinion Update* 7 (July/August 1983): 76-77; Hans N. Weiler, "Education, Public Confidence, and the Legitimacy of the Modern State: Do We Have a Crisis?" *Phi Delta Kappan* 64 (September 1982): 9-14; George H. Gallup, "The 14th Annual Gallup Poll of the Public's Attitudes toward the Public Schools," *Phi Delta Kappan* 64 (September 1982): 37-50; *Gallup Report*, no. 216 (September 1983): 19-31; "The Politics of Education: What the Public Thinks," *Newsweek* 101 (27 June 1983): 61; Geoffrey Isherwood, Tom Williams, and Robin Farquhar, "Public Participation in Education," *Education Canada* 21 (Spring 1981): 4-8.

INDEX

Act on Workers Codetermination (Sweden), 180

AFDC. *See* Aid to Families with Dependent Children

AFL-CIO, 167, 169

AFT. *See* American Federation of Teachers

Aid to Families with Dependent Children (AFDC), 14, 193

Alberta, 129, 154

American Federation of Teachers (AFT), 169, 170

American Medical Association, 110, 125

American Medical International, 125, 141-42

Angle, John, 79

Austria, 51

Banks: influence of, 58, 60, 140, 159, 165-67, 171-72, 181; nationalizations of, 139-40, 157

Barre, Raymond, 157, 185

Belgium, 24

Benefits. *See* Social service programs

Blue Cross, 90, 125

Blue Shield, 125

Britain. *See* United Kingdom

British Columbia, 129, 154

British United Provident Association (BUPA), 141

Bundesbank, 159

Bundesrat, 132

Bundestag, 34, 132

Bureaucracy. *See* Civil service

Business organizations: in Canada, 162; in France, 186-87; in Italy, 140, 183; in Sweden, 175, 177, 178; in United Kingdom, 171; in United States, 162; in West Germany, 181

Business sector: attitudes toward labor of, 23, 168-69, 172, 175-77, 180-81, 184, 198; economic role of, 23-24, 48-49, 53-54, 60-61, 124, 159-67, 170-78, 180-88; and joint business/labor groups, 176-77, 180-81, 184; legislation toward, 164; and multinational corporations, 48-49, 60, 159, 165; party ties of, 171, 172, 178, 181; political access of, 162-63, 165, 167, 172, 177-78, 181, 183, 187; profits of, 164, 171, 177; and small business strength, 165, 183, 186; and state enterprises, 124, 128-29, 134, 139-40

Caisse Nationale d'Assurance Maladie des Travailleurs Salariés (CNAMTS) 114-15, 141-42

Canada: business/labor role in, 23-24, 162-63, 165-70; effectiveness of policies in, 92-93, 97, 190; efficiency of policies in, 22-23, 55, 108, 116, 197; equality of policies in, 97, 105-6, 130-31; government policy role in, 128-31, 143, 162; health insurance in, 89-90, 97, 105-6, 109, 126, 130-31, 162; party policies in, 38-39, 53, 149, 154, 162, 167; policy administration in, 112, 116, 128-31, 143-45, 162-63, 166-70, 188; policy attitudes in, 29, 38-39, 70, 89-90, 117-18, 198-99; policies and economy in, 23-24, 26-29, 38-39, 43-45, 48-51, 55-60, 190; policy-related expenditures in, 10-19, 107-12, 126, 130-31, 154, state enterprises in, 128-29

Canadian Labour Congress, 169, 170

Capital formation. *See* Investments

CHARLES F. ANDRAIN is Professor of Political Science at San Diego State University. His current research interests focus on comparative public policy.

INSTITUTE OF INTERNATIONAL STUDIES
UNIVERSITY OF CALIFORNIA, BERKELEY

215 Moses Hall   Berkeley, California 94720

CARL G. ROSBERG, *Director*

Monographs published by the Institute include:

RESEARCH SERIES

1. *The Chinese Anarchist Movement.* R.A. Scalapino and G.T. Yu. ($1.00)
7. *Birth Rates in Latin America.* O. Andrew Collver. ($2.50)
16. *The International Imperatives of Technology.* Eugene B. Skolnikoff. ($2.95)
17. *Autonomy or Dependence in Regional Integration.* P.C. Schmitter. ($1.75)
19. *Entry of New Competitors in Yugoslav Market Socialism.* S.R. Sacks. ($2.50)
20. *Political Integration in French-Speaking Africa.* Abdul A. Jalloh. ($3.50)
21. *The Desert & the Sown: Nomads in Wider Society.* Ed. C. Nelson. ($5.50)
22. *U.S.-Japanese Competition in International Markets.* J.E. Roemer. ($3.95)
23. *Political Disaffection Among British University Students.* J. Citrin and D.J. Elkins. ($2.00)
24. *Urban Inequality and Housing Policy in Tanzania.* Richard E. Stren. ($2.95)
25. *The Obsolescence of Regional Integration Theory.* Ernst B. Haas. ($6.95)
26. *The Voluntary Service Agency in Israel.* Ralph M. Kramer. ($2.00)
27. *The SOCSIM Microsimulation Program.* E. A. Hammel et al. ($4.50)
28. *Authoritarian Politics in Communist Europe.* Ed. Andrew C. Janos. ($8.95)
30. *Plural Societies and New States.* Robert Jackson. ($2.00)
31. *Politics of Oil Pricing in the Middle East, 1970-75.* R.C. Weisberg. ($4.95)
32. *Agricultural Policy and Performance in Zambia.* Doris J. Dodge. ($4.95)
33. *Five Classy Computer Programs.* E.A. Hammel & R.Z. Deuel. ($3.75)
34. *Housing the Urban Poor in Africa.* Richard E. Stren. ($5.95)
35. *The Russian New Right: Right-Wing Ideologies in USSR.* A. Yanov. ($5.95)
36. *Social Change in Romania, 1860-1940.* Ed. Kenneth Jowitt. ($4.50)
37. *The Leninist Response to National Dependency.* Kenneth Jowitt. ($4.95)
38. *Socialism in Sub-Saharan Africa.* Eds. C. Rosberg & T. Callaghy. ($12.95)
39. *Tanzania's Ujamaa Villages: Rural Development Strategy.* D. McHenry. ($5.95)
40. *Who Gains from Deep Ocean Mining?* I.G. Bulkley. ($3.50)
41. *Industrialization & the Nation-State in Peru.* Frits Wils. ($5.95)
42. *Ideology, Public Opinion, & Welfare Policy.* R.M. Coughlin. ($6.50)
43. *The Apartheid Regime: Political Power and Racial Domination.* Eds. R.M. Price and C. G. Rosberg. ($12.50)
44. *Yugoslav Economic System in the 1970s.* Laura D. Tyson. ($5.95)
45. *Conflict in Chad.* Virginia Thompson & Richard Adloff. ($7.50)
46. *Conflict and Coexistence in Belgium.* Ed. Arend Lijphart. ($8.95)
47. *Changing Realities in Southern Africa.* Ed. Michael Clough. ($12.50)
48. *Nigerian Women Mobilized, 1900-1965.* Nina E. Mba. ($12.95)
49. *Institutions of Rural Development.* Eds. D. Leonard & D. Marshall. ($11.50)
50. *Politics of Women & Work in USSR & U.S.* Joel C. Moses. ($9.50)

LIST OF PUBLICATIONS *(continued)*

51. *Zionism and Territory.* Baruch Kimmerling. ($12.50)
52. *Soviet Subsidization of Trade with Eastern Europe.* M. Marrese & J. Vanous. ($14.50)
53. *Voluntary Efforts in Decentralized Management.* L. Ralston et al. ($9.00)
54. *Corporate State Ideologies.* Carl Landauer. ($5.95)
55. *Effects of Economic Reform in Yugoslavia.* John P. Burkett. ($9.50)
56. *The Drama of the Soviet 1960s.* Alexander Yanov. ($8.50)
57. *Revolutions and Rebellions in Afghanistan.* Eds. M. Nazif Shahrani & Robert L. Canfield. ($14.95)
58. *Women Farmers of Malawi.* D. Hirschmann & M. Vaughan. ($8.95)
59. *Chilean Agriculture under Military Rule.* Lovell S. Jarvis. ($11.50)
60. *Influencing Mass Political Behavior in the Netherlands and Austria.* Joseph J. Houska. ($11.50)

POLICY PAPERS IN INTERNATIONAL AFFAIRS

1. *Images of Detente & the Soviet Political Order.* K. Jowitt. ($1.25)
2. *Detente After Brezhnev: Domestic Roots of Soviet Policy.* A. Yanov. ($4.50)
3. *Mature Neighbor Policy: A New Policy for Latin America.* A. Fishlow. ($3.95)
4. *Five Images of Soviet Future: Review & Synthesis.* G.W. Breslauer. ($4.50)
5. *Global Evangelism: How to Protect Human Rights.* E. B. Haas. ($2.95)
6. *Israel & Jordan: An Adversarial Partnership.* Ian Lustick. ($2.00)
7. *Political Syncretism in Italy.* Giuseppe Di Palma. ($3.95)
8. *U.S. Foreign Policy in Sub-Saharan Africa.* Robert M. Price. ($4.50)
9. *East-West Technology Transfer in Perspective.* R.J. Carrick. ($5.50)
11. *Toward Africanized Policy for Southern Africa.* R. Libby. ($7.50)
12. *Taiwan Relations Act & Defense of ROC.* Edwin K. Snyder et al. ($7.50)
13. *Cuba's Policy in Africa, 1959-1980.* William M. LeoGrande. ($4.50)
14. *Norway, NATO, & Forgotten Soviet Challenge.* K. Amundsen. ($3.95)
15. *Japanese Industrial Policy.* Ira Magaziner and Thomas Hout. ($6.50)
16. *Containment, Soviet Behavior, & Grand Strategy.* Robert Osgood. ($5.50)
17. *U.S.-Japanese Competition-Semiconductor Industry.* M. Borrus et al. ($7.50)
18. *Contemporary Islamic Movements in Perspective.* Ira Lapidus. ($4.95)
19. *Atlantic Alliance, Nuclear Weapons, & European Attitudes.* W. Thies. ($4.50)
20. *War and Peace: Views from Moscow & Beijing.* B. Garrett & B. Glaser. ($7.95)
21. *Emerging Japanese Economic Influence in Africa.* Joanna Moss & John Ravenhill. ($8.95)
22. *Nuclear Waste Disposal under the Seabed.* Edward Miles et al. ($7.50)

POLITICS OF MODERNIZATION SERIES

1. *Spanish Bureaucratic-Patrimonialism in America.* M. Sarfatti. ($2.00)
2. *Civil-Military Relations in Argentina, Chile, & Peru.* L. North. ($2.00)
9. *Modernization & Bureaucratic-Authoritarianism: Studies in South American Politics.* Guillermo O'Donnell. ($8.95)